RINSED

GERRY ROSE

The Book Guild Ltd

First published in Great Britain in 2017 by
The Book Guild Ltd
9 Priory Business Park
Wistow Road, Kibworth
Leicestershire, LE8 0RX
Freephone: 0800 999 2982
www.bookguild.co.uk
Email: info@bookguild.co.uk
Twitter: @bookguild

Typeset in Minion Pro

Printed and bound in the UK by TJ International, Padstow, Cornwall

ISBN 978 1911320 302

British Library Cataloguing in Publication Data.
A catalogue record for this book is available from the British Library.

*To Lesley, who knows what it feels like
to be rinsed but come out the other side.
Thanks for sharing the journey!*

Urban Dictionary: Rinsed

Used up, all gone; To have lost a cuss battle without a comeback; When someone has been thoroughly beaten at a certain sport or activity; If you are rinsed, you have been 'done', so to speak; You may also have been fooled by someone.

Fact and Fiction

In this novel, references are made to a number of historical facts.

However, in the time-honoured tradition, the actual story is, of course, entirely made up.

MAY 2007
PROLOGUE

PROLOGUE   MONDAY 7 MAY 2007

Still buzzing from the adrenaline created by the business that she had just concluded, the thirty-eight-year-old woman stepped out into the early evening London sunshine and headed purposefully for the Underground.

If she was lucky, she would be home in less than two hours and be able to spend some time with her young twins, have a glass or two of wine and get to bed reasonably early for a change.

Reflecting on the fact that she had just bawled out two of her relatively incompetent subordinates, one by telephone and one face-to-face, she chuckled to herself. That would teach the shit-heads, show them not to mess with her again.

Crossing the busy street, she headed up a small alleyway, her heels clicking loudly in the enclosed lane, and only hesitated slightly on seeing the three young men, faces half-hidden in blue hooded jackets, coming towards her down the alley.

Panic struck, however, when they surrounded her and one tried to grab her leather handbag. Striking out, she tried to scream but by now another of the gang had a gloved hand over her mouth. Now terrified by their obvious youthful strength, she saw the knife late and could not believe what was happening to her as she felt the first efficient and excruciating stab pierce her light clothing and enter between two of her left ribs.

As she began to fade into unconsciousness, the gang released her, letting her fall against some railings, and as she slipped to the ground, the tallest of the group leaned over her and whispered in her right ear. They were the last words that she wanted to hear – the last words that she would ever hear.

The gang, without speaking, then retreated back out of the lane and into the busy London rush hour, ensuring, as they ran, that they kept themselves hidden behind their blue hooded jackets. A large white Ford Transit, its rear doors open, gathered the gang in and sped off into the traffic. The Ford would be found two hours later, but no forensic evidence would be lifted from the vehicle; the perfect crime, the perfect getaway and not a single drop of evidence.

The CCTV camera had captured the killing in all its efficient detail and that worried Colm Elliot a lot, an uneasy feeling rising intuitively in his gut. On the face of it, it looked like just another stabbing by drug-crazed youths looking for quick and easy cash to support their desperate addiction. However, what was the big bastard doing leaning over his victim, appearing to talk to her as she lay, bleeding to death on the ground?

Switching the machine to pause, he turned to his two younger colleagues and asked, 'What do you guys make of this helpful little movie?'

'Looks like another pointless, stupid waste of an innocent life,' began Mark Atkinson, his recently appointed detective constable.

'What about you, Hannah?' probed Elliot, turning to his detective sergeant who had been working with him for a couple of years now, and in whom he had high hopes.

'Couple of things bother me,' she began.

'Like what?'

'Like the big guy talking to her as the others took her bag. What was all that about?' she continued, thinking out loud.

'Anything else?'

'Well, the bloody camera bothers me too. I looked at it when I was in the alley, and it is not exactly hidden.'

'So, where does that take you?'

'Nowhere as yet, but...' She ran out of steam.

'It's the "but" that is bothering me too.' Elliot stood and walked to the window of his office and looked out at the rear buildings and goings on behind Marylebone police station in London. As always, lots of hustle and bustle, the underbelly of the capital keeping him and his colleagues fully occupied.

The victim was known to him and had been declared dead on arrival at the hospital. A nasty, aggressive woman who Elliot had found very challenging to relate to, to handle, when he had been the unfortunate sod who had taken the call a couple of years back.

'This does not bring back happy memories, Hannah,' he finally concluded as he headed for his office door. 'I need to go for a decent coffee and clear my head.' He left them to take another look at the CCTV footage.

Elliot's mood was not great as he left the building and headed for a nearby Starbucks and a better coffee than was available in the police station. The original Hillman case had landed on his desk in early July 2005, at the start of a week that London would never forget...

JULY 2005

CHAPTER I   MONDAY 4 JULY 2005

The whisky that had followed last night's bottle of red was drumming painfully at his temples as Malcolm Hillman came awake in the guest bedroom of his house in St John's Wood, London. It was 5.55am and the alarm had taken him from a weird dream, a dream that his house was being broken into by some threatening but mysterious being, unseen but scary nevertheless.

As his consciousness rebooted, the dreadful memory of last night's post-dinner argument with his beautiful Swiss wife Anna came flooding back. They had stood almost nose-to-nose in the kitchen, arguing again over money and her desire to buy a second home in London, the spite and venom palpable on her lovely face, her perfect white teeth gritted in fury.

How he had wanted to punch the bitch in the mouth; how he had kept control of his rising temper and stopped himself from putting his hands around her throat he would never know.

But he had, and had managed to extricate himself from the fury, taking himself from the house and going for a long walk, calming himself down, trying to make rational sense of what was going wrong with his relatively new second marriage. It was always about money, how she never had enough, how the things she wanted were always promised but never delivered. Stupid cow – did she not get the fact that half of his hard-earned wealth had gone in his divorce and that shitloads more was needed in maintenance and the school fees for his grandchildren?

He had returned to the house to find the master bedroom door locked and the place in silence. It was becoming a regular pattern, at least once every couple of weeks. So, he had taken himself off to bed in the guest bedroom, still angry and still half drunk from the wine and the whisky.

Rising from the guest room bed, he shaved and showered. He had a full schedule at work and was due to complete a new ten million pound deal for a client in France. As he dressed, he resolved to go to Anna and apologise, kiss and make up, give her permission to go to the West End and buy something nice.

Entering the room, however, it was clear that she was still in a foul mood and was not going to be easy to placate.

'Off to work are you? Leaving me in this miserable hole all day?' she began. 'With nothing to do but clean up your fucking mess, make your bed, pick up your big shitty Y-fronts?' she continued.

'Funny, I thought our cleaning lady did that,' he countered, feeling his blood beginning to boil. 'Still going on about money are you? Poor bitch.'

'It's all about money, you mean old man. Do you think I married you for your looks? No, you are mean, mean and selfish, everyone says so!' she shouted and with that, he lost it. The red mist descended. *The bitch! he thought. The fucking selfish bitch!*

Knocking her onto the bed, he clambered on top of her, slightly aroused as her short nightdress rode up to reveal her tiny silk panties, his hand over her nasty mouth. Beneath him, she started to wriggle and kick at him and to stop her he reached for one of the many pillows surrounding them on the king-sized bed and covered her face with it, holding ever tighter until she was still. Setting the pillow down, he punched it hard. 'Shut up now, you fucking bitch,' he muttered to himself as he climbed from the bed.

4

Breathing heavily, he carefully wrapped her still body in a light cover sheet and dragged her into the en suite bathroom, where he placed her on the floor before covering her body with a number of towels from a nearby shelf.

Leaving his wife there, he returned to the bedroom and checked his appearance in the mirror before choosing a tie from his closet, pulling on his suit jacket and leaving the house to travel to his office in the city. As he walked to the nearby Underground station, he called their cleaning lady and told her not to work today, that his wife was unwell and did not want to be disturbed.

Detective Chief Inspector Colm Elliot was pissed off. It was a lovely summer's evening and he had been on his way to play a round of golf with his good friend, the author Barry Piers. At forty-six, Elliot was at that moment beginning to feel too old for this life; twenty-four years of cleaning up the carnage of the modern world.

As he turned into the leafy St John's Wood street, he could see the patrol cars at the cordoned-off end of the road as he guided the car up the rows of expensive townhouses. Some of these places would set you back five or six million and from where he sat in his Vauxhall, you didn't get a lot for your money in this part of town.

His detective sergeant, Hannah Bellamy, a pretty, smart and hardworking honours graduate from some midlands university, approached as he stepped out of the car.

'Bit of a strange scene going on here, boss,' she began as they walked together towards the house.

'Geezer walked into Marylebone an hour ago claiming that he might have killed his wife before going to work this morning.'

'And?' asked Elliot in his softening Ulster accent.

'Seems the bastard was telling the truth,' she continued.

'Jesus Christ,' reflected Elliot, shaking his head as they passed through the police tape, past the scene of crime officers, and entered the elegant hallway of the townhouse.

There was no nice way of saying it, but ever since she had first discovered the sensation, since the first time that it had happened, Julia Hillman liked it from behind. And, without exception, the boys and then the men in her life had seemingly had no problem in obliging.

This evening was no different and as she lay face down on the bed, she began moaning with pleasure as her Viagra-enhanced fiancé, Lucas, knelt behind her, giving her what she wanted as she wriggled her ample posterior towards his throbbing manhood.

The interruption of the telephone was not greatly appreciated, but Julia Hillman was not someone who could not multi-task. So, as Lucas continued with his manly duty, she reached out and lifted the receiver to hear her mother's frantic voice down the line telling her that her father had been arrested and was being held in custody at Marylebone Police station.

For the first time in her life, all thoughts of her impending orgasm were suspended and she leapt from the bed, leaving her aging boyfriend with his semi-permanent problem, before heading out of the bedroom to discuss her father's latest predicament with her mother.

'What do you mean he has been arrested?' she demanded incredulously and, as was her want, continued before a reply was possible. 'What has the shit-head done this time?'

The incessant noise coming from the direction of the front desk was driving Colm Elliot to distraction. Who or what was causing such a rumpus at this time of the night? Leaving his bland coffee unfinished, he opened the door of the small interview room and went in search of the source. At the front desk, he was confronted by a vitriolic large-chested woman dressed in a frumpy twin-set and another, more gentile older lady that Elliot took to be the mother of the noise creator.

'What the hell is going on here?' demanded Elliot in a manner indicating that he was not best pleased by either the nature or the volume of the fracas.

'We are here to see my father and this oaf is refusing to let us speak to him,' gesticulated the source of the rumpus, pointing dramatically at the duty officer, who merely spread his hands and shook his head at the senior detective.

'And who might your father be?' continued Elliot quietly, as if to make a point.

'Malcolm Hillman; we have been told that he is in custody and we want to see him, speak with him at once,' she continued.

'Well, I can confirm that Malcolm Hillman is in custody and that he continues to help us with our enquiries,' offered Elliot.

'Then we demand to see him,' ranted the woman, almost spitting on Elliot as she spoke.

'Well, you can demand as much as you like – sorry, I don't know your name,' continued Elliot, trying to calm the situation down.

'Julia Hillman and this is my mother,' offered the younger woman.

'Well, as I was saying, Julia Hillman, you can demand as much as you like, but you will not be seeing or speaking to your father tonight. He is in custody and will be helping us with our enquiries until mid-morning tomorrow at the earliest,' stated Elliot firmly.

'Does he have his solicitor present?'

'His solicitor will be attending at ten am tomorrow morning at the request of your father. So, can I suggest that you calm yourself down and take your mother home until tomorrow – there is nothing you can do to help this evening.'

'This is bloody outrageous!' fumed Julia Hillman.

'Maybe, but your father is here voluntarily and we are trying to get on with our job.'

'I will take this to the highest level; you can't treat people like us in the same way that you treat the bloody plebs that you normally deal with.'

'Indeed, Julia Hillman, but it is not every day that someone walks in off the street after a day at the office and claims to have killed his wife,' Elliot said, bringing the exchange to a sudden halt.

'Bloody woman,' she hissed. 'What was he thinking of marrying that bloody woman?'And with that Julia Hillman led her mother out of the police station and into the dark London night.

'Jesus H Christ,' reflected Elliot as he returned to his interview room, not exactly looking forward to a rematch in the morning.

CHAPTER 2   TUESDAY 5 JULY 2005

Gary Ruthven was excited at the prospect of his day. This morning, he was due to meet with Kate Ross from his firm's auditors to go over any issues highlighted during their recent review of last year's accounts, and this afternoon he was scheduled to spend his time committing adultery with a new lover, a former model that he had fallen for a couple of weeks earlier at a booze-fuelled party in Notting Hill.

As Chief Executive of RuthvenCampbellStuart, a renowned boutique brand consultancy, he was conscious that his focus was not what it should be as he parked his BMW in the underground car park and took the elevator to his firm's fifth-floor office in London's expensive West End.

The first person he met that morning was his chairman, Lucas Hunt, who asked if he could have an urgent word before Gary had even had a chance to switch on his desktop and check his emails.

'Of course, grab a seat. What can I do for you?' he asked as he removed his light summer suit jacket and put it on a hanger behind his office door.

'It's a bit of a tricky one, I am afraid. Don't really know where to begin,' opened Hunt and Ruthven was immediately aware of the tears welling in his colleague's eyes.

'Try the beginning,' offered Ruthven, hoping that they were not in for another of the long personal sessions that were becoming too often the case with Hunt these days. They had known each other for some fifteen years, but to many at RCS, his chairman was now considered to be well past his sell-by date in terms of contribution to the business.

'Okay, cutting to the chase, Julia's father was arrested for the murder of his wife yesterday and is being held in Marylebone Police Station, helping them with their enquiries,' began Hunt quietly.

'Christ, Lucas, what's the story?'

'Well, it seems like he killed her, but we have not really got the full details yet. Julia and I are seeing our lawyer later today.'

'Bloody hell, mate. And you're planning to marry into that crazy bloody family in September? It might be a good time to reconsider,' continued Ruthven with a gentle smile on his handsome face, hardly able to make any sense of what he had just heard.

'You could be right, but in the short term I am going to have to take some time off, look after Julia, see what needs to be done.'

'Sounds fine by me. How long do you think you will need?'

'No idea at the moment, but I guess that I will be missing for the remainder of this week at least,' suggested Hunt.

'Fine, and if you need anything, give us a bell,' concluded Ruthven, rising to escort his chairman from his office.

Kate Ross and her new assistant, a recently qualified young Asian woman who Ruthven thought looked about twelve years old, were waiting for him in the largest of RCS's three meeting rooms when Gary arrived a few minutes late following his shocking discussion with Hunt.

There, they were joined by David Lane, shareholder and Head of Strategic Finance, and Rosie Calder, the firm's part-time independent accountant and bookkeeper. After brief introductions and the distribution of tea and coffee, they all settled down around an oval-shaped American oak table as Kate took control of proceedings.

'The purpose of this morning's meeting is to take you through our draft accounts for the financial year which ended 31 March 2005, and to highlight areas of concern and points of clarification that we require following our recent audit,' she began as her assistant handed copies of the draft report around the table.

'I will begin by providing an outline of the key headlines, then highlight some concerns, before going through our detailed notes at the rear of the document,' she continued professionally. Ruthven had known Kate Ross for some eight years, since the time she had been assistant to the now retired founder of the accounting firm she now ran. Kate also looked after Gary's personal financial planning and probably knew more about the state of the Ruthven family money than he did himself.

'Okay, let's go,' suggested Ruthven as he began flicking through the draft accounts in search of the key strategic numbers.

'To begin, I would like to inform you that our audit has thrown up a number of fairly significant issues that we believe will require urgent attention by your Board, and that will need to be acted upon during the coming months,' she began, somewhat too formal for Ruthven's liking.

'Regarding revenue, the business has shown an overall growth for the year versus last, of just under fourteen percent, and whilst that would normally be seen as positive progress, it needs to be put into perspective by an explosion of costs of just over forty-seven percent against last year.'

Ruthven looked at Lane, not surprised by this information. It was, after all, almost exactly the same as the draft numbers produced internally by Rosie Calder.

'Obviously, these might be expected while your business continues to expand, but the net-net is that profitability is very poor when compared to previous years.' She hesitated to look around the room for reactions.

'What are the implications?' asked Lane quietly.

'Well, we will be recommending that no bonus payments are made and believe that no dividend will be payable this year.' Again Ross stopped to let the room digest what she had just said.

Inwardly, Gary's belly was doing flips; he had been banking on his hard-earned bonus to pay for a kitchen remodel his wife Vicki had just commissioned for their Beaconsfield home, and the dividend was usually earmarked for his daughter's school fees. Externally however, he remained calm and in control.

'Okay, that's the top line. Kate, would you mind getting to some of the issues of concern that you alluded to in your introduction?' requested Ruthven, suddenly very focused on the meeting.

'Of course,' agreed Ross, moving some papers around on the table in front of her.

'To begin, we are concerned about the way in which the Hamburg office setup has been structured.'

'Say more please,' encouraged Ruthven, conscious of David Lane shifting in his seat beside him.

'Well, the strategic model for expansion that we approved some time ago does not appear to have been adhered to in the case of your new German office.'

'Is that right, David?' queried Ruthven of his colleague.

'Technically, the principles are the same, it is just that, with capital tight, the initial financing was indeed structured in a slightly different manner,' began Lane in a voice that was difficult to hear.

'What do you mean by slightly different?' challenged Ruthven, feeling his blood pressure beginning to rise – this was news to him.

'Well, rather than the agreed two hundred and fifty thousand in start-up capital that the model requires, we supplied one fifty backed up by a one hundred overdraft facility arranged through a local German bank,' explained Lane.

'Who the hell is we, David? I do not recall this being discussed,' challenged Ruthven.

'Uli Muller, Lucas and myself agreed the slight amendment to conclude the deal when you were in New York working with Dell,' explained Lane, who was well used to his boss's energy.

'Okay,' sighed Ruthven, looking directly at Lane, 'we can come back to that later. What else do you have for us, Kate?'

'Still on the topic of Hamburg, we have suspicions that another business may be being run from that location,' she continued tentatively.

'Say more,' requested Gary again.

'Well, we are not certain about this, but we feel that Uli Muller may be running a parallel practice with his wife as his business partner.'

Ruthven looked at his two finance people before raising an eyebrow and asking, 'Rosie, David, any thoughts or reactions?'

'You know where I stand on Hamburg,' began Calder, who had often voiced her opinion in private to Gary about how the German office was being run.

'David?' persisted Ruthven.

'I would be very shocked if this was the case; can we explore your evidence, Kate?' he replied, still looking relatively confident and calm.

For the next few minutes, Kate Ross and her assistant outlined the reasoning behind their speculation and after she had finished, it was agreed that Lane and Calder would investigate the matter further in Hamburg during a scheduled visit the following week.

'The next key issue I want to discuss relates to the company's cash flow for the current year...' Again Kate's assistant handed out a pre-prepared spreadsheet for perusal. 'As you can see from this, if your patterns continue this year as they did last year, the firm is projected to run out of cash at the bank sometime next January.'

'Is this a worst scenario projection?' asked Lane.

'No, it's based on projections and uses the actual model achieved last year,' replied Ross.

'So, if our satellites do not grow as planned, it could be much worse,' suggested Lane.

'Exactly,' confirmed the auditor.

'Thanks,' concluded Lane, looking again at the spreadsheet.

'So,' began Ruthven, getting to the point, as was his style. 'How much cash are we likely to need to see us through this expansion phase?'

'We project that you will be looking at needing to inject four to five hundred thousand pounds before the start of the New Year,' stated Ross firmly.

'Wow,' reflected Ruthven quietly. 'That's a big concern and as you know, we have never needed external support before and only run a modest overdraft facility with Barclays.'

'Indeed,' agreed Ross.

'Okay, and I can't say that I am enjoying this session, Kate. Are there any more major issues for you to highlight?' requested Ruthven, hoping quietly that his afternoon was going to prove a lot better than his morning had so far been.

'No. The rest is the standard stuff for clarification from Rosie and I am sure we can get through it fairly quickly,' she responded.

'Good, let's get it done.'

Half an hour later, all other matters had been discussed and agreed and it was Ruthven who began to wrap the meeting up. Looking at his tiny handwritten notes, he began.

'To summarise then, we have grown our revenue, lost control of our cost base and worked our socks off for a chicken-shit profit,' he began. 'We have set Hamburg up by ignoring our fundamental expansion model; our German director may be shafting us by running a parallel business out of our Hamburg office, and we may run out of cash sometime early in the New

Year.' He stopped and looked around the room. 'Other than that, we don't seem to have a lot to worry about. Does that sum things up?'

There was a ripple of nervous laughter around the table before Kate Ross agreed that it did indeed capture things quite succinctly.

'Plus,' began Lane, 'there will be no bonus payments and no shareholder dividends.'

'Not unless you want the business to run out of cash in November,' concluded Ross.

'Thanks, I was trying to forget those two little gems,' joked Ruthven, gathering up his papers into a tidy bundle, the meeting over.

'Thanks, Kate,' he began, pushing back his chair, 'as always an excellent piece of work. Leaves me and David with lots to think about.'

Vicki Ruthven stood waist deep in the chilly swimming pool doing her early morning workout. A plastic-coated weight in each hand, she raised both to her slim shoulders simultaneously before dropping them back to her side. So far, she had completed a two-mile run and twenty lengths of the fifteen-metre pool and would soon be ready to face her day.

Upstairs in the small Spanish villa that overlooked the old course of the San Roque Golf Club, her daughters Emma and Molly lay sleeping following a very late night in the pubs and bars of Sotogrande. Vicki knew that it would be nearer midday before the girls would surface, but was determined to get on with her day while her daughters slept.

They had travelled from their home in Beaconsfield the day before, taking an early morning Monarch flight from London Luton to Gibraltar, and were looking forward to spending the next eight weeks in southern Spain. Gary would be joining them for four weeks in August and a couple of long weekends before then, but in the meantime, Vicki and the girls intended to relax and take full advantage of the excellent Spanish weather.

They had bought the house three years earlier, after Gary had sold a 20% stake in RCS to David Lane and Lucas Hunt and as projects go, it had not been the smoothest. Their developer, a local firm, had proved to be both unreliable and difficult to deal with and it had taken their excellent solicitor in Marbella to finally get the purchase completed without the customary need for a paper bag full of Euros being paid to bribe the completion.

Climbing the steps from the pool, Vicki could hear the telephone ringing in the house and wrapping herself in a towel, entered through a sliding door and rushed across the marble floor to take the call.

'Good morning,' she began, recognizing the RCS number on the telephone display.

'I hope I didn't wake you,' began Gary.

'Not at all; you might have disturbed the girls, but I've been up for ages.'

'Everything okay at the house?' enquired her husband.

'Yeah, the setup seems to have worked this time,' replied Vicki. After trying two local firms, they had at last got a maintenance company that appeared to be doing what they were paid to do.

'Good, just thought I would call and give you the latest gossip before you read about it in the *Daily Mail*,' continued her husband conspiratorially.

'Not like you to gossip, Mister Ruthven,' began Vicki, trying to get herself dry whilst holding the telephone receiver.

Half an hour later, her eldest daughter Emma, who at eighteen had just left school and was hoping to begin her law degree at Leeds University in late September, joined Vicki in the kitchen. As they snacked on some fruit, Vicki updated Emma on the shocking Lucas Hunt story and together they speculated on what the impact might be on Hunt's forthcoming wedding plans. Hunt was not one of Vicki's favourite people, too smarmy and grovelling for her liking, and Julia, whom she had only met once, was in her humble opinion, even worse.

London had a pumped-up and energized feel to it as Gary Ruthven rode a black taxi cab across the city later that day. Saturday had seen a major Live8 Concert demanding action against global poverty that had been put together by the same old crew of mega-rich rock stars who wanted to put the world to rights. The timing was scheduled to precede the arrival of many of the western world's leading politicians for the next G8 Summit, which would be held later that week at the beautiful Gleneagles Hotel in Scotland. Ruthven struggled to get his head around the cost of such a jamboree especially given the extraordinary cost of security required to keep the politicians apart from the thousands of protesters threatening to march on the Perthshire hotel and cause anarchy. As always the tabloid newspapers were whipping up a frenzy in a cynical attempt to sell more copy.

In Trafalgar Square, a large stage and screen had been erected and on Wednesday lunchtime, massive crowds were expected to gather to hear the voting and eventual announcement of which city would be the host of the 2012 Summer Olympic Games. According to the news that morning, Tony Blair, the British Prime Minister, had joined Lord Coe and his team, which included a host of sporting celebrities, in the Far East for a final lobbying push aimed at winning the games for London. It was not something that Ruthven had ever thought possible, although the idea of a London Olympics in his lifetime felt really inspiring, and could prove good for business. That said, the bid would probably fail; the Olympic Committee would surely go for somewhere like Madrid, a beautiful city that could at least be able to guarantee a few weeks of summer sunshine in 2012.

He had lived in the south east of England for almost twenty years, having moved from his native Edinburgh to join the exciting marketing agency BBH only two years after finishing at university. During that time, he had always worked in London and the city still held him spellbound. Every day that he arrived either by car or by the Chiltern Line into Marylebone, he felt that he was living his dream, working where the action was, mixing with the big boys.

As was his style, he turned his mind to finding solutions to the issues and potential problems highlighted by Kate Ross at the audit report meeting. His philosophy was that every problem had a solution and in his mind's eye, he began prioritizing, sorting them into bite-sized items in need of attention.

To begin, where the hell were they going to get half a million in cash from? Barclays would probably agree to an increase in the firm's relatively modest overdraft limit, but would want a corresponding increase in the security that he and Vicki had already provided against their Buckinghamshire home. Drawing down some equity by increasing his relatively small, by London standards, mortgage was also an option although Vicki would take some convincing of that as an idea. His shareholders could be asked to contribute, but Lucas Hunt could probably not afford to help and David Lane, who already owned fifteen percent of RCS, would probably want a bigger stake in return.

'Fuck that for a game of soldiers,' he mumbled to himself as his cab eventually began to free itself from the heavy traffic and pick up speed as it headed for his illicit hotel rendezvous.

No, he would have to get together with Lane and fully explore their options. After all, that was David's role within the firm. Taking his mobile phone from his Zegner suit jacket pocket, he dialled his personal assistant, Jenny, and asked her to fix a two-hour meeting with Lane for Thursday morning.

That done, he then began to ponder what to do about the situation in Hamburg. In his heart, he did not believe that Uli

Muller would be ripping off the firm. Although a bit odd and quirky by nature, Ruthven considered Muller to be a man of integrity, one of the good guys. They had known each other for many years, since their days at Guinness where Uli had been Head of Marketing for Germany and then Europe, and Gary had been a young and ambitious brand director after having been headhunted from BBH. Letting his business head take over, he decided to park that issue for the now. Let Lane and Calder do their investigation, see what they found and deal with the matter then.

Of more pressing importance, however, was the lack of bonus or dividend. Last year he had banked a combined six figures and he had been hoping for more of the same. In fact his own fee income had increased significantly on last year, so he would be aggrieved to get no bonus. The dividend was another matter; the firm was building for the future, so needs must on that front. That said, he suddenly felt anxious: the new kitchen was due to start in August, Molly's school fees would be due in early September and Emma's university accommodation would need paying then too. A quick calculation brought him to a total of seventy-three grand.

'Shit,' he mumbled. 'I will need to get creative to solve that little challenge.'

Julia Hillman, followed closely by her fiancé Lucas Hunt, arrived at the opulent offices of Trevellion & Co in the City of London just after midday. Dressed in a dark grey business suit, she looked like a city lawyer turning up for work. Lucas, on the other hand, looked like he had just been pulled through a bush backwards in his scruffy chinos and tweed jacket that had two buttons missing and the stains of a rushed breakfast down the front.

'I am here for a twelve o'clock meeting with Jonathan Trevellion,' she announced herself to one of the receptionists sitting behind a slab of marble that would have looked equally at home in a cathedral.

'Of course, can I have your names please?' smiled the immaculate girl from behind the desk and a pencil-slim computer screen.

'Julia Hillman and Lucas Hunt,' she stated, turning as if surprised that Lucas was still with her. The girl typed in both names before handing over two visitor passes in plastic wallets embossed with the law firm's logo.

'Please take a seat and I will let Mister Trevellion's office know that you have arrived,' suggested the girl, directing the couple to a bank of deep leather sofas that offered a panoramic view over the square mile that was reputed to be the hub of the great British economic revival.

Julia led them to a seat, seeming to notice Lucas's appearance for the first time.

'Jesus, Lucas, you might have smartened yourself up. You look like a hobo,' she began, trying to wipe the coffee and egg stains from the front of his jacket.

'Sorry, darling, but I have been up since four-thirty. I wanted to get into RCS and grab Gary before the day got underway,' replied Hunt sheepishly.

'What a bloody nightmare this is,' continued Hillman. 'Why did Father marry that bloody woman?' It was a question that Lucas had already heard a hundred times and he knew that he was not required to provide an answer.

Jonathan Trevellion had eighteen months until he left the firm and London for his retirement home in Provence and days like these made him delight in the prospect of his escape. Julia Hillman and her ageing fiancé sat opposite and he knew that the next hour or so was not going to be particularly pleasant.

Julia was his second cousin and to Jonathan, as to the rest of the family, her aggressive intellect and complete self-obsession were to be avoided at all costs, family weddings and funerals apart, of course.

A fourth-generation Trevellion lawyer, the firm had been founded by his great-grandfather William, who had gone on to achieve greatness as a cabinet minister in some long-gone Conservative government. He knew that he had not achieved the greatness that had been expected of him when he had left Cambridge with a First in Law. To Jonathan, that did not matter; his theatre work and playwriting were far more important than being a partner in one of the city's most revered legal firms. Indeed, two of his plays had reached the West End and achieved more than a modicum of critical and financial success. No, his average career as a lawyer was not something that kept him or his partner Rupert awake at night.

Dressed as always in his black Savile Row with its butcher-size pinstripes, pink shirt and green silk tie, he brought his concentration to bear on his cousin, lifted his large Mont Blanc and began taking notes on his yellow legal pad. With Julia's tirade almost at an end, he looked at Lucas, who merely shrugged his rounding shoulders and rolled his weary eyes at the lawyer.

'So, Jonathan, how soon until we can get my father out of police custody?'

'Well, that all now depends on a number of rather important issues,' he responded, dropping his expensive pen onto his notepad.

'Oh for God's sake, Jonathan, no need to be so bloody dramatic. What issues?'

'Well, Julia, to start we might do well to remember that your stepmother has lost her relatively young life,' continued Jonathan, trying to bring some sanity to his cousin's ranting.

'Of course, but surely we can get him out on bail. After all, he did walk in and admit his wrongdoing. Surely that must count for something?'

'Not until he has been formally charged and my understanding is that he is currently, on a voluntary basis, helping the police with their enquiries.'

'What if they charge him?'

'When that happens, we can apply for bail, but in the circumstances that application may be opposed.'

'Christ, what a mess,' concluded Hunt.

'Indeed,' agreed the lawyer, getting ready to wrap up the meeting. 'However, our criminal partner has been with your father and the police since ten o'clock and I expect that we shall have a full briefing on progress soon.'

'But what can we do to hurry things up?' implored Hillman impatiently.

'In unfortunate circumstances like these, Julia, I am afraid that things are not for hurrying. The police will want to complete their initial investigation, and procedures will need to be followed.'

'Oh for God's sake, man, there must be something we can do.'

'Patience and some decorum might be a good place to start,' suggested the lawyer, pushing back his chair, the meeting obviously over.

To the uninitiated, The Hempel Hotel in London's swish Notting Hill comes as something of an architectural surprise. Behind its traditional exterior, the interior is contrastingly minimalist by design; it takes some getting used to and whilst Gary had stayed at the place before, he still resented the surly nature of the service provided by the stick-like reception staff who, in their black Prada uniforms, preferred talking to one another rather than focusing on their guests.

Having had his credit card balance significantly reduced, he made his way to the elevator and took the contraption to the third floor, where despite the near darkness, he guided himself to his room using the lighted room numbers projected onto the dark wooden floor, and cracked the absurd entry system to let himself in.

'What a fucking ridiculous place this is,' he muttered to himself as he tried with some degree of difficulty to find the bathroom, which was concealed behind the same white panelling used to decorate the rest of the room. *Five hundred pounds for the night and you need to be able to read Braille before you can take a piss. This bloody woman better turn up!*

The liaison had been carefully planned. Gary would arrive by no later than 1.30pm and Tandy would get to the hotel around two after having had lunch with an old friend with whom she had told her husband she was staying the night. All a bit cloak and dagger, but to Gary it would be worth it; the woman was bloody gorgeous and with all the stress at the agency and with Vicki and the girls in Spain, a bout of illicit afternoon sex was something to look forward to. Stripping, he had a quick shower before pulling on some light jogging bottoms and a t-shirt, poured himself a glass of chilled Sauvignon Blanc, stuck his iPod in the player provided by the hotel and started to relax in anticipation of his guest's arrival.

He had known Tandy Brozek at a distance for a couple of years; had met her with her husband Tomas, who worked as a director of one of London's top soccer clubs, on a number of booze-filled occasions and no doubt like most men, found her to be very attractive but clearly out of bounds given how close she seemed to be to her partner. Two weeks earlier, however, he had attended a dinner party hosted by one of his clients and found himself sitting next to Tandy, who as the night had progressed, had become more and more amorous towards Gary, who although normally faithful to his wife, had occasionally slipped off the straight and narrow during his twenty-three-year marriage. One thing had led to another, cell phone numbers were exchanged and before either of them knew it, they had met for lunch three times and now planned to consummate their relationship in the big low bed at the Hempel.

He heard her shoes clicking on the dark wooden corridor before the buzzer echoed in the room, and rushing to open it, she stood before him in a light Burberry coat, high heels and exotic fishnets.

'Well, look at you all relaxed in your jogging gear.' She began leaning against the doorframe, a bottle of Möet & Chandon champagne in her right hand. 'Can I come in, or are you just about to go for a run?'

Gary laughed, a nervous, excited laugh. 'Of course you can come in.' He waved her in and for a moment she stood swaying slightly as she surveyed the room.

'Nice room, nice big bed, lovely man. I think I might stay.' And with that she undid her coat and slipped it off to reveal her near nakedness to a stunned but highly impressed Gary.

'You look nice, but how did you manage lunch dressed like that?'

'Oh, I didn't. I slipped my dress off in the cab.'

Seconds later, they were both on the bed, their tongues investigating each other's perfect teeth while Tandy removed Gary's jogging bottoms and he forgot all concerns about what might be going wrong with his business and instead indulged in an initial exploration of Tandy's magnificent body.

Later that evening, as Gary and Tandy ate a room service dinner in their near exhausted post-sex state in the Hempel Hotel, Colm Elliot, accompanied by Hannah Bellamy, formally charged Malcolm Hillman with the murder of his wife Anna. Hillman, who was seated next to his solicitor, a bright young criminal law partner from Trevellion, listened in silence as the charge was read out and he was then informed that he would appear before magistrates in the morning and that police would be opposing any bail application.

Hillman was then taken back to the cells as Colm Elliot made his escape for the evening to drive home for an early supper with his long-term partner Susan Lamont, at their small but stylish home in Northwood, Middlesex.

CHAPTER 3   WEDNESDAY 6 JULY 2005

Ruthven was shaving in the minimalist bathroom at the Hempel as Tandy lay sleeping on the low bed, half covered in a crumpled white bed sheet. On the flat-screen television, Lord Coe was delivering an impassioned speech littered with the word 'legacy' to the watching world, as an inspiring film which had been shown earlier was replayed on a large screen behind him. Though he would never admit it to anyone, Gary was moved to tears by the former Olympic champion's plea for the Games to be given to London. According to commentators, the final announcement would be made after midday UK time and Ruthven genuinely hoped that his adopted home city would be chosen. Before that, a number of rounds of voting would take place, with one of the potential host cities being eliminated at each stage.

His shave complete, he turned on the shower and before getting in, was joined by Tandy, who was obviously keen on some early morning exercise of the knee-trembling variety. Gary simply smiled and eased them both into the steaming glass compartment, not being one to look this particular gift horse in the mouth.

Just before 10.30am that morning, Malcolm Hillman appeared before a magistrate in London where, after a brief hearing at which he had merely confirmed his name, was formally committed to trial for the murder of his wife Anna Hillman. No plea was offered and Hillman was remanded in custody after an application for bail was refused after representations by his solicitor and the Crown Prosecution Service. Hillman was then taken by custody officers to a waiting van and was duly transferred to London's Wandsworth prison. His two daughters Helen and Julia were present at the hearing with their mother and Lucas Hunt, and by all accounts the solicitor representing Hillman then headed back towards his city office with his ears ringing after another Julia Hillman outburst that, amongst others, had contained the words 'incompetent bastard'.

The meeting at the Diageo offices in Henrietta Place had lasted slightly longer than Gary Ruthven had expected and he left the building into a cloudy central London with one of his account directors, Ian Blackwell, in something of a dash. Grabbing a taxi, they instructed the driver to get them as close to Trafalgar Square as possible, hoping to make it before the Olympic announcement was made.

'According to the news we have made it into the final two,' announced the cab driver as he hurried them along a busy Oxford Street.

'So it's now between us and the Frogs; hope we can beat them at this...' he continued.

'So do I,' agreed Gary, hoping that they would be there on time. As they travelled, he noticed people gathering outside pubs and bars, excited to hear the announcement.

Trafalgar Square was mobbed and partially closed to traffic, so Gary and Ian paid the driver and rushed towards a gathering throng of people. On the stage, a number of famous former athletes, including Steve Cram, and the double Olympic Gold medallist Kelly Holmes, mingled as they constantly cast their eyes towards the large screen onto which a series of pictures from the International Olympic Committee meeting in Singapore was being beamed. Thousands of people were now present and were angling for a closer view of the screen. Ruthven felt excited as he took in the scene, noticing Union Flag umbrellas and hundreds of flags and banners. To the right of the main stage, a large white sign simply said 'Thank You' and Ruthven hoped that this was not a bad omen – thanks but no thanks. The water fountains in the middle of the square had been switched off and at the back of the square a gantry held television crews getting ready to transmit pictures around the world.

'Christ, this is exciting,' announced Blackwell as he video-recorded the scene onto his mobile phone.

'It sure is.' And with that, a man that Gary knew to be Jacques Rogge, the President of the IOC, appeared on the large screen and began opening an envelope with the iconic Olympic rings on the front. Ripping it open, he drew out a card and began...

'The International Olympic Committee has the honour of announcing that the games of the thirtieth Olympiad in Two Thousand and Twelve are awarded to the city of... London."

All around them people burst into spontaneous cheering as they danced, hugged and kissed friends and strangers alike. The Olympic Summer Games were coming to the East End of London in seven years' time. For a bizarre moment Ruthven thought of Paris, the city that had just lost the vote. How flat would their gatherings be now?

For the next hour, Ruthven and Blackwell made their way on foot back to the offices of RuthvenCampbellStuart taking time to stop on the way for a glass of celebratory beer.

'What a fantastic day to be British and in London,' enthused Blackwell. 'Thanks for making us go to the Square, I would probably would have just headed back to the office and watched the announcement on television.'

'I know, but at least we can tell our grandchildren we were there when the announcement was made,' responded Ruthven.

'Let's all pray for three weeks of good weather in seven years' time.'

'Yeah, that and some British Gold medals,' Gary replied.

When they got to the office, the television in reception was on full volume and staff were watching the Olympic news with champagne flutes in their hands. The celebration had begun and they cheered the arrival of Ruthven and Blackwell. It was indeed, reflected Gary, a great day to be British and in London.

Colm Elliot was in the middle of preparing his detailed report for the Crown Prosecution Service on the Malcolm Hillman case when a member of his team opened his office door to tell him the news about the Olympics coming to London.

'Fantastic,' he smiled at the bearer of the good news. 'Now we will have every lunatic terrorist in the world thinking about the bloody mayhem they can bring to our city.' But with any luck he would be retired long before then. The door to his office closed quietly as the young detective constable left and Elliot returned to his paperwork, keen to get the thing finished before the day was out.

However, the terrorist thought would not leave his mind. Elliot had grown up in Northern Ireland and experienced some of the worst atrocities experienced in the United Kingdom. Indeed, it had been the bombing of the town centre in Omagh in 1998 and the deaths of twenty-nine people that had finally persuaded him to accept the offer of a promotion and move to London to join the Anti-Terrorist Squad. There, he worked for Ian Maitland, the then commander of the squad whom he had first met back in 1981 following an audacious attack on the government of Margaret Thatcher by a breakaway IRA faction. Ireland was more or less at peace these days, but since the 11

September 2001 attacks in New York and other al-Qaeda targets, a whole new terrorist ball game was in play, a game he was glad to be out of following his transfer, again on promotion, to the Metropolitan Police. Trying to focus his attention back on the Hillman report, he just hoped that in seven years' time, when the Olympics came to London, that the world would have become a better and safer place. Somehow, however, he doubted that very much. That said, he was forty-six years old and intended to retire at fifty, which would see him well gone from the force by the time the Olympics arrived.

That evening as Gary Ruthven took the Chiltern Line train from Marylebone to Beaconsfield, having decided to leave his car at the office after too much alcohol, he was still excited by what had happened in the city that day. As he read his *Evening Standard* newspaper, the headlines were all about the Olympics and the forthcoming G8 conference in Scotland. However, on page five he found a short report on the death of Anna Hillman and the subsequent arrest and charging of Malcolm Hillman. Clicking on his cell phone, he called Lucas to see how things were but only got a voicemail request to leave a message, which he did. Before switching his handset off, however, he received a rather saucy text message from Tandy, who was clearly anticipating a repeat of their sexual calisthenics at some point in the not too distant future.

The train took thirty minutes to reach Beaconsfield, a small Buckinghamshire town some twenty-five miles north-west of London, and Gary enjoyed the mid-evening walk to his family home via the local Waitrose store where he bought himself a fresh ready meal for his supper. As he walked, he began to rehearse for his meeting with David Lane in the morning, conscious that some serious decisions were going to have to be made about the business. He also began to concern himself again about the cost of the proposed kitchen refit that was due to start in August and where he was going to get the funds for his youngest daughter's school fess, not to mention Emma's university fees and accommodation charges. Smiling as he entered through his electric gates and headed towards the large house that he called home, he reflected on the last twenty-four hours with a mixture of naughty pleasure and guilt, despite the fact that he knew that he would have to see Tandy again sometime soon.

CHAPTER 4   THURSDAY 7 JULY 2005

Pencil Kane was cool, he always had been. At school he had been the good-looking and smart black guy who unlike most of his kin, stayed out of trouble and did his academic work both on time and to a very high standard. Ever since he could remember, he had always dressed really well, making sure that everything matched, was meticulously clean and pressed. For Pencil, the world was clear and easy to understand. He was smart, articulate and clever, and had been the best all-round sportsman his secondary school could ever remember. Yes, Pencil was sharp. In fact, Pencil was sharp even before he was called Pencil. In fact, Pencil was so sharp his friends told him he would probably one day cut himself.

At seventeen years old, he was now out of school with nine GCSE passes at A-grade to his name and according to people who knew about things, Pencil Kane had the world at his feet, quite literally. Because despite all of his academic prowess Pencil Kane was going to be a football star and had already made his debut in the Premier League, the third youngest player to do so and the youngest for the London club who now paid him six thousand pounds a week with the promise of a new and more lucrative contract on the way when he reached his eighteenth birthday in September. Yes, Pencil had it made, and Pencil was already famous.

Despite everything though, Pencil did not take himself too seriously. Not for him the big flashy cars with the blacked-out windows and loud blaring music; not for him the Rolex watches and the other stuff that he saw the young guys at his club getting up to. No, Pencil had his feet on the ground and could tell you, to an accuracy of plus or minus ten pounds, how much he had in his two bank accounts. No, Pencil was sharp and Pencil was going to be rich beyond his wildest dreams. In fact, he had calculated how much money he would gross if he just managed to be a Premier League footballer until he was thirty-two years old, in fifteen years' time. And it was a lot of money and he intended to invest it wisely and become rich. Yes, Pencil had read about the great players of the past – George Best, with his talent and looks and alcohol problem who had died a broken man before he was sixty; Paul Gascoigne, the England World Cup star who now cut a sad and lonely figure and followed rock bands in an alcoholic daze. No, Pencil was not going to drink booze, Pencil was not going to waste his cash, Pencil was going to give his talent every chance. Pencil was going to be as good as he could be.

Entering the Underground, his music playing gently in his ears, Pencil boarded the next train, excited to be meeting his recently appointed agent Paul Ruthven to discuss his new Nike contract. Who would believe it? Nike were going to pay Pencil Kane a big amount of wonga to wear their football boots and trainers.

Paul was not like a lot of the other agents. Paul had been a good player himself, even played for Scotland and Liverpool, and he knew what was best for his young client. Pencil was happy with Paul Ruthven, knew that he would learn what was right from the guy. Pencil Kane would be a hard-working talent and be as good as he could be.

Just then, however, Pencil Kane's world went dark. Pencil Kane's life changed forever as the first explosion ripped through the Underground carriage, knocking him off his seat and into a deep and very dark oblivion.

In his office early to prepare for his 10am meeting with David Lane, Gary could not help but notice the worry on his PA Jenny's face when she knocked on his opened office door and entered to stand in front of his designer glass-topped desk.

'The BBC are beginning to get worked up about a series of incidents on the Underground, looks like it might be a terror attack,' she interrupted him gently.

Rising to follow her from the room, he joined a number of others in front of the television screen where only yesterday they had been celebrating the Olympic announcement.

'Has everyone who is supposed to be here today arrived?' asked Ruthven calmly.

'Only David Lane has yet to arrive,' announced Jenny.

'See if you can get him on his mobile,' suggested Ruthven, a sinking feeling forming in his belly. What the fuck was going on?

Susan Lamont had once been the victim of terrorist activity; a long time ago, her then lover had been assassinated at the hands of the Provisional IRA. Although over the death by now, she still could not but be drawn to the story as it was unfolding on the BBC that morning. Walking through to the main bedroom, she shook Colm Elliot awake suggesting he would want to see the news. Another scarred by the IRA, Colm dragged himself from the bed. He was due in Marylebone in the afternoon and had been catching up on much needed sleep.

The news programme was informing the world that up to six explosions had now been reported with significant casualties being taken to numerous London hospitals. Five explosions had been triggered on the Underground and one on a London Transport bus in Tavistock Square.

'Fuck, fuck, fuck,' began Elliot realizing that he would be needed in London. 'I thought I would be long gone before this happened again in London.'

'Who do you think...'

'Suicide bombers, probably al-Qaeda; timed to perfection with the G8 and the Olympic announcement – maximum publicity. Fuck, fuck, I better get dressed.'

Susan crossed the room and they embraced, a warm tight hug of people who had seen the dark and devastating effects of terrorism on innocent people.

David Lane was not happy to be back living in the United Kingdom, was unimpressed by what had happened in the ten years he had lived in the USA, and generally could not understand what had happened to society and the general behaviour of people. Everywhere he went he felt like he was confronted with rudeness and loutish behaviour, from road rage drivers, to drunken soccer fans, to the newly titled ladettes. It was getting worse and he craved for his house in France and his beloved golf course at Pont Royale.

Returning to the UK, at least part-time, had been his wife's idea, as she wanted to be closer to their two grandchildren. However, no sooner had they bought their home in Windsor than their only son Mark and his wife had announced that they were moving to Brussels to take up a promotion with the logistics company that Mark worked for.

Lane had found the situation infuriating but by the time of his son's promotion, had got himself involved in two small and relatively new companies as an adviser and an investor.

One of those companies was RuthvenCampbellStuart and Lane was enjoying the challenge of working with Gary, whom he had met via Lucas Hunt. That morning, however, he knew that he was in for a hard time as Gary seemed less than pleased with the Hamburg issue when it had come up at the auditor meeting the day before. He was also grappling with what to do about his boss's bonus for the year. Ruthven's performance in fee creation had been outstanding and he had beaten his annual target. He would need to get something, as the last thing the firm needed was a demotivated Gary. Without Gary on his game, RCS would not stand a chance. At least not until the business expansion was well progressed. No, he would have to find a way of getting a bonus past the Board for his boss.

Arriving in London by train from Marlow, he knew immediately that something was not right; panic seemed to be etched on the faces of everyone he saw – what was going on? Flipping open his cell phone he called his wife in Windsor to see if there was anything on the news, but she did not answer his call. He then tried Lucas Hunt, but that call went straight to voicemail. Next, he called Jenny at RCS, to be shocked by what was unfolding in London. He was right, the bloody country was in total decline.

Rushing outside to the taxi cab rank, he wished that he had not had as many gin and tonics last evening, conscious that he was still drinking too much, despite his doctor's warning that he needed to cut down. That said, he didn't really care. He was old and grey and as a handsome man all his life, now noticed that fewer, if any, women paid him much attention these days. Not that he couldn't still perform in the bedroom department, it was just a fact that the same opportunities did not arise anymore. What made it worse was at RCS he could not help noticing how all the good-looking women paid attention to Gary and basically ignored him, despite his shareholding and seniority. No, for David Lane life back in England was not great, and now there were no fucking taxi cabs to be had. Shit, he was going to be late for Gary and he could feel his blood temperature rising as he headed off on foot, sweat already forming on his forehead.

On the day of the infamous 9/11 terrorist attacks in the US, Paul Ruthven had been in a specialist clinic in central London being told that his soccer career was over. Mr Bryan Jones had broken the news to him in a cold, matter-of-fact manner that Paul had appreciated; his cruciate knee ligaments were not going to repair well enough for him to compete in the cut and thrust of the English Premier League. At the age of thirty-four, he was being advised to accept his substantial insurance payout and start planning for his future away from playing.

The terrorist attack unfolding in London that morning was bringing that same sinking feeling to the pit of his stomach, and he was not sure how to react. His first thought was of Pencil Kane, who was now late for their meeting regarding his Nike contract. Then he thought of his brother Gary and made a quick call to RCS to discover he was safely at work.

Unlike his older brother Gary, Paul had never been married; had never felt the need to settle down and have children with any of the many women he had been in a relationship with. He now lived, mostly alone, in London, in an apartment paid for with his football earnings and insurance pay-off, and next year as he reached forty, he would be able to start drawing down his healthy pension. Unlike Gary, he had no kitchen remodel to worry about, no school fees to find, no university costs to keep him awake at night. Indeed, worry was not an experience that Paul Ruthven was really familiar with. As Gary's wife Vicki often said, Paul did not do worry. In addition, his new career as an independent agent to emerging young soccer players was going well. He seemed to be able to relate to the players as well as the clubs involved, who seemed to like, trust and respect Paul as one of their own. The money was also good, and on his brother's advice, he too had employed Kate Ross to manage his money and advise him on his new business venture.

Paul had grown up in East Lothian with his mum, dad and big brother in the village of Dirleton. The family home, which was on the village green and overlooked by the historic Dirleton Castle, was middle class and comfortable and his only real challenge in his young life was living in the shadow of his smart and academically gifted elder brother. At school, he was used to people saying that he was good, but not quite as good as Gary. And then he had discovered football, and from a very young age, people began to talk of Paul as someone 'who could go all the way' in the sport. At eleven, he was picked for his county, and the following year he was recruited to join one of the two Edinburgh professional clubs, Hibernian, on schoolboy terms.

For Paul's dad, a moderately successful local solicitor, Paul's football was a worry, as he could not see it bringing him the sort of career that he had imagined for his young sons. However, he did recognize that from an early age his younger son did seem to have the focus and dedication that would be necessary to bring success in any career, so with some degree of reluctance, he committed to support Paul in his soccer in the same way he was supporting Gary in his academic work.

At school, Paul achieved modest success in his academic work, but by the time Gary was heading off to Edinburgh University to study English, Paul had gone full-time with Hibernian and had represented Scotland at every level from schoolboy to under-18 and was fast building a national reputation as an excellent attacking full-back. But Scotland was not where the young Ruthven was setting his sights; from a young age he had been a big fan of the English League, where the clubs were bigger, the rewards greater and the demand for Scottish talent was still strong. So, with barely fifty first team appearances at Hibernian under his belt, Paul Ruthven moved south to join London club West Ham United and quickly established himself in England's top division. Three seasons later, he was transferred to Liverpool for a then record fee for a British full-back and his climb to the top of British football was complete. Ten years later, and with forty appearances for his home country at international level under his very successful belt, came the injury that was to put a premature end to his football career. He moved back to London and after a short period of rehabilitation, during which time he lived with Gary and Vicki in Beaconsfield, Paul bought himself an apartment in central London and went about planning the next stages of his career with the same focus and dedication that had been the hallmark of his playing career.

A period followed when he tried his hand at television punditry, but he grew restless with the hanging about that seemed a big part of television life; he got involved in journalism, but didn't feel like he had the talent for it; he studied for his football coaching badges and enjoyed working with young kids, but had no desire to coach professionally, although this involvement got him intrigued by the world of representation and agent work. This led to a short spell with one of the larger sports management firms, but his purpose for working there was clear to him. He was there to learn how the industry worked, to establish his network before moving on to work as an independent, and represent up and coming talent, bringing his own experience to bear on the profession. In early 2004, less than three years after the end of his own playing career, and with the support of Gary and Kate Ross, Paul Ruthven opened his own agency and began the slow process of garnering young talent to his firm. In the eighteen months he had been in business, he now had ten young players on his books as clients and perhaps his prize acquisition to date had been the rising young Arsenal star Pencil Kane. Paul loved Pencil; the boy's focus reminded Paul of his own levels of dedication and commitment. He was in no doubt that with the right coaching and representation, Pencil would go on to play for England, perhaps in the not too distant future. Getting Nike hooked had been a breeze, and he was in no doubt that Kane's salary would be significantly lifted when his eighteenth birthday arrived later in the year.

But for now, the young man was late – very late. He had obviously been caught up in the chaos and panic that was now spreading across London that morning. Trying his cell phone again, the system seemed to be down. That sinking feeling was nagging again at Paul, but there was no need to panic, the young man would be there soon.

By eleven that morning, London was close to a complete meltdown. Public transport was halted, cell phone services were unavailable and confusion was rife as to what had actually happened. Gradually, television news bulletins began to piece together the events that had taken place, and similar to the 9/11 attacks in the USA in 2001, there was real fear among government officials that the UK was under a severe terrorist attack. The unbridled joy of the day before when the summer Olympic announcement was made had been replaced by a sense of shock and outrage across the country in general and the capital in particular.

For Julia Hillman, however, it was just another pain in the arse as her plan to visit her father in prison was totally compromised. With Lucas in tow, she had chosen to ignore all advice not to travel and set out for Wandsworth in their somewhat aging BMW. However, by the time they reached the notorious city orbital that was the M25, it was clear that the traffic was not going to be flowing in their favour.

'Jesus, Lucas, we are never going to get there on time,' she began, and as was his role, Hunt could only try to pacify the woman he was due to marry in September.

'Don't panic, honey. London has been thrown into disarray this morning.'

'Disarray my arse! What this country needs is more of the spirit we had during the war. Christ, how would Hitler have failed if five or six little explosions had been able to bring the country to its knees?' continued Hillman, as she accelerated the car every minute or so into any ten yards of space that opened in front of them.

'Would you like me to drive, honey?' offered Lucas, concerned at the damage she might be doing to the car.

'Don't be a dopey fuck, Lucas. You know I am a better driver than you.'

'Okay, honey. Just trying to help.'

'Well, you're not. Why didn't we get the radio fixed? We could end up sitting here for days at this rate. Try your mobile again, maybe you can get a signal.'

Lucas tried his phone, but the network was still not responding. How had his life come to this? He would be seventy next June and his plan for a peaceful retirement with his second wife Cathy had disappeared three years earlier when she had gone for a girly break in Tunisia with two fellow doctors and had not returned for three months after falling for a Tunisian waiter. When she had come home it was to demand a divorce from Lucas and an equal share of his hard-earned retirement plan. After months of legal wrangling, Cathy had flown back to Tunis with seventy percent of their marriage cash, leaving Lucas with the other thirty percent, minus legal costs, and a bunch of shares in his former business that eventually turned out not to be worth the heavy duty paper that they were printed on. He had bought a small house in a rather shabby part of Tufnell Park and at the age of sixty-six, had set about finding himself a job that would help him keep the wolves from his door. Eventually, that had led him to the role of Chairman at RCS, working with Gary Ruthven, who had long admired some of the communications work that Hunt's company had done for him when he had been with Guinness. Initially, the work with RCS had gone well, but on his way back from a visit to a family friend in Hong Kong, Lucas had been taken very unwell with an aneurysm and fallen into the unusually helpful arms of Julia Hillman, a woman half his age, who saw him safely home and who, surprisingly to Lucas, took a continued shine to him after he was released from hospital.

Indeed, Hillman was also at a hiatus in her life, having just left a job in the city to take some time out and enjoy some of her hard-earned bonus. A round-the-world trip had followed and Hong Kong was her final stop before she was due to return to her home in West Sussex. If the trip had not been all that she had hoped for in terms of relaxation, the one thing that it had done for her was highlight the fact that she was broody for a child. However, given her nature, she had not been too successful thus far with the men in her life. True, she was not too bad to look at, and her crown jewel of a chest always ensured attention, but she knew in herself that she would always be difficult to live with. No, what she needed was a man who could donate some sperm and do, more or less, what Julia Hillman wanted, so that she could, in turn, get on with what she wanted to do. So, when the somewhat frayed but nevertheless debonair Lucas Hunt arrived somewhat fortuitously in her life, there was little chance that Julia was going to let him escape. Not that Hunt, who could not believe his luck and who had always been attracted to strong women, was even thinking about escape.

After an hour of tediously slow progress on the M25, Hunt and Hillman decided reluctantly to abort their planned visit to Wandsworth to see her father. But that was not before Lucas was bombarded with another tirade about the lack of justice in her father being locked in prison, and all because he had married that bloody awful woman. Hunt felt it prudent not to mention that was not the reason for his detention.

'Okay, let's map out the options,' suggested Gary Ruthven to David Lane.

'As far as I can see there are two or three,' began Lane,

standing at a flip chart with a smelly purple marker pen at the ready in his hand.

'Write them down then, David.'

'Firstly, we could extend the company overdraft with Barclays.' Lane simply jotted 'Overdraft extension' on the flip. 'Secondly, we could apply for a government loan scheme award via Barclays.' This was also jotted in shorthand.

'Thirdly?' prompted Ruthven.

'Thirdly, we could raise more capital in a share offer.'

'Any more?'

'Well, we could stop our expansion plan and focus on building what we have.'

'Okay, let's look at the pros and cons of those you have written up.'

'Well, we could get the overdraft. I have already had an initial off-the-record chat with the bank, the downside being that they would require security.'

'Property?' asked Ruthven.

'Yes, and your house is their preferred option.'

'Okay. Government loan?'

'That is doable, but a bit more complicated regarding terms,' continued Lane, who had obviously been doing his homework.

'Such as?'

'Well, for example, the scheme would look to security from married shareholders, so you and Vicki would be in line for that,' replied Lane.

'Unless Vicki were to transfer her shares to me before we applied,' suggested Ruthven.

'An option,' conceded Lane.

'Okay. Share offer?'

'Well, I would be prepared to buy more shares, and perhaps Lucas as well.'

'Lucas? I didn't think he had a pot to piss in,' queried Gary.

'Well, Julia has some cash, so it might be a possibility.'

'Not sure I would want the money that much, and wouldn't any share sale mean that any cash raised would belong to Vicki and me?'

'Sure, but you could lend it back to the company on to-be-agreed terms,' suggested Lane.

'Fine, so what about stopping the expansion plan?'

'We could do that, but we would still have to raise some capital to support what we have already committed to,' Lane offered.

'Yes, but we could do that through a share sale; keep it in the family as it were.'

'True, and if we needed say half what Kate Ross suggested, then that might be the answer.'

'Let's sleep on this until tomorrow, although you should be aware that I am not keen on providing more security. In fact, let me be clearer, I am not going to attach more to my house. Not that Vicki would agree to that in any event.'

'I understand that, so we are tending to favour slowing down the expansion plan and raising more cash via a share sale,' summarized Lane.

'Let's sleep on it. I need to get my head round it, and as I said, I am not keen on having Julia bloody Hillman as a shareholder,' concluded Ruthven.

Just then Jenny entered the room to tell them that the Prime Minister was about to appear on television to provide an update on the day's atrocities in London. Their meeting over, Lane and Ruthven joined the others, for the second day running, in front of the television screen in the RCS reception area.

With the television news confirming that London was going to be gridlocked well into the evening, Gary called his brother and made arrangements to stay the night with Paul at his apartment. He then called his family in Spain and updated them as best as he could on the situation in London. Vicki and the girls were clearly distraught from the images that they had managed to watch via Sky television and were keen for Gary to get out of the UK and join them in the relative safety of southern Andalucia. Having placated his family he called his parents in Scotland before spending the remainder of the afternoon working on an updated proposal for Levi's in Brussels whilst intermittently checking the television for any more news on the terrorist attack.

At six o'clock, he left the office to join the throngs of people slowly making their way through the London streets without the use of public transport despite the fact that some buses now seemed to be running again. Gary could sense the tension in people that he passed and was aware of the fact that he himself was being particularly diligent when in close proximity of young Asian men carrying backpacks. He was also conscious of how alert his senses were to the noises around him as he walked. For example, the amplified and strange ticking sounds that parked cars along his route seemed to be making, sounds he had never previously noticed, his senses heightened by the shock of the day. *Christ*, he thought to himself, *will I ever be able or indeed willing to travel on the Underground again?*

Although still shocked by the day and the somewhat perverted feeling of being part of a dark day in the history of London, his mind also replayed the meeting he had had earlier with David Lane. For the first time, he could feel himself doubting the wisdom of embarking on the growth strategy, of bringing in Lane and his money to the company. Life had certainly been a lot easier before his arrival, and what the man knew about the industry was a lot less than Ruthven had originally thought. For sure, the company could not have been allowed to stand still – what company ever did successfully? But with Lane and Hunt as his main advisers, was the business in the safe hands he needed it to be? Two things that he was certain about were the fact that he would not add any more security to his home, and nor would he allow Julia Hillman to become a shareholder in the company. Anyway, with her father now facing a murder rap, it was unlikely that she or Lucas would be in the frame of mind to discuss that option anytime soon.

The walk to Paul's apartment, which was just off Marylebone High Street, took him less than thirty minutes and when he got there, there was no reply from the apartment intercom. He therefore retrieved a key from the man in the foyer and made his way to his brother's home on the fourth floor. On entering, he found a note from Paul informing that he gone to the hospital to see one of his clients who had been injured in one of the blasts that morning. *Shit*, thought Gary, *this thing has been too close for comfort*. Removing his jacket, he dumped it along with his bag in the spare bedroom and went to the kitchen and searched the television channels hungrily for more updated information.

From the BBC, he was able to put together a fairly clear picture of what had happened that morning. The first bomb had exploded on an eastbound Circle Line train travelling between Liverpool Street and Aldgate at 8.50 and the next two explosions had ignited within the next fifty seconds. The second bomb had exploded in the second carriage of a westbound Circle Line train as it was leaving Edgware Road and headed towards Paddington and that explosion had seemingly damaged another, eastbound train, as it approached platform 3 at Edgware Road. The third bomb exploded on a southbound Piccadilly Line train travelling between King's Cross St. Pancras and Russell Square. Exact details of deaths and casualties were still not clear although at least forty people were known to be dead and many hundreds injured and taken to various hospitals around the city. A further explosion occurred in Tavistock Square on a double-decker bus travelling its route from Marble Arch to Hackney Wick. That explosion had ripped the roof off the top deck of the vehicle and destroyed the back of the bus. According to the BBC, eyewitnesses reported seeing 'half a bus flying through the air'. That particular detonation took place close to the British Medical Association building in Upper Woburn Place, and a number of doctors in or near the building were reportedly able to provide immediate medical assistance at the scene.

Gary felt morbidly fascinated by the details being reported and watched as the Metropolitan Police Commissioner Sir Ian Blair stated that the terrorist attack had been perpetrated by four apparent suicide bombers who had been working as a unit, having travelled into London that morning. Initial reports suggesting that there had been six rather than three explosions on the Underground were understood to have been considered because the trains had been damaged between stations, causing wounded to emerge from different exits, giving the impression that there had been incidents at both stations. Gary made himself some toast and a mug of tea and reflected on the scale of the attacks, wondering as he ate what it took to convince four people to carry out such horrible acts and what was so wrong in their existence that they would willingly sacrifice their own lives? An anger coupled with deep confusion swept over him as he got lost in his own thoughts and awaited the arrival of his brother.

Just then, Paul Ruthven strode purposefully out of the main doors of the Whitechapel hospital in east central London. Shocked and sickened by what he had just seen, he needed to get home and to start making plans for his young client. Pencil Kane had been travelling to Russell Square and his meeting with Paul when a bomb exploded in the carriage in front of the one he was travelling in. Pencil had and would survive, but had suffered major damage to his right foot and some minor injuries to his left. His mother and sister were still by his bedside and it would be some time before doctors could assess the long-term extent of his injuries. However, one very kind and gentle young female medic had privately indicated to Paul that Pencil Kane would in all probability no longer be heading for a stellar career in professional football. That, thought Paul as he headed towards his parked car and driver, was going to be the least of the young man's worries. First though, he needed to liaise with the people at Pencil's club and make sure that the boy received the best care and treatment possible. Then there would be the challenge of rebuilding him psychologically. One minute he had literally had the world at his feet, the next he was lucky still to have feet. Fucking hell, why had he not sent his driver to pick him up? Why had they not arranged the meeting for tomorrow? Shit, thousands of people across London would be asking themselves similar questions and blaming themselves in some way for the carnage and damage to loved ones and friends.

Reaching the car, Paul opened the door and slumped into the passenger seat of the Mercedes. Jorge, the Portuguese driver normally assigned to him by the car firm, looked at him with raised eyebrows.

'It does not look too good, Jorge,' sighed Paul as the car pulled gently away from the parking slot in the lane it had been waiting in for the last three hours.

'How is he?'

'He will survive, but he has severe injuries to his lower legs and feet. We will know more tomorrow.'

'Ah, that is so sad. I am sorry, Mister Paul. What comes of this world?'

'That is a great question, Jorge. A great question,' reflected Paul as his mobile telephone sparked surprisingly to life, the network having been severely disrupted for most of the day.

'This is Paul,' opened Ruthven, not recognising the caller's number. It was Arsenal's head coach, a well regarded and highly successful Frenchman with a rare reputation for sophisticated thinking and leading edge approach to his job. Paul updated him and they agreed to meet in the morning and visit Pencil together. After another brief reflection on what the world was coming to, the call ended, leaving Paul to travel in silence with his sad thoughts.

Whitechapel had been like a war zone, which perhaps was what it was, and during his time there, Paul must have seen close to a hundred injured people being brought in or moved around. Some had minor cuts and abrasions, others would be in hospital for months, rebuilding their bodies and their lives after the trauma of the day.

Arriving near his apartment, he got dropped off in Marylebone High Street and went to a Sainsbury's to pick up something for his supper with Gary who would be wondering where the hell he was. When he reached his home, his brother was talking to their parents on the telephone, doing his best to reassure them that they were both safe. Opening himself a bottle of beer from the fridge, he took the proffered telephone from Gary and did his best to calm his mother, who like most mothers had no doubt been imagining all sorts of things throughout the day when the only news on the bombings had been available via radio and television.

Across London in one of three major incident rooms set up in New Scotland Yard, Colm Elliot sat with thirty or so other senior officers awaiting the arrival of the Met Commissioner and the latest update and briefing. As expected, Elliot had been taken off his existing cases and attached to the Met response team dealing with the terrorist attack. His previous experience in Northern Ireland and within the Anti-Terrorist Squad meant that he was considered a key contributor to this new investigation. That said, Elliot had made it clear that he did not want to be put on this particular detail for any longer than necessary, and it was agreed that his contribution would be for the first few days only.

As he waited, he listened to the chatter going on around him, chatter which ranged from genuine concern for the future of

Britain to the sadly normal calls for all foreigners to be shipped back to where they belonged. Elliot had heard it all before, the racism, the nationalist jingoism, the fury at government interference, to the downright ignorant calls for what amounted to nothing short of ethnic cleansing in the ghettos of the UK's largest cities. Despite his personal opposition to most of the claims, he did feel a certain sympathy for the men and women sitting around him. At the end of every atrocity, it was people like these who had to deal with the aftermath; it was them who had to face the abuse that they would get in the press for not keeping the country safe; it was them who would be accused of heavy-handed policing when going into the streets to investigate the cells who plotted their campaigns.

His personal reflections on the day seemed to keep coming up with the same word, and that word was tolerance. Tolerance had perhaps become the greatest British malaise; London was described by many as the most tolerant city in the world from a racial integration perspective, but how many British people really understood what they were being tolerant of? How many really knew what was going on in the communities that were building up across the country? How could it be right that in major towns and cities such as Bradford, the Asian community accounted for some eighty percent of the population and of that eighty percent reports suggested that fifty percent did not speak English? To Elliot, this day was potentially a major turning point for the country. Perhaps now people might pay attention to the underlying problems associated with this rather lazy British approach and tolerance. An opportunity for politicians to start asking the right questions; to try and understand what causes young Asian men to leave their loved ones, travel into London and blow themselves and hundreds of others up on an Underground train or on a bus full of people going about their normal daily business.

A stir at the front of the room brought him back from his reverie. The commissioner and a couple of his senior cohorts had arrived and the briefing was about to commence. *This should be good*, thought Elliot, drifting for a moment back to his investigation of Malcolm Hillman and the killing of his young wife. What possessed a man to suffocate his wife and then go to work? *Jesus*, he smiled wryly to himself, *the human race really is fucked up.*

CHAPTER 5   FRIDAY 8 JULY 2005

Pencil Kane was not playing nearly as well as Pencil had come to expect. In fact, he was having real difficulty in getting into the pace of the game; it was frustratingly passing him by. No matter what he tried, the ball seemed to elude him, causing him to experience a real feeling of panic. Why could he not get on the ball; influence the play in the way he normally could? Then Pencil relaxed – it was just a dream. Yes, he had been asleep and dreaming. Then Pencil Kane began to panic – where was he sleeping? His last memory was of being on the train to meet Paul Ruthven. Then there was nothing. Why was Pencil no longer in control?

Opening his eyes, he realised that he was in a hospital somewhere, the sights and sounds familiar from that *Casualty* programme on the television. From outside he could hear the sirens as ambulances brought more people to the hospital. But why was he here? Then he remembered – the blast, the wind, the sudden darkness. Pencil realised that he had probably been involved in a train crash. Yes, that was it. His Underground train had been in a crash and he was now in hospital.

Then Pencil started to panic again. If he was in a hospital bed he must be injured, so raising his head he was relieved to see his hands lying by his side with a drip attached to the back of his right hand, a yellow-looking fluid coming from a bottle hanging above his bed. Looking further down, he could see his feet under the sheets and he could feel his toes move as he instructed them. Pencil relaxed. Whatever had happened, he was going to be okay. Pencil had just had a minor mishap on his way to international stardom. Pencil was good.

Just then a young nurse appeared by his bed and smiling asked him how he was. Pencil replied that he was good, returned her smile and fell back into a deep sleep, hoping that in his dream, he could get the ball and start to influence the game.

Gary, wearing one of his brother's shirts, which was sadly a little tight around the waist, was walking toward his company office with many thoughts swirling around in his active brain. He had never been jealous in any way of Paul's sporting success, quite the opposite in fact; he was as proud as any brother could be of what Paul had achieved in his career, and in many ways how Paul led his life. For example, Paul managed his finances better than Gary had ever done, his mantra being 'spend today's money tomorrow', which was in many ways opposite to the way Gary and Vicki led their lives. No, they were like the rest of the world, spending tomorrow's money today. That was one of the reasons he was getting so worked up at the prospect of no bonus money – that money was accounted for. God alone knew how much Paul had stashed away from his career and it was not a topic they discussed, but he could guess that it was well into a couple of million at least. He also had no mortgage on his apartment and that had got to be worth another million and a half, minimum. *Christ*, he thought, *why was I not as careful with my money?* He could and did earn a small fortune, but his family lifestyle was very expensive and if anything went wrong with the business, it would not take long for his house of cards to crumble. Aware of his growing financial anxiety, he decided that he needed a plan and committed to call Kate Ross that morning, to see if she was free for lunch so that they could start developing a way forward that would put himself and his family on more secure footing.

His thoughts then turned to his personal client list. In no particular order of importance he began reviewing their current status. At Levi's, he was working with the European Brand President on the impending launch of a new and exciting vintage jean. Levi's would always keep BBH as their main agency, but they regarded RCS well enough to entrust them with a few exciting new product launches. At Diageo, some of his old colleagues still felt loyalty to Gary, and he was enjoying a project with them that was concerned with the concept of sensible drinking; a company with many of the world's leading alcohol brands encouraging consumers to manage consumption was both counterintuitive and business smart. In New York, he was assisting the new CEO at a company owned by the Dell family, to work on its market positioning prior to international launch, and at the BBC in London, he was working on a campaign aimed at maximizing the potential of a significant joint venture in movie making. Add to that a couple of smaller projects and it was clear that his client plate was pretty full and very rewarding. It was the running of the business that was getting him down, taking up too much time, and as he walked he realized, perhaps for the first time, that he might need to make a decision soon regarding where he wanted to focus his time and attention.

Today would be better though. His Creative Director, Carole King, was due back from vacation. Carole always returned from a break on a Friday, her logic being that her last weekend away was always ruined by her worrying about what might be awaiting her return to the office. So, by coming back on a Friday, she could find out and therefore enjoy her last weekend to the full. In secret, Carole was the love of Gary's life. She was his closest friend – beautiful, talented and in truth, his soulmate.

They had met at BBH, and she had worked with him ever

since, following him firstly to Guinness, and then to RCS, as his Creative Director. That said, their relationship was, and he suspected always would be, totally platonic. Despite the fact that he loved her dearly, and she him, his loyalty to Vicki and the girls had always meant that he and Carole could get no closer than they were. This was because Gary knew that if he embarked on an affair with Carole it would end his marriage. They had simply come into each other's lives at the wrong time. Indeed, Carole had now made matters more final by going off and getting married herself. Two years earlier, she had met and quickly married Dan Jenner, a very wealthy mobile phone guru, who was seventeen years her senior and who was now enjoying his hard-earned fortune in semi-retirement. As far as Gary was aware, no children were planned and the couple lived a very comfortable life in Holland Park. That said, since the whirlwind romance and marriage nothing had changed between Carole and Gary in any way. They were as close as ever, and Gary probably knew that if he ended his marriage tomorrow and declared his undying love for Carole, then she would almost certainly leave Dan to be with Gary. She knew about his occasional flings of course and mildly rebuked him for straying when he did, but leaving Vicki was not part of the plan, and Gary was just really excited to have his best friend back in the office from vacation.

Approaching the office, his final thought turned to yesterday's horrors in London and to the sadness he felt for Pencil Kane. He had met Pencil on many occasions and liked him a lot, expecting great success to come the young man's way. But that all now looked to be at an end, destroyed by fanatics on the Underground. Tears welled in his eyes as he entered his building and waited for the elevator to take him up to his office.

Unshaven and looking positively dishevelled, Malcolm Hillman sat opposite his two daughters in one of the visitors' areas in

Wandsworth Prison. With tears in his eyes and having obvious difficulty speaking, he listened as his elder daughter Julia outlined plans for a reapplication for bail.

'It is simply unacceptable that they are keeping you in this place.' She looked at her sister for support and getting little reaction continued. 'And I have told Jonathan that he better find us another lawyer or we will be taking our business elsewhere. I have rarely witnessed incompetence like it.'

'Julia,' interrupted her father, finally clearing the emotion from his throat. 'I don't want bail just yet.'

'What? Honestly, Father, you've totally lost your marbles. We need to get you out and start working on your defence as soon as practicably possible for Christ's sake.'

'No, I have people that I need to see, psychiatrists and doctors. What I have done does not make any rational sense,' continued Hillman softly.

'Exactly my point. You must have had some sort of breakdown,' pushed his daughter.

'Julia, I killed my lovely wife. I need help to find out why, so for once in your bloody life listen to what I am saying.' Hillman looked around to check who might be listening before continuing. 'I do not want to reapply for bail until I have spoken to doctors and started to make some sense of this horribly sad situation. Do I make myself clear?'

Julia Hillman looked at her sister, Helen, then back at her father. She was not used to not getting her own way on things.

'Okay, Father. If that is your express wish, then so be it. But you are making another stupid mistake.' And with that she pushed back the metal chair she had been perched on and stood up, the visit with her father clearly being brought to an end.

'We will let Jonathan know; tell him to hold back until you are ready.' Her father and sister both stood and after brief embraces, Julia left with her sister, an anger welling inside her that she would have to vent on someone.

Watching his daughters leave, Malcolm Hillman was led wearily back to his cell and his thoughts – thoughts that made no sense, a sense of desolation, sadness and shock having overwhelmed him.

Outside the prison, Lucas came towards the sisters.

'How did it go? How was Malcolm?' he began nervously.

'Oh, he was fucking fabulous, Lucas, on top of the world. How do you think he was, you stupid man?' Julia responded, having found the ideal person to vent her anger on.

Paul Ruthven and the Arsenal head coach sat in a small room listening intently to the young surgeon as she described the extent of Pencil Kane's injuries. The pair had met up in Paul's office and had travelled together to the hospital, both shocked by what had happened to London in general and to Pencil in particular.

Despite the fact that Pencil had survived the blast in much better shape than many others, the doctor was less than optimistic about the long-term likelihood of him making a full recovery.

'In many ways, the boy has been very lucky,' she continued, clipping an X-ray image onto a lighted screen on the wall in front of them. 'To begin, he is still alive. However, he did suffer a high impact trauma to his right foot, causing dislocation between the heel bone and this smaller bone in the foot.' The doctor pointed to the damage on the screen. 'This needed surgery, and the insertion of a screw. He will be in plaster for at least six weeks and will then need significant physio before we will be able to tell how good the recovery might be.' She stopped as if to invite questions.

'What about his other foot?' asked the Arsenal coach, his face ashen.

'Suffered a minor fracture of his long bone, but that didn't need surgery and should heal okay.' She smiled, indicating that that, at least, was positive.

'Long-term prognosis regarding the right foot?' Paul plucked up the courage to ask.

'At best eighty-twenty against him resuming his career,' suggested the doctor, before continuing, 'But who knows how his body will react. Pencil is young and very fit. He may just surprise us.'

'But you are not confident?' guessed the coach.

'I think it's eighty-twenty against him playing in a World Cup for England, but with proper care and the human endeavour, who can tell?'

'So, next steps?' The Arsenal man was getting practical.

'He needs to stay in hospital for a week or so, then lots of rest while the plaster is still on. Then we will see how successful the surgery and the screw have been and then physio.' The doctor studied them before continuing. 'That all adds up to three stroke four months at least, and there are also the psychological challenges to overcome. The boy's had a major trauma.'

'When can we move him to our private care?'

'Probably best that he remains here for a week or so, then he can be moved.'

'Well, Doctor, thank you for everything. We should go and talk with Pencil's mum, give her a much needed update.' Paul shook the impressive doctor's hand; was it wrong in the circumstances that he found her so attractive? He was about to leave the room when she pulled out a notepad.

'Would you guys mind giving me your autographs? My nephew is footy mad and he'd never forgive me.'

They both smiled, signed, said their farewells and went off in search of the Kane family. The news had not been great, but it was far better than either of them had been expecting.

Carole King was in many ways glad to be back at work. Yes, her vacation with Dan had been terrific in terms of relaxation and sunshine, but she was very worried about how matters were evolving at RCS and how Gary was dealing with things. She loved him dearly, and could tell from his demeanour that all was not well with him.

Whilst away, she had reflected long and hard on her life, and concluded she was one of the luckiest people alive. She knew her looks could stop conversations in rooms she entered; she knew she was lucky to be married to Dan, a kind and gentle man with more money than a small African nation; she knew she was very good at her job, but she also knew that she had a duty to care for Gary Ruthven, to be by his side no matter what was going on in his life. She also knew that right now, Gary was beginning to come to terms with some serious errors of judgement that were now coming home to roost at RCS.

He had been genuinely pleased to welcome her back that morning, but acted distractedly with her, his mind clearly on things that she knew to have been troubling him for some time. For the first time in his life, Gary Ruthven was beginning to doubt himself and his decisions. Yes, he had made mistakes, like bringing in David Lane and persisting with the useless Lucas Hunt, and now was continuing with their crazy growth plan for the business. Ruthven's challenge was going to be how decisively he would react to the situation. Carole had known her husband Dan long enough to see how strong seriously successful business people were – decisive and always commercial. She doubted that Gary possessed those attributes. Yes, he was highly intelligent, and the most talented brand guy she had met, but did he have the leadership or business acumen to build RCS for the future? Additionally, his recent talent acquisition was poor, all contributing to the negative things that were building at the agency.

What RCS needed was a really good chief executive, someone to compliment Gary's business development skills and take the strain of the internal business management from

Ruthven's shoulders. RCS also needed a really good finance director to work with the chief exec to get things back in control. What concerned Carole most was this: if she could see these things so clearly, what the hell was blinding Gary?

That, she decided, was what she needed to find out. She would take him to dinner this evening and start to get some answers. It was time to act, time to be there for her best friend.

Meanwhile, across London, Kate Ross was listening as Gary Ruthven outlined his desire to get his family finances into significantly better shape.

'Well,' she began her response, 'that is music to my ears. With all things considered, you are probably sitting here today with a net worth situation of approximately one million. However, your pension has had nothing contributed to it since you left Guinness, and if anything went wrong at RCS, your savings would not see you guys through for much longer than nine months.'

'I know, I know,' countered Gary, putting both palms up in mock surrender. He also did not want to divulge details of his secret cash fund that he had hidden in his Sol Bank account in Spain. He had the best part of three hundred grand in there that not even Vicki knew about.

'Like you,' continued Kate, 'I think that the time is right for a proper and disciplined review and that discussion should involve Vicki, who does play a big part in your financial affairs.' She stopped to take a sip of the sparkling water she had ordered with her salad lunch.

'Intuitively, Kate, I am very worried that we have got the model wrong and that it's going to be very difficult to course correct.'

'Say more,' encouraged the accountant.

'Well, all our investments and commitments seem to be

heavily biased in favour of a continued growth in property prices, and the whole world and his brother seem to be gorging from that particular trough. Every time I drive down the Spanish coast, all I can see is new buildings, apartments by the shed load sprouting up, and frankly, I wonder who is going to buy them all. Christ, when Vicki and I were in Dubai last Christmas, it was even worse. The beachfront is beginning to look like Manhattan. Who has got all that money? My guess is that ninety percent will be borrowed from the banks, and how long can that last?' He sipped his wine, letting his anxiety have a free reign as he was really keen to get this stuff off his chest.

'Of course, you might be right in your assessment, and you are not alone in thinking like this. The big question remains what do you want to do about it?'

'Well, isn't that your job?' smiled Ruthven.

'To some extent, but if you are worried about your exposure, you could start by selling your house in Spain. That would get you what? Half a million? Pay off your mortgage on Beaconsfield, and start to use the savings you would make to rebuild your pension pot.'

'Shit, Kate. Isn't that a bit drastic?'

'I am only saying.' It was her turn to hold up her hands at Gary.

'But, do you think I am worrying too much about things?'

'No, I don't. You have a very successful career, a promising business and you are still relatively young,' she began.

'Thanks,' mocked Gary, who was not feeling relatively young at that moment.

'But,' continued Kate, 'you are heavily exposed if the economy takes a turn for the worse and affects both the property market and your company. Your foundations are built more of sand than concrete at the moment, and that is not a place that you should be happy to be.'

'That's exactly my point. So what to do?'

'Before we consider that little conundrum, it might also be worth thinking about the foundations at RuthvenCampbellStuart.'

'Oh Christ, Kate. You are not going to rock that ship too?'

'Okay, give me your take on the situation.' She sipped her water again as their lunch arrived.

'Well,' began Ruthven, waiting until the waiter was out of earshot. 'I am beginning to get anxious about the firm too.'

'In what ways?' she probed and Gary noticed her use of the plural. She was here today to have a proper discussion.

'Well, two things really,' he began before taking some rocket leaves into his mouth and considering his response carefully. 'Both to do with talent,' he continued.

'In what way?' probed Kate.

'To begin, I will need to make a decision on Lucas as Chairman. He is now adding no value at all. My plan was to wait until after his wedding in September, but with things as they are, he might need to be moved out sooner.'

'Couldn't you do it in stages? Semi-retire him, half his salary, with a view to full retirement at the end of the year?'

'That might work, but then I come to his replacement.'

'David Lane?'

'Yep, and he is another worry.' Ruthven sat back, inviting a response.

'Possibly, but haven't you boxed yourself into a corner with these guys and their shareholding?' She continued her probing.

'I guess, but as you once said, we need to do what is right for the company.'

'Buy their shares back and get rid of them; easy enough if you do not think they are giving RCS what you brought them in for.'

'Great idea, except I bought the house in Spain with that money.'

'As I said, boxed yourself in there, my friend.'

'What's next? I told you so?' smiled Gary, recalling Kate's words of warning before he had sold shares to Lane and Hunt. Of course, he had ignored her advice, had been blinded by the money.

'No I told you so from me, but I do confess to be getting more concerned for you as this conversation develops.' The discussion was rested for a few moments as they both busied themselves with eating their salads, before Ross continued.

'Back to the talent issue. Are those your only concerns?'

'No, I am worried about our distinct lack of business development skill. I still seem to be the only person who is building our order book, the new offices are proving slow to get going and I think that we are very likely to start missing our key targets.'

'I thought Lane was helping build sales plans?'

'That is part of his role, but this is not like selling paint, it is all about relationship building and it takes time, nine months to a year normally.'

'I thought that was in your plan?' she asked.

'What?'

'The nine months timeframe,' she clarified.

'It was, but I am fed up getting half truths about how new business is doing. I need concrete facts.'

'Okay,' she paused. 'Let's see where this is getting you.'

'It is telling me that I have got a ton of issues building both in my private finances and with the business. Issues that will need attention very soon, although I do not know where I am going to get the time to deal with them, my client work is full-time as it is.'

'Fortunately, your situation is not unusual, Gary. You are simply becoming a victim of your own success and what got you here will not get you to the next level. You are going to have to undergo a new career spurt, develop new ways of coping.' She spoke these words gently.

'But it all feels so overwhelming, Kate. This is not what I imagined.'

'I get that, but to progress you are going to have to focus and prioritise,' she encouraged.

'What do you think is top priority?'

'Good question,' Ross replied, careful to consider her next response.

'So?' implored Ruthven.

'Well, that is difficult. Where do you feel most anxiety?'

'I am very worried regarding personal finances,' he began, 'and if the company hits some kind of buffer, I need to know we are okay at home.'

'Good, so that is where we will start and as I said earlier, we need Vicki involved in those discussions.'

'Agreed, but she is in San Roque already.'

'No worries, I am happy to come down one weekend, get a better sense of how much that place might be worth.' She smiled, but Gary knew she was being deadly serious.

'Mmm, that is not going to be an easy conversation. Vicki loves that place.'

'I am sure she does, but I am also sure she'll want to know what is going on and be part of whatever decisions you might make.'

'Of course,' agreed Ruthven, not really looking forward to that meeting.

'Otherwise, how are things between you two? Still being a good boy?'

'What else?' shrugged Gary, feeling himself blush slightly.

'That's good, the last thing you need is your wife getting upset on any other stuff. After this little chat, seems to me that you're in quite enough troubled waters.'

Gary Ruthven nodded his agreement, privately writing himself a mental note to end the thing with Tandy immediately. Kate Ross was right. His life was in enough of a mess without any more shit of his own making.

Colm Elliot had not slept for twenty-four hours and badly needed a shower and a shave. However, he had been promised a return to his real job once his current strategic assessment was complete. Elliot and his temporary team had been given responsibility for pulling together an accurate and detailed account of the movements of the four suicide bombers who caused so much devastation on the London Transport system on the day that was already becoming widely known as 7/7.

With an enormous amount of information and CCTV footage available, Colm was now confident that their initial draft would be completed before the day was out and that he could then be released back to the Met. Their investigations had focused on a group of four men, three of whom were from Leeds in Yorkshire, and were reported as being primarily cleanskins, meaning that they had been previously unknown to the authorities who widely monitored potential terrorist cells operating within the UK. On Wednesday the 7th of July, all four men travelled to Luton in Bedfordshire by car, then on to London by train. The men were recorded on CCTV arriving at King's Cross station in London at 8.30am that morning and early indications suggested that property associated with the four men was found at two of the explosion sites.

Elliot and his team now knew the names of the culprits to be Mohammad Sudique Khan, aged thirty, Shehzad Tanweer, aged twenty-two, Germaine Lindsay, aged nineteen, and Hasib Hussain, who was aged just eighteen. His team also now knew where the men had been living prior to the suicide bombing of London and special forces were now preparing raids on at least six properties in Leeds, Aylesbury, and in Hyde Park, London.

Elliot and his team also took time to study similarities between the London bombings and the 11th of March 2004 train bombings in Madrid before concluding their draft report by suggesting that the attacks and their synchronised nature bore all the hallmarks of al-Qaeda or an organisation closely related to al-Qaeda.

With the report completed in draft format, Elliot called his temporary boss and told him that he was ready to submit the document for review; he was told to deliver the report in person and went to find the Deputy Chief Constable, glad to have the job done.

Concern was still etched on Gary Ruthven's face when he returned from his lunch meeting with Kate Ross, and his mood was not much improved when Jenny informed him that Lucas Hunt was in the building and hoping to have a meeting with him before the afternoon was out.

'Give me five minutes and then tell him that I will see him now. But, I want you to come and interrupt us at two-thirty, drag me away. I don't care what excuse you use, just get me out of there.'

Jenny smiled in understanding, her instructions clearly understood.

Gary quickly went to his office, picked up a note from Carole inviting him to dinner after work, and prepared himself for whatever Lucas wanted to see him about. One thing that he was sure of, whatever it was, it would add no value to RCS.

Still in shock from the week's happenings, Paul Ruthven had returned to his own office only moments later and determined to call the guys at Nike; see what their response would be to the difficult and uncertain news about Pencil.

To his pleasant surprise, his Nike counterpart suggested that they get the contract signed that afternoon, so Paul signed as Pencil's agent and arranged for a courier to collect and speed it over to Nike's London offices.

That settled, he called his brother to see what plans he had for that evening and the weekend. Gary informed him that he was having an early dinner with Carole but would then be driving home to Beaconsfield, and that he intended spending most of Saturday getting some catch-up on much needed sleep.

Paul then decided that he would take the train to Scotland; visit his parents, play some golf with his father.

First though, he called Pencil Kane's mum to see if she was going to be okay over the weekend. She said that she would, so Paul rushed home to pack before catching a taxi cab to King's Cross, where he joined the throngs of people trying to escape London, already cursing his impulsive decision to go home for the weekend.

The Square in London's Bruton Street was one of Gary Ruthven's favourite restaurants and as he awaited the arrival of Carole, he reflected on what had been a quite unique week in his life. He was also still incredibly anxious about his financial situation. What the people who knew him did not know was that he was deeply in debt to his credit card companies. Of the six cards that he carried in his wallet, four were definitely maxed out and the other two were tottering close to that position. In all, his credit limit on all six cards was ninety thousand, and he calculated that this month's bills would show a total debt of eighty-six or seven thousand. Of course, he could always repay the total from his secret stash in Spain, but that was his rainy day money, accumulated by doing private client work in the USA and having invoices paid into a private business account on the Isle of Man. *Needs must*, he thought as he watched Carole light up reception as she entered The Square. *I will transfer fifty grand next week and get some pressure off.*

As Carole walked towards him, he was conscious of male heads turning and females shifting uncomfortably. *God*, he smiled to himself, *this woman is getting even more beautiful as she gets older.* Standing, Gary kissed both of her offered cheeks as the waiter hovered to settle her in her seat.

'You look drop dead, Mrs Jenner,' whispered Ruthven.

'Why, thank you,' she smiled back. 'It is amazing what a very expensive vacation and a very rich husband can do for you.'

'Indeed, tell me about your break,' he began before clarifying, 'but please miss out any bedroom bits or I might just be forced to go kill myself.'

'Bedrooms are so last century, Gary. I thought even you would know that.'

'Stop right now,' he was giving up already, 'and tell me why you so urgently needed to take me out to dinner this evening.'

'That's a shame, I thought I could have more fun with you first.'

'Fun?' mused Ruthven. 'Yes, I think I remember what that is.'

'And so you should. You are becoming a very dull boy.'

They ordered some wine and still water before Carole got to the point as requested.

'I have decided to take you in hand, Mr Ruthven,' she began.

'That sounds promising,' smiled Gary.

'Yep, it's time to map you out, tell you what you need to do to fix things at RCS and start getting your life back, your fun back.' She stopped as Gary was invited to sample the bottle of Sancerre that they had ordered.

Two hours later, as Gary Ruthven guided his BMW out of the underground car park at his office, he was reflecting heavily on the time he had just spent with Carole King. Kate Ross at lunch, Carole over dinner – they were more or less telling him the same thing. That it was time to act; remove Hunt and Lane and get some better calibre and much younger talent into RCS. He knew that they were right, but intuitively he also knew that it was not going to be that easy, that there was likely to be a heavy price to pay for the mistakes that he had made.

Colm Elliot arrived home in Northwood just before midnight; his draft report had been accepted by the Deputy Chief

Constable and his temporary team had been dismantled immediately, most being reassigned to work elsewhere on the suicide bombings. Elliot, however, as had been promised, was released back to his job at Marylebone.

Susan had a light supper ready for him and after a quick shower – the shave would wait until the morning – they ate, chatted and finally collapsed into bed.

'What a freaking week that was,' were his final words before he fell into an almost instant deep sleep.

'You are not wrong,' sighed Susan as she quietly switched off the bedside lamp and snuggled up against her exhausted partner.

SEPTEMBER 2005

CHAPTER 6   MONDAY 19 SEPTEMBER 2005

London was enjoying a surprisingly balmy and still evening despite the forecasted threat of night-time ground frost as the limo carrying Pencil Kane and his agent Paul Ruthven pulled to a silent halt outside the main entrance to Arsenal's Highbury Stadium in the north of the city. Paul and the driver exited simultaneously, both keen to help Pencil out of the vehicle and safely onto his light metal crutches.

Quickly, they were surrounded by press photographers and fans alike, flashing cameras and cheering Pencil as he carefully climbed the steps before entering the famous marbled halls with their bust of Herbert Chapman, a long gone but still revered former club coach.

Pencil had been at the ground on numerous occasions since the bombings in July but tonight was going to be very different. Tonight Arsenal was playing Everton in the Barclays Premiership and the match in front of a capacity crowd was being broadcast live on Sky television. And Pencil Kane, who had become a heroic national symbol of courage and determination, was to be presented to the crowd before the match, his way of saying thank you for all the support he had been given since that fateful day.

For Pencil, it was not an evening he had been looking

forward to. In his mind he wanted to be running onto the pitch as a fully recovered player. That said, and because Pencil Kane was still sharp, he knew that he had to take full advantage of his considerable fame, just in case he didn't fully recover and might need to take his career in another direction. Pencil loved his public and knew he might need them long after his physio and podiatry was completed.

So five minutes before the scheduled kick-off time, and with the players from both teams lined up in a sort of guard of honour, the stadium announcer silenced the massive crowd before inviting them to give a heartfelt welcome home to one of Highbury's finest young players, a young man who had shown the courage of a lion since his tragic injuries in London during the 7/7 bombings.

Pencil hobbled onto the hallowed turf on his crutches, dressed in his maroon Arsenal tracksuit and wearing black Nike trainers, making his way towards the centre circle. As he did so, the crowd went into raptures in an eruption of noise and emotion that would later be reported as one of the most touching welcomes that the old ground had seen in its ninety-three-year history.

Pencil threw his shoulders back and stretched to his full six-foot-three-inch height, dropped his crutches and began returning the applause to the fans. There he stood for a full two minutes, before bending to pick up his crutches and slowly making his way back to the edge of the pitch, very aware and somewhat embarrassed to see so many people, players, staff and fans alike, wiping tears as they continued to applaud his exit into the tunnel and away from the public spotlight. As he was embraced by Paul Ruthven, he could hear the crowd as they began chanting his name – the cry of 'Pencil, Pencil, Pencil', reverberating around the stadium.

'Well done,' said Ruthven as he guided Kane up the stairs and into his stand seat to watch the match.

'Thanks. That was one of the most amazing moments of my life,' replied Pencil eventually, as he settled down to enjoy the game that Arsenal eventually won two–nil with two surprising goals from the club's centreback and captain.

Colm Elliot had been planning on watching the Arsenal match on television, but could no longer get focused enough to do so. Earlier that day, he had been very upset to hear that Malcolm Hillman had been released from Wandsworth Prison on bail, after a special plea to be allowed to attend his daughter's wedding the following Friday.

Elliot was keeping a close eye on developments in the case, very worried that Hillman, who had dispensed with the services of Trevellion & Co and was intending to defend himself, was going to manage to escape the punishment that Colm felt he fully deserved for the cold-blooded murder of his wife. There was also a rumour that with the help of his daughter, Julia, and a Harley Street specialist, no doubt paid a handsome fee, that Hillman was claiming to be suffering from the early stages of Alzheimer's disease.

'If that fucker has Alzheimer's, then I am a freaking Chinaman,' he said aloud to Hannah and anyone else listening in the canteen earlier that morning.

'Surely the CPS can get an alternative opinion,' countered his subordinate, trying to calm her boss down.

'You would hope so, but I am not going to take any chances with that slippery little lot.'

'What are you going to do?' asked Hannah, getting concerned.

'For starters, I am going to get my best suit on and go to a wedding on Friday; let the shits know that they are being watched.'

'Need a partner?' she laughed, half seriously.

'Why not? Get your best frock ready and find out where the nuptials are happening.'

'It's a date,' concluded Hannah, thinking to herself that Friday should be fun.

By the time Elliot got home that evening, he had worked himself into a sense of total dedication. If it was the very last thing that he did in the Met, he was going to ensure that Malcolm Hillman and his very difficult daughter did not manage to manipulate a jury to let him off with his crime. No, Malcolm Hillman was going to do time for killing his wife, and for Detective Chief Inspector Colm Elliot, that meant a life sentence. Anything else would, he strongly believed, be an absolute travesty of justice.

Turning on the television, he and Susan watched in silence as the national news reported the emotional reception given to Pencil Kane at Highbury. They too, had tears in their eyes by the end of the report and accompanying footage.

Vicki Ruthven was a very worried lady. Her daughter Emma was due to travel to Leeds the next day to enrol at the local university for her first year studying law and her husband Gary was being somewhat vague about how they were going to pay Unite for her accommodation. Unite were the company who specialized in the provision of student halls of residence and since Gary had done some brand work for them he was showing great loyalty to the firm. However, with their kitchen remodel just completed, they had struggled to find the full payment for that and had been holding back the cheque for Molly's school fees, waiting for the school bursar's office to send them a reminder.

She and Gary had always had a fairly volatile relationship. They often joked that they had argued themselves around the world. Vicki admitted to being difficult at times and calm as her husband was, there were days when she knew that she pushed him too far. Tonight was almost one of those and she knew that they would have ended up arguing had he not finished his light dinner and taken himself off to the gym. He was on a new regime, after deciding in Spain that his waistline was expanding quicker than he liked. Waiting for his return, Vicki had probably had a glass or two of wine too many, and that only made her more anxious about their financial situation.

Of course, Kate Ross had visited them in San Roque, and had done her best to reassure them that if they made the right decisions now, then all would be fine. That said, the fact that Gary had felt it necessary to fly Kate down in the first place only fed her anxiety more than they had imagined. Vicki's father Tom had been self-employed, so from an early age her mum and dad had tried to educate her in best practice husbandry, as Tom had so quaintly called it. However, since she had been with Gary, their disciplines around money had been at best overconfident, and at worst too risky.

They were both planning to drive Emma to Leeds in the morning in her Mercedes, and the stuff waiting in the hall to be loaded was, in Vicki's opinion, quite ridiculous. There was everything from television to laptop to music system to a box of shoes; two boxes of clothes, photo-frames, bed linen and five pillows and scatter cushions. Emma clearly intended to use the Unite room as a right little home from home. *So let's pray that my bloody husband can afford to pay the bill.* Otherwise, they would have to consider packing one of the many tents that were stored in the garage.

On Friday, they were due to attend Lucas Hunt's wedding to the less than delightful Julia Hillman, and Gary had informed her over supper that Julia's father had been released from prison on bail to attend.

'Not too sure I want to be in the same room as an axe murderer,' she had stated on hearing the news.

'Hardly a bloody axe murderer, Vicki,' Gary had replied.

'Only because he killed his wife in the bedroom. Who knows what he might have used if they had argued in the garden shed,' she had persisted.

'Fair point,' her husband had conceded, recognising her mood, before going to grab his gym bag and making his escape.

No, she thought, deciding one more small glass of wine wouldn't do any harm, thinking that she would not miss this ridiculous wedding for anything. It was promising to be one of the highlights of the year. Just then, she heard Gary drive up in front of the house and she set off to greet him; to seek reassurances about money in general and tomorrow's impending bill in particular.

In St John's Wood, a small gathering of the Hillman family, including the soon-to- be new member, Lucas Hunt, welcomed Malcolm Hillman when he returned from Wandsworth prison after his surprise release on bail.

Not surprisingly, Hillman himself was not feeling too comfortable at the thought of returning to his home and the scene of the killing of his wife back in July. However, at the insistence of his daughter Julia, they all gathered in the kitchen for a glass of champagne and nibbles bought earlier from Fortnum & Mason.

'Christ, Julia, you really know how to take insensitivity to new heights,' her father opened on entering the kitchen and being greeted by his family members.

'Nonsense, Father. It is a big week for this family and I am not going to let this ongoing saga surrounding that bloody woman spoil it for us,' opened his daughter, sipping her drink with a flourish.

'For God's sake, you really take the biscuit, Julia,' voiced her sister Helen, who was usually the last person to challenge her elder sibling.

'Oh shut up, Helen. If it wasn't for me Father would still be languishing in Wandsworth and not home and able to get ready for Friday.'

Lucas, somewhat embarrassed by the exchanges, simply offered more nibbles before attempting to change the subject.

'Everything considered, Malcolm, how are you bearing up?' he asked gently, much to the annoyance of his soon-to-be wife.

'Not too great, Lucas, to be honest. If only I could turn back the clock,' he began, tears welling in his eyes, and Lucas could not help but notice the obvious weight loss and greying pallor of Malcolm Hillman's facial skin.

'Well, I am sure a few nights at home will do no harm,' continued Lucas, who had been convinced of the argument that it had been Anna's own fault that she had been killed. Julia had banned the use of the word murder by any member of the family.

'Not sure I agree with that, Lucas. This place feels tainted, so the sooner we sell the better,' reflected Hillman.

'Another of your bloody stupid thoughts, Father. This was your home before that woman and should remain so now. You need to stay in touch with your roots,' interjected Julia in her usual style; a style that had led to the resignation of Trevellion & Co and the decision that Malcolm Hillman should defend himself rather than depend on a 'bunch of incompetent wanker lawyers', to quote Julia accurately on the topic.

'We will see, Julia. Things will be clearer after the trial in November.'

'After you are acquitted in November,' pronounced his daughter categorically.

'As I said, we will see.'

After another half an hour of the Hillmans basking in the milk of human kindness, everyone but Julia and Lucas took their leave, suggesting that Malcolm Hillman should get some sleep. However, with the rest of the family gone, Julia told her father to take a seat, suggesting that they needed to go over the details for the wedding.

'Do we need to do that tonight?' quizzed Lucas, catching the frustrated look on the other man's face.

'Of course we do, and I particularly want Father thinking about his speech. We want nobody seeing any sign of weakness,' responded Julia before Lucas told them that he would get to bed and let them get on with it.

CHAPTER 7   TUESDAY
20 SEPTEMBER 2005

Pencil Kane was awake very early. Today was Pencil's birthday and the day that his player salary at Arsenal was rising to a terrific twenty grand a week, an incredible one point zero four million pounds per annum. On top of that, Paul Ruthven had negotiated another two hundred and sixty thousand for image rights, bringing his grand total to one point three million. Pencil liked to think about the money with such precision. Pencil also hoped to God that his foot would recover and that Pencil Kane would be able to repay the club for the faith that they were showing in him by agreeing the contract despite the injuries that he had sustained.

Struggling from his bed, he pulled on a T-shirt and some boxers and hobbled to the plush new bathroom in his plush new apartment knowing that his mum would be arriving soon to help him prepare for the day; he also expected her to bring his birthday cards and presents. Not that he expected anything special from his family.

Pencil was worried by how much his right foot still hurt. The left was okay now, but with the plaster cast removed from the right, the pain was still excruciating until he managed to pop some of the painkillers the club doctor had prescribed.

As well as being his eighteenth birthday, today Pencil was going back to see the specialist at Whitechapel, the young medic who had so cared for Pencil during that first week after the 7/7 bombings.

While having a quick shave, Pencil reflected on being eighteen. Today, he could legally go into a bar and order a drink; today he could get married without having to ask for his mother's permission, and from today he had the right to vote in elections. Yes, from today Pencil Kane was officially an adult, a man as well as at the start of his plan to become very wealthy.

The apartment buzzer sounded and Pencil hobbled to let his mum into the block. She would be happy today; it was a big day for Patricia Kane, the only parent that Pencil had known, the woman who had worked herself to exhaustion making sure that her son Pencil and her daughter Davina had everything that they had needed to live happy in their childhood. Patricia was still beautiful, and at thirty-six could have any man she wanted, but Patricia had been badly hurt when her husband had run off when Pencil had been just two and Davina hardly six months old. Pencil loved his mum and had long vowed to repay her for everything that she had done for him, and now Pencil was going to be able to afford to start that repayment.

'Happy Birthday, my big man,' she began on entering the apartment and giving her son a tight hug. 'What's it like to be a man at last?' she continued, pushing him to arm's length so that she could look at him properly.

'Pencil is cool, Mum, Pencil is cool,' he replied, deliberately trying to sound like some cool street gangster from some American movie.

'Well, you sure as hell looked cool on the news last night.' She was opening a M&S carrier bag and extracting a bundle of envelopes of all colours, birthday cards from the family. 'It had me in tears watching my boy, the national hero, with all them people calling your name. Were you okay?'

'Pencil was good, Mum. It was very emotional, but really nice, really humbling.'

'I am sure it was. Now let me get the kettle on while you get these cards opened. You don't have too much time. When are you leaving for the hospital?'

'Paul Ruthven is picking me up at ten, so a couple of hours yet,' replied Pencil.

'And how is that right foot this fine morning?' His mother stopped to check the expression on her boy's face.

'Pencil's foot is still sore, but Pencil is going to recover.' He smiled widely, his most charming smile, the smile that made everyone who knew him just love Pencil Kane.

With Gary Ruthven out of the RCS office for the day, taking his eldest daughter to university in Leeds, David Lane had suggested that he and Lucas Hunt should meet to go over the agenda for the meeting scheduled for the following day. The purpose of that meeting was to make a final decision regarding the additional cash funding of the business. Lane had just returned from his preferred home in Provence and looked tanned, well and a little slimmer, after three weeks of golfing and swimming every day.

Lucas Hunt, by stark contrast looked like he had been up all night, which was not strictly true, although he had experienced real disturbance to his sleep, having slept in the master bedroom in which Anna Hillman had been killed – not murdered, he reminded himself.

As Chairman, it should have been Hunt's responsibility to pull together the agenda for the Wednesday meeting, but with the Hillman bail application and his impending wedding, David Lane had taken it upon himself to make sure the prep work got done.

Tea and biscuits were at the ready; Hunt couldn't operate without a Hobnob or two. Lane got some pleasantries out of the way before pressing on.

'Well, to begin, the purpose of tomorrow's meeting is for us shareholders to agree on the route we are going to take to fund the business from December,' he began, passing the agenda to Hunt, who was making a mess of dunking a biscuit in his tea.

'I thought the Ross girl said we didn't need an injection until the New Year,' queried Hunt, showing a surprisingly accurate recollection of their July meeting.

'True,' answered Lane, 'but that was before we agreed to pay Gary his contracted performance bonus and before we failed to meet our end of July revenue numbers.'

'Okay, so how much are you looking to position?'

'Well, with the expansion plan halted and taking what I've just mentioned into account, I believe that we need three hundred grand by first of December,' explained Lane, finding it very difficult not to laugh at the mess Hunt was making of the table, crumbs and tea drips now everywhere.

'And your proposal?'

'Well, I would like to suggest that we both contribute fifty thousand each through a further share purchase that Gary would then loan back to the company, and that we then raise the remaining two hundred thousand via Barclays and the government's small enterprise loan scheme,' outlined Lane.

'Okay, and have Barclays agreed to the loan scheme?' asked Hunt, his tea and biscuits now finished.

'They have in principle, but we had to wait for Vicki to transfer her company shares to Gary to avoid the married shareholders clause regarding the provision of security.'

'And is that all done now?' asked Hunt, his mobile telephone now vibrating on the table. 'Just let me get this, David, it's Julia.'

As Hunt went about responding to his bride-to-be's latest whim, Lane went in search of someone to come and clear up the mess and remove their cups.

'Can we continue?' asked Lane impatiently after a five-minute interruption.

'Of course, David. Sorry about that, Friday is looming,' apologised Hunt.

'So, where were we?'

'You had outlined your proposals for raising the additional funds, explaining that we had been waiting for the Ruthvens to transfer shares.'

'So I was, and yes, that has all been done now. Technically, at least, Gary is the sole owner of seventy-five percent of the company.'

'Okay, and when do you need you and me to complete the next batch of share purchases ?' asked Hunt, opening his diary in order to note down the reply.

'Ideally at the beginning of November; get the paperwork cleared and Companies House informed before the start of December. The loan scheme money can be paid in two tranches, the first in December and the second at the beginning of February,' replied Lane, reading the details from his notes.

'Sounds good, David. And when will the company need to start repaying the loan scheme money back?'

Lane again referred to his notes before replying that it was April 2007.

'And Gary is happy with this solution?'

'On two fronts very happy. Firstly, he has not needed to increase his personal guarantees and secondly he is not being asked to input any cash of his own,' replied Lane.

'Good, so are we aligned?' asked Hunt, obviously keen to be getting on his way.

'If you are happy with the proposals, then tomorrow should be short and sweet,' concluded David Lane, not sure that he had been given a full commitment from Hunt.

'I think so. I will just need to double check with Julia this evening.'

Despite the fact that Paul Ruthven had been seeing Dr Lucy Campbell since early August he had neither asked for nor been given an update on the progress of Pencil Kane's injury. So, it was with some degree of trepidation that he entered Whitechapel Hospital with Pencil for their ten o'clock appointment that morning.

In reception, three people approached the young footballer, all politely asking for Pencil's autograph. As always, Pencil Kane showed a degree of respect and real presence when talking to strangers showing an interest in him. For his part, Paul had started to get used to the fact that younger fans no longer recognised him, not asking him to sign the magazines or envelopes proffered to Pencil. For Paul Ruthven, that no longer mattered; what did was getting the right contracts for his clients, contracts that generally earned him a fee of between ten and fifteen percent.

Trying to stop what was turning into a celebrity fest in the hospital reception, someone from security arrived and invited Paul and Pencil to a private waiting room where they waited to be joined by the Arsenal head coach and the meeting with Dr Campbell.

At ten precisely, the waiting room door opened and the young medic, having said her quick hellos, invited them to follow her along a lengthy corridor and into an examination room. On crutches, Pencil did his best to keep up and Paul was very conscious of how nervous the young man now looked.

On entering the room, the first thing that the medic did was to wish Pencil a very happy birthday, reaching to give him a gentle peck on his cheek.

Turning quickly to the business in hand, she switched on the X-ray light on the wall and pulled a couple of X-ray images from an envelope that she had been carrying with her.

'Okay, gents,' she began. 'Let's get down to business.'

'God, Pencil is nervous this morning,' responded Kane honestly.

'Quite understandable in the circumstances, Pencil, but let's begin with the good news.' She clipped the first X-ray to the light machine before continuing. 'This is a picture of your left foot, and as we can see the fracture has recovered well, the healing near completion. Your left foot will be as good as new after another five of six weeks of physio and light training.' She stopped and the three men were smiling; the Arsenal coach even had a small tear in his eye.

'Let's now take a look at the more damaged right foot.' Again she stopped to clip a new image to the screen. 'And unfortunately, the news on this foot is not so good.' Again, the surgeon paused to make sure Pencil was sitting comfortably before continuing. 'As we discussed before, this foot took the brunt of the blast and suffered what we might call a high-energy trauma; the medical term is a dislocation of the talus between these two bones.' Again, she pointed to the screen. 'With the cast now removed and some early physio, we can say that it has failed to heal properly and may result in degrees of arthritis.'

'What do you mean, failed to heal properly?' It was Pencil who was sharpest to the question.

'Well, to an extent, the surgery and the insertion of the screw was successful. You will be able to walk again without crutches, but early prognosis is that you're going to face a very uphill struggle to recover enough to resume your career in football.'

Christ, thought Paul, *she is not backing away from the truth*. She was doing what she was trained to do, saying it like it was. Looking at Pencil, the young man was clearly struggling with what he had just heard.

'Are you saying that full recovery is not a possibility?' asked the Arsenal coach gently.

'Not definitive at the moment, but what I am saying is that recovery to the level of fitness required of a top-level sportsman is highly unlikely. I am sorry to be so blunt, but I think Pencil needs to hear things as I believe them to be.'

'Pencil really appreciates you being so honest, Doctor,' began the birthday boy, 'but are you telling me that Pencil should not even try to get his full fitness back?'

'No, I think that we should all continue with that as the goal, but I don't want anyone leaving here today under any false impression as to how difficult the challenge is looking. If Pencil was not a footballer, we would all be celebrating today. After all, after the seriousness of the damage, being able to walk again would be considered a great result.'

'So, what's the next phase of the recovery plan?' It was the coach who was first to get planful.

'More of the same, gentle physio. The pain in your foot will gradually decrease and you will be able to step up your work. Let's give it another six weeks, then come back again and see how things are progressing. All being well, I'll then be able to get that screw out,' concluded the medic, having just put on one of her most impressive performances in a situation that had been causing her sleepless nights.

'However, before you go,' she decided to add, 'please see this process as a journey, not a destination. On that journey, we should set some milestones, the first being to walk again without those things.' She pointed to Pencil's crutches. 'When we achieve that, another milestone can be set and progress can be built that way. It was never possible that this first phase would see a full recovery.' Dr Campbell smiled at Pencil Kane and then held him by both hands before summing up by saying, 'Just remember, fifty-two people died that day; you are going to continue to be one of the very lucky ones.'

Pencil smiled and replied, 'Pencil is cool, Doctor. He will take each day as it comes, but I will not give up on my dream to play for Arsenal again, at least not until I've given it every chance.'

The medic then gave him a hug before replying to Pencil and the others,

'That's the spirit that we all need to show over the coming weeks and months.'

'Stoke Park? Isn't that where they filmed that James Bond movie; you know the one with the golf scene and that OddJob character,' responded Elliot on being told that the Buckinghamshire hotel was the venue for the Hunt-Hillman wedding on Friday.

'Must have been before my time, boss, but I do seem to remember that scene from the first *Bridget Jones* movie. You know the scene on the lake where Hugh Grant recites that rude little poem?' She was getting excited about their visit.

'Hugh who?' asked Elliot.

'You know, the flop-haired posh bloke who got himself arrested with that prostitute in the States a few years back,' continued his sergeant, not quite believing that her boss, a highly regarded and honoured senior detective, had never heard of Hugh Grant.

'Nope, name doesn't ring any bells. We must have very different preferences when it comes to going to the pictures.'

'The pictures?'

'That's what we used to call the cinema where I came from, back in the day, when folk like me still went on a Saturday evening.' Their banter continued.

'The pictures – I'll have to ask my gran about that one next time I see her. Next left,' suggested Hannah. They were going back to the St John's Wood crime scene, Elliot wanting to re-familiarise himself with some of the details before he reconnected with the Hillman family at the wedding. They drew up outside the house, surprised to see the place all lit up, someone was clearly living there.

'Don't tell me that the insensitive sod has come home on

bail, sleeping in the marital bed? Jesus, I've seen it all now.' But Hannah was not listening, she was on the phone finding out what address Malcolm Hillman had given on his bail application. After a few minutes, she got a call back confirming that he would be living at the St John's Wood address and reporting to the local police station every Thursday.

'That blocks my intention to have a wee snoop about,' concluded Elliot, starting the car and heading away from the scene, a limerick swirling around in his head that went something like:

> *'There was an old lady from Ealing,*
> *who had a peculiar feeling, so*
> *she lay on her back and opened her crack*
> *and pissed all over the ceiling.'*

'Stoke Park it is then, Hannah. Didn' you see Daniel Craig in *Layer Cake*?'

'Not sure I did,' she responded, somewhat confused by her boss's sudden mood change.

'Get the DVD before Friday, its just been released. It's cool and a lot of the scenes were filmed at Stoke Park. The place is very close to Pinewood Studios, so handy for the movie boys.'

Now Hannah knew that Elliot had been taking the piss earlier, the shit.

Having got Emma unpacked and settled into her very nice en-suite room in Unite's newest building in central Leeds, the Ruthven family, minus Molly who was at school in Gerrards Cross, had a late lunch in Café Rouge. Much to Vicki's relief, Gary's credit card had afforded the strain of being deducted the four thousand pounds that was the accommodation charge for the forty-five weeks of her first year tenancy.

On leaving Café Rouge, Emma informed them that she wanted to go off and explore central Leeds, and given that she was not due to enrol at the university until the following day, her parents agreed before hugs and kisses were exchanged and Emma wandered off to her new life.

Vicki and Gary walked in silence holding hands back to the car park to collect their car, tears in both their eyes.

'What a pair of soppy sods we are,' suggested Vicki, but Gary found it difficult to respond, not quite sure why he was finding the moment so emotional.

'Rites of passage, I guess,' was all that he could muster and as they reached the car, his mobile phone vibrated in his jacket pocket.

Scanning his device, he was shocked to see that he had a text message from Tandy, the last person that he had been expecting contact from. Replacing the phone in his pocket, he would read as they travelled as Vicki was driving them home. She was a nervous passenger and Gary had long realised that letting her drive was the most stress-free way of getting from a to b in a car with her.

As they navigated their way out of Leeds and headed for the motorway south, Gary perused his phone in general and the text from Tandy in particular. Her message had simply read: 'We need to speak urgently, call me.' Ruthven's nervous system went into meltdown – what on earth could the woman want? Surely her husband had not discovered their clandestine session in the Hempel? *Oh fuck*, thought Gary to himself.

After his July meeting with Kate Ross regarding family finances, Gary had taken the advice to heart and had called Tandy to put an end to their short-lived affair. She had taken his message pretty well and she had even offered one last night of passion as a 'farewell gift', an offer that Gary had refused with, to be honest, some degree of difficulty. Since then, he had not heard from her and had assumed that the matter had been put to bed, so to speak. But now this. Why on earth could she need to speak to him so urgently? Fearing the worst, Gary scanned his other messages, made a couple of calls as Vicki drove them home, then texted Tandy back to say he would call her that evening. With over eighty miles still to drive, he just wished to God that his heart would stop its palpitations.

'So how many more shares will we get in RCS for this extra fifty thousand?' queried Julia Hillman later that evening after Lucas had updated her on his meeting with David Lane.

'You know, that is a good question. I don't think David said. My assumption is that we will get another five percent of the company,' responded Hunt honestly.

'Jesus, Lucas, you need to get a grip. If you want me, or more realistically Father, to write a cheque for fifty grand, you could at least have the decency to know what the fuck we are paying for, and if we got another five percent, doesn't that just value the company at one million? It's surely worth more than that!' ranted the future Mrs Hunt.

'Let me go and call David, he may have mentioned it. I've just had so much on my plate lately,' said Lucas, standing to go and find his telephone.

'Your plate?' scoffed Julia Hillman, near incandescent with rage.

'Yes, my bloody plate,' muttered Lucas leaving the room, frustrated that he had left his mobile in the car.

Dr Lucy Campbell and Paul Ruthven sat in a local Italian restaurant in Marylebone enjoying an end of day chat and a glass of fine wine. Paul had finally plucked up the courage to call the medic on his return home from Scotland the week after the 7/7 bombings. Lucy had been delighted to receive his call but had informed him that she was currently in a relationship with someone at work. Crestfallen, Paul had apologised but had finished the call by inviting her out anytime in the future, if and when she was free to do so.

To his pleasant surprise, he was delighted to receive a text message at the beginning of August from her saying that if he was still interested, she was free that week. Paul had called straight back, and they had met up that very evening for a drink. Things had developed from there, and although not officially living together, the couple had become very close over the month or so that they had been dating.

'So, how was young Pencil after our discussion this morning?'

'He was putting a brave face on things. He is a very focused and determined individual, so if anyone can do this, Pencil can,' reflected Paul.

'You guys did get my message this morning?' she checked, putting down her wine glass and making full eye contact with Paul.

'Oh yes, the message was received loud and clear. Pencil is aware that his playing days are most likely over. That said, I am going to support and encourage his rehabilitation in any way I can. The fitter he gets the better for whatever else life may throw at him.'

'Good, now tell me about this wedding on Friday,' Lucy said, changing the subject.

Gary sat in his car outside his gym waiting for Tandy's call. He had sent her a message saying that she could call him now and was waiting anxiously for his phone to ring, all kinds of horrible thoughts running through his mind. Moments later it rang.

'I bet that you are wondering what is so urgent,' began Tandy, all sweetness and light down the line.

'I have to admit to being a bit curious – not that it's not nice to hear your voice,' he replied nervously.

'Well, we seem to have a little problem,' she began.

'Really?'

'Yes, really.'

'Well, you better enlighten me before I have a strawberry,' invited Gary, using the Cockney slang for a heart attack.

'Are you sitting comfortably?' teased Tandy further.

'I am outside my gym in my car, so comfortably is relative.'

'I am pregnant,' she then stated, and Gary did well not to let out the inward groan that he was feeling.

'And?'

'And you will be pleased to hear that you are the proud sperm donor,' she replied.

'I am assuming that you are sure about all this, Tandy?'

'As positive as my pregnancy tests, yes.'

'But what about…'

'What about my lovely husband?' she guessed.

'That's where I was going,' said Gary gently.

'Oh, he doesn't know yet and frankly I would like to keep it that way.'

'Sorry, you've jumped ahead of me – what about him as the potential father?'

'Had the snip eight or nine years ago, when his first marriage ended,' she said, confirming one of Gary's fears. 'And you are the only other man I have slept with, so one and one comes up with two I am afraid to say.'

'Christ, Tandy, this is a shock. How are you keeping?' he asked, remembering his manners.

'Oh, I am glowing. I just don't want to glow any more, if you get my drift.'

'Indeed, how do you want me to help?' asked Gary finally, in total panic.

'Well, I've booked myself in for a termination next week,

and it would be nice if I had someone to chum me to the clinic; someone who might be just as keen to keep this little secret as I am.' Tandy had matters under control. For that at least, Gary was grateful.

'Of course, and you are sure that's what you want to do?'

'No, I want you to leave your lovely wife and daughters and do the honourable thing and marry me before my baby is born,' replied Tandy, obviously getting a little rattled.

'I had to ask,' reasoned Ruthven.

'Fine, but don't be so fucking stupid. Of course it's what I want to do. So just get your sexy ass and your credit card with me to Harley Street next Wednesday. I will text you the address and appointment time.'

'Don't worry, I'll be there.'

'Oh, I know that you will,' she stated firmly.

'And, Tandy, I am sorry.' He tried to say something gentle, kind. Take responsibility for this latest mess in his life.

'Stop being so soft, Gary. I am a big girl and in case you hadn't noticed, it took two to tango.' And with that the call was ended.

Ruthven started his car and headed for home. *Jesus*, he thought to himself, *I am one dumb fucking stupid bastard. What was I thinking of?*

CHAPTER 8

**WEDNESDAY
21 SEPTEMBER 2005**

Call it his Catholic guilt bag, but Gary Ruthven had not managed a great deal of sleep by the time that he climbed out of his bed in Beaconsfield just after five that morning. He was trying to come to terms with the fact that somewhere in London, not thirty miles away, a woman who was not his wife was carrying his child. That child, a sister or brother to Emma and Molly, was soon to be no more; would next Wednesday cease to exist and all because he and Tandy were both petrified of being caught for their selfish indiscretions, their wanton sexual desire, their base need for a duplicitous fuck.

If ever Gary Ruthven was being given a wake-up call, this was it. He had lost his way, become so far removed from the well-intended, high-integrity human being that he so hoped that he was. Add that to his abject carelessness with his family money and his failure to do proper due diligence at RCS before grabbing Lane and Hunt's share money and diving into the overheated Spanish property market. Christ, when was he going to stop this carelessness and get himself back on track, back to the man that he felt he really was?

Realistically though, he thought as he walked to the station to catch a 6am train in to Marylebone, he had no choice but to go along with Tandy. The termination, he couldn't bring himself to use the term abortion, needed to happen if he was to save his marriage, save himself from this disaster.

On the train he reflected further on what he had become and realised that for the first time in his life that he no longer liked himself, that he had lost all sense of self-respect, and that, for Gary, was a very sad and dangerous place to be, to have arrived at. He then had the insight that it was not his Catholic guilt bag that was worrying him at all, it was his fucking pathetic fear of being caught. He had become a total twat, and all that was really worrying him was being found out and his stupid little fantasy world being disrupted, his fantasy world that allowed Gary to believe that he could go on behaving in such duplicitous ways and keep getting away with it.

Leaving the train in London, Gary Ruthven determined that it was time to stop this dangerous merry-go-round that he was on, and get off. It was time to be who he really believed he was, to stand for what he believed in. His big problem was, he was not sure what that really was any more, or where the fuck to begin.

That, he muttered to himself, *is step one. I need to find the space and time to reflect on who I am and what I stand for.* From there, he decided, he could start to put matters right, to pay for his sins. Sins that in all honesty he had really enjoyed committing.

As always, Carole King was one of the first people to arrive into the offices of RuthvenCampbellStuart. Looking her usual immaculate self, in her designer suit and thousand-pound killer heels, she was ready for the business of the day; ready, as she would often say to herself, to kick ass.

With a busy schedule that day, she made herself a herbal tea and went for her early morning briefing with Gary, who was already at his desk looking busy and somewhat distracted.

'Good morning, boss. How are you this fine day?' she began, cheerfully entering Gary's office and pushing his office door closed with her behind.

'All the better for seeing you, that's for sure,' responded Ruthven, walking from behind his desk to join her at a round working table that was completely clear of clutter, holding only a few recently published professional magazines.

'Why, what's up? Did Emma get settled in okay yesterday?'

'Oh yes, she was good. Couldn't wait for me and Vicki to leave to be honest,' he reflected, noticing how amazing Carole looked, even for this early in the day. 'Christ, Carole! What time do you have to get up to look like that in the morning?'

'That's for me to know. So, what's up?'

'You don't want to know, you really don't want to know.' Ruthven was shaking his head.

'Try me, it can't be that bad,' urged King, intrigued.

'Only if you swear not to utter a word to anyone,' he began conspiratorially.

'I promise, you know me.'

So Gary Ruthven shared his dark and depressing situation with his best friend and long-term soulmate, without interruption, as she sat watching him, sipping her herbal tea. When he had finished, she took a few moments to respond.

'You do know that I am going to be really cross with you over this?' she began, putting her mug down on an RCS coaster on the table.

'I would expect so. I am really cross with myself and that is putting it mildly.'

'What the fuck were you thinking of?' she questioned, ironically using the same phrase that he had used the night before when he had left the gym to drive home.

'I don't know the answer to that,' he replied.

'Well, you have reached a new level in your attempts at self-destruction. What sort of programme are you on?' Gary had never seen Carole so angry. She was going pale with fury, taking deep breaths before continuing. 'If you don't start to sort your freaking self out, Gary, you are going to blow everything that you have worked for!'

'I know, I know, it's just that I don't know where to start. It's like one bad decision has followed another, as if my lucky streak has run out,' he reflected sadly.

'It's not about luck, you twat, it's about getting a grip and getting advice from the right people, not those stupid fuckers you've employed to run your company.' She was furious like he had never seen before. 'And about learning to keep your freaking pecker in your pants!' With that she stood and looked at him through harsh eyes. 'I am done listening to this self-pitying crap from you. Get things sorted or I am out of here, out of RCS, out of your life. I am not liking what you've become!' With that, Gary Ruthven's best friend and soulmate stormed from his office, slamming the door as she left.

Christ, thought Ruthven, as he returned to his desk, *that was not the reaction that I had been expecting. Jesus, what a mess.*

In the office early for the meeting with Gary and David, Lucas had been sitting quietly looking at a porn site on his laptop when he heard Carole and Gary begin their conversation in the office next door. Conscious of the flimsy walls, he determined not to listen, but could not help himself when he heard his boss tell Carole what was up with his life. As someone who himself had never been able to keep his pecker in his pants, as Carole had so simply put it, he was not completely surprised to hear of Gary's situation. That said, condoms had been long invented, and this was information that might come in useful – information that he was sure Julia would like to be privy to. *Well, well,* he thought to himself, *the smart and articulate Gary Ruthven was not so smart after all.* Lucas intuitively knew that his jacket was on a shaky hook at RCS; Gary had grown distant and impatient with him. This news could buy him some time. *Like to see you fire me now, Mr Ruthven,* he smiled to himself, an unlikely insurance policy having just landed in his lap. Disengaging from his porn, he went in search of a cup of tea and maybe some Hobnobs, a renewed jaunt in his step.

Overnight, Pencil Kane had decided that he might need to start thinking about his backup plan. Not that Pencil was going to give up on the idea of making a full recovery and playing again for Arsenal. No, Pencil needed a backup plan because he knew that he was now one of the most famous young people in England; knew that everyone in the country loved him for what had happened to him. And Pencil was sharp enough to know that this was his moment, his opportunity to build his fame and fortune. So, he would need to sit down with his agent, the person he trusted completely, and explore his outline backup plan in more detail.

Meantime, Pencil had to get to the Arsenal training ground and continue with his physio and podiatry. Desperate as he was to get rid of his crutches, do some bike work, he knew that doing that was many weeks off. Pencil though, needed to show his loyalty and his professionalism. After all, Pencil was getting paid one point three million pounds a year, and Pencil could not yet walk without crutches.

The first part of his backup plan was to get a television company to follow his progress. Paul Ruthven had suggested that a while ago but Pencil had said no. Now, however, things were different. Pencil might not recover and it would be good if his fans could see how hard he tried, his effort and dedication. Then they could do a book, a sort of diary of Pencil's progress from the bombings to wherever he ended up. Pencil Kane would still be famous, would still have the world at his feet.

Even if those feet would no longer be good enough for football.

His buzzer went and he let his mum into his apartment as he left to be driven to his club's high-tech training facility in London Colney, and his physio work. On his way, he texted Paul Ruthven simply saying that it was time for the backup plan; time for the television programme and the book. Paul replied saying that he would get onto it, wishing him good luck with the physio.

Pencil Kane was happy. He needed to keep progressing, needed the backup plan just in case.

Another day, another dead body, thought Colm Elliot as he and Hannah entered an old warehouse at the back of London's Paddington station. The call had come in just as he was about to head home, another fairly routine occurrence in the world of the Metropolitan Police.

Elliot had been born in County Antrim in Northern Ireland, the second son in a small family. His mother had taught in a local Catholic primary school and his father had been a self-employed painter and decorator, a kind, loving man with two fatal flaws, the drink and the bookies. Colm's elder brother Liam had aspired to follow in his father's footsteps and had done so in more ways than one, first as a painter and decorator, then as an alcoholic gambler. Elliot's father died at the age of thirty-eight from a brain tumour, and his mum had died of cancer just six years later. Liam Elliot was still alive, if only just, and now lived a sad and lonely alcoholic life in a care home in Antrim that was paid for by Colm. His trips home tended to be rare; for family funerals, and the odd visit to the few family members that he still stayed in touch with.

From a very early age, the younger Elliot boy had wanted to become a policeman, a detective being his private ambition. However, being a Catholic and a policeman was not easily achieved back in the days when Colm was growing up. But, Elliot had gone to university in Manchester and upon graduation, with a First in Criminology, had applied and been accepted to join the Greater Manchester police force. After a year as a bobby on the beat, Elliot was identified as having high potential and was sent to London for assessment for entry to an accelerated promotion programme. Success there saw him sent back north to Liverpool as a young detective constable before his recruitment to the highly secretive security forces in Northern Ireland, where his accent and local knowledge was seen as being highly beneficial to a seriously over-stretched force in the province. There, the young Elliot, who was already a sergeant, soon impressed his superiors and was often involved in dangerous projects and missions. One day, he might take the time to write about his experiences, or, he thought as yet another corpse loomed in front of him, he might just retire to somewhere sunny and play golf every day.

Carole had never known herself to be angry with Gary, but she was absolutely furious with this latest revelation. *Stupid, stupid man* was the mantra that she kept repeating to herself all day, finding herself drifting from her usual focus while in a variety of client and project meetings.

By 4pm that afternoon, she had decided that she needed to confront him, tell him how she was feeling, but did she really know why she was so angry? Why had this situation caused her so much hurt and to some extent heartbreak?

After asking Jenny to fix her a slot on his schedule, she went to her room, still in a spin, still in a furious strop, but why?

Sitting at her desk, her emails on the screen in front of her just a blur, she considered her reaction and found the answer. She was jealous. *Jesus*, she thought, *after all these years?*

Pushing back from her desk, she pulled on her cashmere

coat, told Jenny to cancel her meeting with Gary and left the office to go and do some shopping. 'Fuck,' she muttered to herself as she went out into the fresh early evening. *I am jealous and the twat has really hurt me this time.* It was time for some serious thinking, some serious rethinking about herself and that asshole. Before that, it was time to hit the shops, time for some serious retail therapy.

CHAPTER 9

THURSDAY
22 SEPTEMBER 2005

Like Paul Ruthven, Lucy Campbell had been the second child in her family. As the middle of three daughters, she had always wanted to be a doctor, ever since the time that she and her elder sister Lesley had both been ill with chickenpox and their town's first female GP had come to their home to visit the sick sisters.

Her father had worked in Bradford as an insurance actuary with Bradford & Bingley, while her mother busied herself keeping their immaculate semi-detached home in Harrogate. At school she had excelled at most things that she put her mind to, her academic work and sport, with the modest exception of swimming, and despite the fact that Lesley had led the way into medicine before her by going to Dundee University, Lucy's hard work and natural ability had got her a much sought-after place to study medicine at the University of Edinburgh.

At university, she breezed through her early years, attracted to and experimenting with all aspects of university life. She worked hard and for the first three years, tended to play hard as well. Young men came and went as she enjoyed her sexual liberty too much to stick with just the one partner; she experimented with alcohol and even illicit drugs before deciding that neither were for her and giving both the drink, with the occasional exception of a glass of wine, and the drugs the boot. As for the sex, well that was something that the young and attractive medical student decided she could not live without.

On her graduation day, she was the only one of the students in her year who was surprised when she won the gold medal awarded for surgical excellence and after her foundation programme that lasted three years, Lucy did her core surgical training at Edinburgh's Royal Infirmary, with her themed speciality area being orthopaedics. That in turn led to her applying and being accepted for a Speciality Registrar role in the surgical wards of the same hospital. At the age of thirty, and with four years' speciality experience under her professional belt, the highly regarded registrar was appointed to her first fully fledged consultant orthopaedic surgeon's role in Whitechapel in London, where she had built her reputation as a renowned specialist in lower limb surgery over the three years she had been there.

In her private life, after her forty-eight hours per week at the hospital, the young surgeon continued to be experimental as a somewhat slower stream of men entered and left her life, without any one of them threatening to become anything resembling permanent. Her love of life and endless energy continued, and her vacations would take her, sometimes with her sisters to whom she remained close, on cycling tours of the Alps, or walking in south-west France along the foot of the Pyrenees, or on one occasion halfway up Mount Everest on a charity event.

Living her life to the full, with a deeply satisfying and fulfilling career, Lucy Campbell had no room for marriage or the thought of settling down with children. She had never met a man that she could in any way see herself committing to on a permanent basis.

All that changed, however, on the 7th of July that year, when the serious and dashing Paul Ruthven arrived at Whitechapel hospital to visit his young protégé, the badly injured Pencil Kane. Tall, handsome, polite, and much to her delight, Scottish, she felt her heart miss beats like never before. People at the hospital had told her that he used to be a footballer, but that had meant nothing to the young medic, knowing nothing about that particular sport.

When he had called a few days later to ask her out, she had to refuse as she had been dating a colleague at the time, someone who took a little longer than she had expected to finish with and so clear the path for Paul.

So, as she arrived at Whitechapel that morning, it was with a very special feeling in her heart, a feeling that she was in love and a feeling that Paul Ruthven could in fact be the one for her. Tomorrow, she was having a day off to attend the wedding of one of Paul's friends, a colleague of his older brother, where she would meet the other Ruthven boy, someone she knew was going to be her brother-in-law some time in the not-too-distant future. For Dr Lucy Campbell had set her mind on Paul Ruthven and when she set her mind on something, it would inevitably happen.

Just after nine that morning, Paul Ruthven arrived at the offices of IMG in central London to meet an old friend of his, Charles Tonkins. Charles used to produce football matches for Sky Sports and had just returned from a job in Jordan to take up a new post as head of UK television with IMG.

'So, you've now gone over to the other side,' began Charles as they settled into the untidiest office that Paul had ever had the displeasure to visit. 'Sorry about the mess, not had time to get things organised properly,' he continued, noticing Paul taking in the chaos.

'I have indeed,' replied Paul, before continuing, 'How are things here?'

'Really busy, there is just so much television,' expanded Charles.

'Room for another bit of work I hope.'

'Christ, plenty of room, three hundred channels in the UK at the moment. I remember the good old days when there were only two,' laughed the IMG man.

'Ah well, you have a good few years on me there, Charles,' laughed Ruthven.

'Bastard. So what do have in mind?'

Ruthven took the next ten minutes to outline his initial thinking regarding Pencil and his rehabilitation programme.

'Sounds interesting. I saw his little cameo at Highbury on Monday evening; not a dry eye in our house,' responded Tonkins eventually.

'So, what next?' pushed Paul, as always keen to get moving.

'Christ, I can see why you hated being a TV pundit. Ever heard of patience?'

'Sorry, just appreciate that time is short for you TV moguls,' laughed Ruthven.

'Let me run the idea past a few people here; we need to act quickly or we will miss key events. Christ, Monday would have been a cool behind-the-scenes moment,' mused Charles, his mind already on the programme, and who he could sell it to.

Ten minutes later, Paul Ruthven was back in the car and being driven back to his office by Jorge. He had the parents of another young player coming to meet him at midday. They had heard good things and were looking for the right person to look after their son's best interests. More often than not, thought Ruthven, that meant their best interests.

Julia Hillman was getting stressed. It was the last day before the wedding and people did not seem to be taking things as seriously as she felt that they should. Her father, for example, was refusing to let her read his draft speech, saying that it still needed a few tweaks and refinements.

'That would indicate to me that the silly bugger's not got it written yet,' she stated to Lucas, who was busying himself on a final draft of the table plan.

'I am sure that he has it all in hand. After all, he's had plenty of time to think about it,' replied Lucas, realising immediately that he had made a big mistake.

'Lucas! Never, ever let me hear you say something like that again!' she exclaimed. 'My father has been through hell and you think it's okay to sit there and be flippant? You are such a stupid bloody man at times!'

'Sorry, darling, but you know what I mean.'

'No, frankly I don't know what you mean!' she near shouted, leaving the room.

Just then, Lucas's mobile phone rang in his pocket. It was Julia's father, who wanted to know if he needed to attend the police station in St John's Wood that day as per his bail conditions. Lucas informed him that he was not sure given that he had just been released on Monday, but that he would speak to Julia and call him back if he needed to attend. Cutting the connection, Lucas went back to the final draft table plan and promptly forgot Malcolm Hillman's request.

Colm Elliot received the call later that afternoon informing him that Malcolm Hillman had in fact missed the first of his bail conditions. Smiling to himself, he informed the caller, a duty officer who knew of Elliot's close interest in the case, that he and Hannah would look into it and get back to him by end of play on Friday. Now he had the perfect reason for being at Stoke Park, and if anyone thought otherwise, he would simply threaten to take Hillman back into immediate custody.

Later that evening, the Hillman party began arriving at the venue for the wedding. Malcolm Hillman was leaving no expense spared when it came to his daughter's big day and had booked a number of bedrooms at the upmarket hotel. The wedding service, a civil ceremony due to the fact that this was Lucas's third marriage, was due to commence at 11am and would be followed by a reception for just over a hundred people, friends and family all more than a little intrigued to be attending an event where the bride's father was awaiting trial for the murder of her stepmother.

Malcolm Hillman checked in for the night at just after 8pm, totally oblivious to the fact that by being away from his home address that night, he was in breach of the second of his bail conditions.

Paul Ruthven received a call from Charles Tonkins at IMG at 8.30 that evening to inform him that IMG wanted to take up the option on making what he now called the fly-on-the-wall documentary on Pencil Kane.

'That sounds terrific,' replied Paul. 'When do you want to get started?'

'Let me pull my team together tomorrow. Perhaps we can then meet to map things out on Monday. Ideally, we would like to start filming later in the week; get Pencil doing a video diary when we are not around, that sort of stuff.'

'Sounds good, Charles. Can I inform Pencil?' he checked.

'Yeah, that's cool. Tell him he's going to be famous.'

'He's famous already, Charles, this will just take him into orbit,' reflected Paul.

'Think of all those juicy fees, Ruthven. You really are the luckiest of shits,' teased the TV man.

'Just doing the best for my client, Charles, and if you call getting blown up on the Underground lucky, then Pencil is the lucky one,' remonstrated Ruthven.

'Fair point, fair point. I will call and arrange a time on Monday. Are you around tomorrow?'

'Until ten-thirty, then I am at a wedding. But that, my old friend, is another story.'

Ruthven then called Pencil to let him have the good news. Pencil had been at the training facility all day and his foot was killing him; Paul Ruthven's call did enough to lift his spirits.

CHAPTER 10   FRIDAY
23 SEPTEMBER 2005

After an overnight ground frost across the country, early morning sunshine greeted Colm Elliot and Hannah Bellamy as they turned into the drive at the Stoke Park Club that fine Friday morning. Driving the Vauxhall, with golf courses to either side, Hannah pointed to Hugh Grant's lake.

'This is the opening scene in *Layer Cake*,' she continued, referring to the drive towards the hotel buildings.

'So, you got the DVD?' asked Elliot, slowing the car to admire the beauty of the place, the large dome of the mansion house now in view.

'I did, and it had a couple of endings but I only watched the one. What's the point?'

'Does seem to be a bit pointless. This place is amazing,' reflected Elliot, taking in the golf views.

'Golfer are you, boss?' asked Hannah, watching his eyes wander the fairways.

'Occasional golfer; loved to play as a boy, not that my family encouraged it,' replied Elliot. Golf always took him back to his boyhood days with his mates in Portrush.

'You should've brought Susan, she'd like it here,' offered Bellamy.

'She would. Might bring her for a romantic break, book the Hugh Grant suite.' He smiled at his sergeant before continuing, 'Not on a copper's wage though.'

'How did Hillman make his money?' asked Hannah suddenly, the thought crossing her mind, not for the first time, but the first time to Elliot.

'Part of some sort of investment fund, seems to have gone under suspiciously a while back but not before the owners had made themselves a tidy packet.' Elliot had done the research.

Elliot found them a parking space in a car park heaving with expensive models, and as they climbed from his modest Vauxhall, he recommitted to make sure that Hillman got his just rewards for murdering his wife in cold blood. *Some things*, he thought to himself, *should be beyond how much money a person has in the bank.*

They walked together and climbed the steps leading to the entrance to the mansion, to be met by an official-looking young man in the reception area.

'Good morning, can I help you?' he asked quietly, discreetly.

'Yes,' replied Elliot, showing the man his police identity. 'We would like to speak to your general manager.'

'Of course, let me find you a place to sit while we try to find him.' They were led through a grand hall to what the man called the orangery, where he seated them and asked a hovering waitress to take their order for tea or coffee.

Five minutes later, they were joined by a man introducing himself as Marc, the general manager, and for the next five minutes, Elliot explained the situation; why he was there and the co-operation that he would appreciate from Stoke Park.

Julia Hillman and her sister Helen, who was going to be one of Julia's bridesmaids, had spent the last two hours being pampered in the Stoke Park Spa and were making their way through the orangery to a private room that the family had booked for breakfast when she spotted Elliot and Bellamy enjoying their coffee. Storming to confront the detectives, she was shaking with rage by the time that she reached them.

'What the hell do you think you are doing coming here today?' she began, sitting and trying to keep her voice low enough so as not to be overheard by the other guests.

'Good morning, Julia Hillman,' began Elliot, the slightest hint of a smile on his face.

'I asked you a question and if I don't get the right answer, I will have you for harassment,' she continued, venom in her voice.

'We are here to check up on your father, see how he might perform at your wedding,' responded Elliot before being interrupted.

'Like fuck you will,' she fumed. 'I am going to get security, get you thrown out. You can't do this to me and my family! This is outrageous!'

'Oh, I think that you will find that we can. You see, your father is in breach of his bail conditions, and if you don't calm yourself down and listen, then we just might be inclined to take him back into custody straight away,' offered Elliot quietly but firmly.

'What do you mean, in breach of his bail conditions?' Julia Hillman hissed through gritted teeth.

'Two counts. The first failing to attend St John's Wood Police Station yesterday before 4pm, and secondly, not being at his agreed address last evening,' explained Elliot, now fully enjoying himself.

'That's just been a silly misunderstanding, can easily be rectified.'

'Well, that depends on the deal we strike,' suggested Colm.

'What deal? I am doing no deal. This is my wedding day, for Christ's sake, do you have no heart?'

'Oh yes, Julia Hillman, I have a heart. Which is why my colleague Sergeant Bellamy and I are here and ready to do you a deal, without which by the way, we will be taking your father into custody with us when we leave,' explained Elliot, conscious that they had been joined by an elderly man who was hovering behind Julia Hillman.

'This is my fiancé, Lucas Hunt. Lucas, these two are police officers. Father has breached his bail conditions,' she began by way of introductions.

The elderly man took a seat, growing paler by the second.

'Surely,' he began, 'we can come to some arrangement.'

'Exactly what I was trying to say to Julia Hillman before you arrived,' replied Elliot.

'So, what can we do to help?'

'Well, we would like to be given permission to observe your wedding ceremony, hear the speeches, that sort of thing,' began Elliot, feeling victory in his grasp.

'Never in million years,' fumed Julia again. 'That is not going to happen. This is police harassment, nothing else. You will get suspended for this little trick. I will go to the very top to have you punished.' The rant continued.

'Very well, if that's your final word, Sergeant Bellamy and I will go find your father and be off back to Wandsworth, let you get on with your nuptials,' sighed Elliot, beginning to stand.

'No, wait,' urged Hunt. 'Please sit and let's see if we can work this out.'

Ten minutes later, and much to the chagrin of Julia Hillman, they had a plan. Elliot and Bellamy would attend the civil ceremony and would be allowed to watch the speeches during the wedding breakfast. In return, Elliot and Bellamy would report back to the duty officer that Malcolm Hillman's bail breach was an oversight and he would be allowed to stay for the duration of the wedding celebration.

As Julia Hillman, her sister Helen and Lucas Hunt left to

complete their preparations, Elliot and Bellamy could hear Hunt being lambasted with questions from Julia about how her father could have forgotten his bail conditions.

Just after 11.45, Gary and Vicki Ruthven, accompanied by Paul Ruthven and Lucy Campbell, arrived at Stoke Park where after a quick glass of champagne, they were guided to the room in which the civil wedding ceremony was to be held. Finding four seats on the groom's side of the room, they chatted quietly while waiting for the service to begin. Vicki saw Lucas Hunt chatting to a young man she took to be Lucas's son. The young man was due to be best man at his father's third wedding.

'I can't wait to see the axe murderer,' she whispered to Gary, who smiled back before putting a finger to his lips in a signal to his wife to be quiet.

'Do you think his suit will be covered with arrows?' persisted Vicki, the midday glass of champagne clearly having gone to her head.

Just then, there was movement at the front of the room and a rendition of the bridal march began playing through the room's music system. Moments later Julia Hillman walked in slowly, arm in arm with her father.

Wearing a grey silk suit and carrying a modest bouquet of lilies, Vicki thought Julia looked as good as she had ever seen her. The man with her, however, also dressed in grey, looked pale and nervous, clearly overcome by the moment he had probably thought he would miss. Vicki could not help but think of the crime that the man had committed, feeling that it was wrong that he was allowed to be there.

Forty minutes later, the ceremony completed, the new Mr and Mrs Hunt left the room and the guests followed out into the great hall where a string quartet were playing and more champagne and canapés were being passed among the guests. Looking drop dead in a Stella McCartney creation, Carole King and her husband Dan Jenner had slipped into the wedding ceremony a few minutes late. Dan looked equally elegant in his suit and white silk shirt although he could not be persuaded to wear a tie, so it was his usual tan, stubble, fashionably long hair and open-neck shirt. As a couple, they looked a million dollars, which was a very low estimate of their actual net worth.

Carole loved being with Dan. He was so calm and relaxed about everything and with everyone, carrying, as he went about his life, the air of a very successful and contented person. That morning, she was still carrying real resentment and anger towards Gary for what he had told her about his situation with Tandy, was still trying to privately analyze her sense of jealousy.

Seeing the Ruthvens standing near the foot of a grand staircase, she indicated to Dan to join them as a waitress offered them a glass of champagne from a tray.

'Well, this looks like a nice family gathering,' she began, joining them and being introduced to Lucy Campbell. Dan quietly shook hands with the men and pecked the women on their cheeks with his usual ease.

'What a lovely place for a wedding,' continued Carole, taking in the surroundings and looking for the newlyweds. 'I guess they have gone outside for photographs.'

'I guess so,' agreed Gary, who was looking very distracted and being much quieter than normal.

'Interesting to see Julia's father here,' said Dan quietly.

'Feels very odd,' responded Vicki Ruthven, admiring how healthy and wealthy Carole and her husband looked, hoping to herself that one day in the not too distant future she too could go to events knowing that money was not an item on her 'things to worry about' agenda.

'So,' asked Carole to Lucy, 'how did you two meet?'

'In fairly unique circumstances,' began the very natural and pretty doctor, who was thrilled to be meeting friends of Paul and his brother.

'We met on 7/7,' interjected Paul Ruthven. 'Lucy is treating Pencil Kane, and we first met in the war zone that was Whitechapel hospital on the day of the bombings.'

'Blimey, and you got Ruthven to ask you out?' smiled Carole, clearly avoiding eye contact with Gary.

'I did,' replied Lucy, taking hold of Paul's arm before adding, 'but I made him wait a few weeks before accepting.'

'Good for you,' smiled Carole again, really warming to the young medic and her soft Yorkshire accent.

'How is Pencil doing?' asked Dan to Paul.

'On the mend. He was very lucky, but his injuries were very serious,' replied Paul quietly.

'Bloody terrible thing to happen,' reflected Dan accepting, another glass of champagne from a waitress.

'The whole situation was a nightmare,' agreed the younger Ruthven just as an announcement was made inviting the guests into the hotel's Fountain Room for the wedding breakfast.

So, after a brief inspection of a board containing the table plan, the group who would be sitting at the same table made their way into a beautiful room with magnificent views out onto the Stoke Park grounds and gardens.

Colm Elliot and Hannah Bellamy were seated at a hastily arranged table at the back of the Fountain Room watching as the guests made their slow way into the room and began to find their respective tables. At the front of the room, Julia Hillman and Lucas Hunt arrived at the top table, accompanied by Malcolm Hillman, his ex-wife and Julia's sister, Helen.

Elliot was fascinated by the dynamics in the room in general and within the inner family circle in particular; amazed that this grand event was taking place within the Hillman family when the trial of the patriarch was still imminent.

'Not much evidence of early Alzheimer's on show, Hannah. What do you think?'

'I'm finding this whole thing very creepy, boss. It's like the death has been forgotten.' Bellamy seemed to shiver in reply.

'The murder, Hannah. Let's not forget what it really was,' corrected Elliot.

'Trust me, boss, I've not forgotten, even if this lot would like to.'

'Glad to hear it, Hannah, glad to hear it.'

The wedding breakfast in the spectacular south-facing Fountain Room, with its views of the terrace, fountains and Capability Brown landscaped gardens was a very elegant affair. Paul Ruthven was feeling really good as he enjoyed his roasted duck breast topped with seared foie gras and served with apple and potato rosti and truffle sauce. He felt good being with Lucy who, although seven years his junior, made him feel like he was the luckiest man alive. Sure, he had been with more than his fair share of beautiful women in his time, but she was different. Bright, energized, career focused and absolutely killer in bed, she had totally transformed his long-held desire to stay single. Paul wanted to be with Lucy every waking moment and the fact that he couldn't because of her career, because of her independent spirit, just made being apart from her all the more vexing.

Paul was also worried about his brother, who seemed to be well out of sorts. He would have to have a quiet word with him, see what was going on. His telephone vibrated in his jacket, and he checked the incoming message under the level of the table top, hoping not to appear rude. It was from Charles Tonkins at IMG, confirming their agreement to do the documentary on

Pencil and that the Arsenal publicity team had approved the idea, in principle, subject to clarification of the process and the proposed terms. Paul smiled at Lucy, switched his phone off, and returned to his meal.

'Good news?' she asked quietly.

'IMG approval,' he winked in reply. 'You might become a reality television star by the end of this project.'

'Not going to happen,' she smiled back, taking only her third sip of wine since their arrival at Stoke Park.

'I hope you are not getting drunk,' he teased.

'Mmm... might've just reached my monthly quota,' she replied, her glowing cheeks making her look even more beautiful to the besotted Ruthven.

'So,' began Vicki Ruthven to Lucas Hunt, who had joined their table to say a proper hello to his colleagues and friends. 'Where are you two off to on honeymoon?'

'We're staying here tonight, then going to Vienna from Heathrow tomorrow,' began Hunt, obviously very happy that the wedding ceremony was done and that the lunch was proving an obvious success. 'Julia and I both adore the opera and we've got tickets to the Vienna State Opera, *La Bohème*, tomorrow evening,' he concluded.

'Sounds lovely,' replied Vicki. 'How long are you there for?'

'Just four days. Julia needs to get back for her father.'

'It must be very difficult,' suggested Carole King quietly across the table.

'It's been incredibly challenging and now he's decided to act for himself, the preparation is enormously time-consuming.'

'I am sure,' replied Carole, her eyes straying to Julia and her father sitting at the top table.

'Anyway, is everyone okay here?' Hunt changed the subject.

'Very nice, thanks,' seemed to be the unanimous verdict.

'Good,' said Hunt, eyeing the next table, keen to get on with his rounds.

Julia Hillman – she had decided to retain her maiden name – was trying hard not to let the very presence of the two police detectives spoil her big wedding day. However, inwardly she was seething. How dare those shit-heads come here on a day like this? Fortunately, her father seemed not to have noticed, or at least was not letting it be known that he had noticed Elliot and his sidekick. *Perhaps*, she thought to herself, *he really does have early Alzheimer's.*

Dismissing that as unlikely, she monitored the lovely room. The hotel bumph said it was two hundred years old and she agreed that it was the perfect setting for the occasion. Her eyes landed on the RCS table, the handsome Ruthven brothers, Vicki and Paul's new woman, and wondered what they were discussing with Lucas. She had also been surprised by David Lane's late withdrawal – he was odd, she thought. *I bet my father is a topic of speculation.* She concluded her attention returning to those who had turned up, wondering how Malcolm was going to perform with his speech.

She then eyed the two police, sitting chatting quietly at their table, a couple of glasses of wine on the small table in front of them. What asshole gave them wine? She fumed but then saw Lucas move to another table and guessed that she had found the answer. *What a stupid but lovely man I have just married*, she concluded with a smile on her face.

Her father was chatting with Helen, and Julia began to speculate about babies. How long would it take her to get pregnant? Not long she hoped. Then, with a sudden panic attack, she calculated that if the first baby was born within a year, Lucas would be seventy-eight by the time it started school. *Oh Christ*, she thought, *I hope the dear man stays healthy.*

Twenty minutes later, Malcolm Hillman got to his feet in front of just over a hundred family and friends in the Fountain Room to deliver his much anticipated father of the bride speech. Searching in his suit pocket, he pulled out what appeared to be his notes before putting on his reading glasses and clearing his throat.

'Ladies and gentlemen,' he began, and continued to speak eloquently and articulately for four or five minutes before it was time to salute his daughter.

Just then, a young girl of seven or eight, who happened to be Helen's youngest child, walked to the front of the room and handed him a green Harrods bag, which he took before kissing the girl on the top of her head.

'Which brings me to Julia,' he continued, 'and a present that I've been meaning to get for you for no less than thirty-one years. Let me share the story first.' He stopped to take a sip from his water glass before continuing. 'Thirty-one years ago, in August 1974, Julia's mother, Julia, Helen and I were heading for our holiday cottage in Cornwall. It was a beautiful day, baking-hot sun, and Julia and Helen, who was just two at the time, were getting restless in the back. The traffic was busy and we were probably travelling at fifty or sixty, when Julia, complaining of the heat, said that her teddy Tom was overheating, so could I open our sunroof. To keep things calm I duly obliged and Julia soon had Tom poking out through the car roof. A little later, and to our horror, Julia began to scream in the back of the car but with the traffic so bad, it was a few minutes before I could pull over into a lay-by, only to discover that Tom had gone.' There was a ripple of sympathetic laughter and a number of ohhs and ahhs around the Fountain Room before Hillman continued.

'Yes, Tom was gone for good. Somewhere on the old A5, hopefully to a good home. Julia, as you can imagine, was distraught, but no new Tom was found.' Again, he stopped for water before continuing. 'Until now that is.' With a flourish, he pulled a beautifully wrapped gift from the Harrods bag and handed it over to his tearful daughter who took no time in ripping the gift open to reveal a vintage Steiff teddy bear. The two embraced, before Hillman concluded by simply saying, 'Ladies and gentlemen, please raise your glasses in a toast to the bride.' To a person, everyone in the room was touched by the emotionality of the moment, and as they toasted, Colm Elliot whispered to Hannah Bellamy.

'As I said before, Hannah, if he's got Alzheimer's, then I'm a freaking Chinaman.'

Hannah, a tear in her eye, busied herself with her telephone, making sure that her recording of Malcolm Hillman's touching speech was safely stored on her Nokia.

Across the room, Vicki Ruthven leaned towards Gary and whispered, 'He's going down for murder.'

The formalities of the day over with, Colm Elliot and Bellamy decided it was appropriate for them to take their leave. However, not before Colm had his last little bit of fun at the expense of the new bride. Motioning for Lucas Hunt to join them at their table, he asked him if they could have a quiet word with himself and Julia in the great hall before they departed. Leaving the Fountain Room, they found two empty sofas behind a grand piano and waited for the newlyweds to join them.

As seemed to be normal, Julia Hillman arrived in an aggressive and nasty spirit.

'You shit-heads are doing your best to really piss me off,' she began, sitting opposite the two police officers.

'I'm very sorry to hear that. And here was me thinking I'd shown to you that I had a soft side to my nature,' countered Elliot, more than a hint of a smile on his face.

'I will find a way to report this,' hissed Hillman. 'This is unacceptable,' she continued.

'Whatever,' waved Elliot with his right hand. 'We just wanted to thank you both for your co-operation.'

'Our co-operation?' fumed Hillman. 'Our co-operation?'

'Yes, and to warn you to make sure that your father keeps to his bail conditions in the future – no more slip-ups. Because, if there are any more, we'll have him back in Wandsworth quicker than you can say, "Welcome home, Tom the teddy." Am I making myself clear, Julia Hillman? Or should I be saying Julia Hunt?'

'Julia Hillman is fine as far as you're concerned,' she replied, going pale as she realized that this was not an argument she had any chance of winning.

'So, have I made the position clear?' Elliot was standing, ready to take his leave.

'You've made yourself very clear.' It was Lucas Hunt who tried to close the discussion.

'Good, so we'll be off and leave you to your celebrations.' Bellamy stood, and followed her boss back towards the reception and the exit.

'I think that's been a very worthwhile few hours, Hannah, don't you agree?'

'I do indeed, boss, but if I were you, I wouldn't be expecting a thank you card any time soon.' They were descending the steps at the front of the building.

'Really? And here was me thinking I'd just done the lady a big favour,' smiled Elliot as they went to retrieve his Vauxhall from the car park.

It was a beautiful late afternoon and Vicki had suggested a walk in the grounds to see the old St Giles Church that stood opposite the hotel across the lake. Gary and Dan went to their respective cars to collect coats and jackets to guard them from the chill as Lucy, Vicki and Paul waited for them at reception.

The women walked in a threesome some fifteen yards in front, and Gary, Dan and Paul took up the rear. Gary watched the women in front of him. Vicki, tall, slim, blonde and attractive, his wife of twenty-odd years who had no clue of the anguish her husband could be about to bring upon her if the Tandy situation ever erupted; Carole, about the same height as Vicki, but dark haired and even more beautiful, the soulmate who was feeling badly let down by him on so many fronts; and Lucy, smaller than the other two but just as pretty, someone he knew he was going to really like although he had only been introduced to her earlier that morning. Yes, he had met a few of Paul's women in the past, but Lucy seemed different.

Stopping on a bridge that spanned the two sections of the lake, Gary took in the magnificence of the mansion house and its dome, admiring the golf course and the grounds that led to the church. Paul was chatting with Dan and the women were laughing at something one of them had just said; probably Vicki, who had a great, if sometimes wicked, sense of humour. Gary was struck by the enormity of his situation. *What if Carole said something to Vicki, what then? Jesus fuck*, he cursed to himself, *what on earth am I doing to my life? Forget that*, he corrected, *what on earth am I doing to the lives of my family?*

A few years earlier, Ruthven had been introduced to the work of Dr Eric Berne, a psychologist who had first developed the concept of Transactional Analysis. This had led to him read Thomas Harris's famous book *I'm OK – You're OK*, and the whole concept of what he referred to as Parent, Adult, Child. Gary had found real help in trying to understand his own personality through that book. As he stood on the bridge at Stoke Park, he suddenly had the massive realization of what was so different between himself and his younger brother. Paul, to put it simply, whether deliberately or not, lived his life in the present, in Adult, for most of his time. *I, on the other hand*, reflected Gary, *while aspiring to live in Adult mode, spend too much of my time in Child, wanting to be liked, wanting to be a good father, wanting things to go my way, not dealing in the here and now, avoiding the facts…* Basically living his life frightening himself with what might happen.

'You look like you are somewhere else.' Paul had approached him unnoticed.

'Just thinking,' retorted Gary quietly.

'Penny for them.'

'No, I was just reflecting on life, how things turn out, often not as planned.'

'Ah, the old life plan panic.'

'How is your life plan, Paul?'

'Don't really have one. I remember reading a quote somewhere that suggested that life is what happens when you are busy planning your life. I kinda liked that, like to take each day as it comes.'

'What happens when you fuck-up though?' They were walking again, following the women and Dan up a short incline towards the church and its ancient graveyard.

'Put it down to experience; see what can be learned and move on,' replied the younger Ruthven.

'I think I might need to try that soon,' smiled Gary, tears forming in his eyes.

'Well, you know where I am if you need to talk,' offered Paul.

'Thanks. Might just do that,' replied Gary, knowing that it was unlikely. How could he share some of these things with his wee brother? That, after all, was not the way it worked. He was supposed to be the wise one, the big brother. Realizing how stupid that thought was, he went to be with his wife, his heart near breaking point for the stupid things he had done, his love for her swelling.

Pencil Kane was as angry as he had ever been with anyone or anything. It was gone 9pm and his right foot was in such pain, he imagined meeting the people who had done this to him and beating them to a pulp. Yes, Pencil knew that whoever he had been was dead, blown to pieces by his own horrible device, but that did not help Pencil at that moment. His physio work at the London Colney had been great. It was fun to be back among the other players, even if they were the injured ones; the banter made Pencil feel normal again. They had even let him spend some time in the pool, having adjusted the floor of the pool to lessen the weight on his feet. But now, before he took his night-time pain killers, the pain was excruciating. *The bastards*, swore Pencil Kane – *what right did they have to do this bad thing to me?*

Just then his telephone rang and he checked the number before accepting the call from his agent.

'Hey, Paul Ruthven. How was your big flash weddin'?' he asked as brightly as possible.

'It was okay, Pencil, as weddings go,' replied Ruthven honestly.

'And how is my TV deal cookin'?'

'That's why I am ringing, we've got the go-ahead. You're going to be the star in your own reality TV show.'

'Hey, that's cool, man. When do we start?'

'Not sure yet. Arsenal wants some input to the ground rules, but IMG are talking about starting filming on Monday.'

'That's sounds pretty soon.' Pencil was pleased.

'It is indeed; they feel that we've got some ground to catch up on. How are those feet today?'

'Been tough this evenin', man. Left one is great, but the right bastard is giving me grief,' replied Pencil.

'Do you want me to get you back to see Dr Campbell?'

'No, man, let's leave it for a few more days. I need to take tonight's pills and get some sleep. Today was a tough one at the club.'

'Okay. If you're sure I'll let you get on with it. I'll speak in the morning after your physio.'

'Good man, speak then.' Pencil broke the connection.

In bed that night, Pencil Kane started on what he called his Plan C. He was going to open a store that sold vintage clothing and cool vintage sports gear. His first store was going to be called Pencil One, the second Pencil Two, and so on. To his knowledge nobody had ever done that before. By the time he reached Pencil Ninety-Nine, he would be really rich; richer than he would have been being a footballer. Smiling to himself he switched his widescreen TV off, his pain and anger subsiding. *Bastards won't beat Pencil Kane!*

NOVEMBER 2005

CHAPTER 11

SATURDAY
5 NOVEMBER 2005

The rain was driving into their faces from a near horizontal angle, but that did not stop Paul and Gary Ruthven from climbing up onto the ninth tee at Aberlady Golf Club in East Lothian. Behind them the waves smashing ashore from the Firth of Forth looked to be rising higher than the point at which they now stood to prepare their tee shots.

Gary went to the tee marker and tried to place his ball on a tee that he had just pushed into the soggy ground, but it would not stay there, being blown off the tee by the ferocious wind and rain. Laughing, he walked back to his brother.

'You know what's crazy?' he began.

'No, what?'

'My wife's out shopping in this,' Gary completed the old but still funny joke.

'Do you want to call it a day?' laughed Paul, knowing that his brother would not be the first to quit their game.

'You gotta be kidding, I am two up,' responded Gary, going back to prepare to make his shot.

Two hours later, they both stood in the piping hot showers in the clubhouse changing rooms, their hands and feet gradually recovering their circulation. They had come to Scotland for the weekend to see their parents, play some golf and have a general catch-up session. Gary was still crowing about his narrow victory as they dried, dressed and took a couple of seats in the warm but near deserted bar before ordering piping hot tea and a couple of rounds of bacon sandwiches. Their dad had declined the chance to join them, claiming he had seen the weather forecast, so the brothers were keen to take the opportunity to have a chat, see what was going on in the other's world.

'So, what's up with you?' It was Paul who got them started.

'Nothing much, same old busy-busy at RCS; same old internal strife,' he began as he ate his sandwich and eyed the wild weather outside the panoramic windows.

'You still got Lucas Hunt in tow?'

'What do you mean?'

'Well, the old bugger looks like he'd struggle to stay awake for a day at work,' clarified Paul.

'He does have his moments. We had a bloody mess with him last week. His computer caught a porn virus and he tried to get Jenny to resolve it for him. She told him to go fuck himself and reported the incident to Carole, who went and tore into him.' They were both laughing.

'Christ, porn at his age?'

'Got a young wife to keep happy I suppose,' reflected Gary generously.

'So, he's with you for the foreseeable?'

'No, I've discussed things with David Lane and he suggests we let him see the year out and then start to wind him down until next summer,' he clarified.

'Is he any better?'

'Christ, Paul, what's this? Get revenge for the golf time?'

'Not at all,' defended Paul. 'I was just checking. How's the expansion plan going?'

'Not great. New business is very slow, the world is changing.

I think we need to review our model and approach,' began Gary thoughtfully.

'Brands will still be around though.' It was a question.

'No doubt in my mind, but the big boys will become mega and need to be very nimble at adapting to the global economy; the weak ones will disappear faster than ever.'

'Examples?' Paul was intrigued.

'Take Apple. They are showing all the signs of becoming dominant in music; how long before they move into other categories?'

'Such as?' Paul finished his sandwich, focused on his brother's insights.

'Telephones. Nokia are dominant now, but there are some interesting things going on with Blackberry and the boys from the Far East. There have been rumours and it's not a great leap from computers to smart phones, as they are now being called.'

'So, should I be buying shares in Apple then?'

'You could do a lot worse,' replied Gary, wishing he had enough cash to speculate with.

'Worse than what?' Paul had the bit between his teeth.

'Well, you could always buy a house in Spain,' laughed Gary.

'Not big into houses as you know,' replied Paul.

'There you go, a few grand in Apple stocks might be a good idea.'

'Any others?'

'Well, this social networking thing is interesting. Not sure how they're gonna make money out of it though,' continued Gary.

'What, like Facebook?'

'Yep, but intuitively if you get a few hundred million people into something, next stage is real commercialisation, the thing they are good at in the States,' he shrugged.

'And how are your financials doing?' This was new territory for the brothers and Gary wondered why it had suddenly come up.

'What do you mean?' He bought himself some time.

'Well, you've got an expensive-looking lifestyle, so I assume all is good.'

'Okay, things could be better. It was much easier when I owned RCS myself, seemed to make a lot more money. Ever since I sold shares to Lucas and David I seem to be working harder and making less.'

'But you got some of that cash out?'

'Oh, yes. However, I've just sold another ten percent to them, but I'm loaning that cash back to the firm to help the expansion.'

'Is that wise?'

'Not sure, but needs must.'

'Yes, but things are okay?'

'We'll see; this next six months is going to be quite tight. We are way behind on our targets and our costs still rise,' explained Gary, feeling uncomfortable with the way the conversation had developed.

'But you're not at risk?'

'I certainly hope not, but only time will tell.'

'Okay, just remind me not to expand my little empire if I ever suggest it.'

'I will, unless I need to persuade you to give me a job,' Gary laughed. 'Want a beer?' he asked, changing the subject and standing to go to the bar.

'I'll have a pint of heavy shandy, but answer me one thing.'

'Go on.' Gary sat down again.

'If things are as you say, why sell more shares to Lane and Hunt? That really confuses me, big brother.'

'That's a great question, and I need a beer before I can begin to answer it,' he replied.

'Get the beers. I am here for a while by the sound of things.'

In London, the damp and dull afternoon weather was what fans might call a perfect one for football. At Highbury, Pencil

Kane took his seat in the stands beside a small number of other first team squad players who were either injured or simply not selected for that day's match. The season was to be Arsenal's last at their old ground and next year the club would be moving to their magnificent new 60,000-seater stadium just a short walk away. The old stadium was to be converted into apartments that would retain the original shell of Highbury and the current pitch would be transformed into gardens. Pencil had put a deposit down on one of the new homes; had considered it to be a good investment but would never the less be sad to see the old ground disappear.

Sitting in the stands, Pencil was conscious of the buzz that was going on around him; people asking for photographs and autographs. The BBC had broadcast the first of their monthly documentaries on *Pencil's 7/7 Recovery: An Intimate Portrait* the previous Tuesday evening and although it had gone out on BBC2, the average audience for the programme had topped an amazing eight million viewers. Critics had been very positive about the film, praising both the sensitive filming and Kane's courage. Pencil had been keen not to present himself as a victim – that was not in Pencil's plan – and he had been very pleased by how he had come across in the show.

On Monday, he was due back at Whitechapel for his review with Dr Campbell and he was at best pessimistic about how his right foot was progressing. Yes, Pencil no longer needed his crutches and his limp was significantly better, but the foot still hurt like shit when the painkillers were nearing the end of their effectiveness. Still, life was going on and Pencil One, his first store, would be opened in London's Covent Garden in early December two days after the next BBC show was due to be aired. All perfectly planned by Pencil and his advisers to keep his momentum on its upward curve. In addition, his first diary was being published in time for Christmas and would include all the material shown in the December TV programme. Paul

Ruthven had secured a six-figure-sum advance on the book and the publisher was anticipating a bestseller to end the year. Yes, Pencil still had the world at his feet.

Arsenal beat Sunderland 3-1 with goals from Robin van Persie and Thierry Henry, but that did not stop the large crowd from chanting Pencil's name for two minutes from the thirty-first minute of the match; thirty-one being the squad number that Pencil had been given at the start of the season. As the crowd cheered his name, Pencil waved shyly from the stands, privately confident that the fans at the game would have *Pencil's 7/7 Recovery: An Intimate Diary* on their Christmas present list for that year at least. His fallback plans were in place. Pencil was sharp and Pencil was achieving great progress, even if his right foot was not playing ball, so to speak.

Before Emma had been born, Vicki Ruthven had held a senior merchandising role in the UK for the American firm Gap. So, when Paul Ruthven had called to see if she might be interested in helping with the new Pencil Kane store project, she had jumped at the chance to join the new project team.

Gary had helped Paul find a store designer, a young guy who had helped a number of premium brands get launched in the London market, and a couple of consultants from RCS were being used to work through what the Pencil store brand was going to be. Vicki was impressed by Pencil. The young man knew what he wanted and hidden behind his bizarre 'Pencil speak' was a very smart business brain. Two private investors had been persuaded to back the project for a modest 25% share in the business and no expense was being spared to get the store to market.

Vicki found the merchandising work fascinating. They were going to be selling everything from vintage Levi's to authentic sports kit, signed by some of the world's top athletes, from football to golf to tennis to baseball. Pencil and the store designer had sourced two gigantic chandeliers from a store that was closing down in Paris, and the dark grey walls would be adorned with framed prints of the most famous stars on earth from Steve McQueen to the legendary Pelé. As the project developed, Pencil Kane's focus and attention to detail became almost maniacal and he was not afraid to get a painter to repaint an entire wall section because the texture 'felt wrong' or an electrician to straighten a light switch that to the normal eye already looked perfect.

Another aspect of the project that caught Vicki's attention was the regular presence of a two-man film crew from the BBC, and on more than a few occasions, a section of a meeting had to be repeated, or an entrance to the site by one of the team had to be retaken to ensure real *authenticity*. Despite the fact that she was not heard saying anything on the first programme, Vicki had been seen in five scenes and felt pleased to have been included at all.

So, with Gary in Scotland, Vicki and her younger daughter Molly were hitting the shops that Saturday afternoon. Not to buy for themselves, but to look for stock and to find product that would help merchandise the store. Pencil wanted it minimalist, but Vicki had to point out that the place needed to have sufficient stock, explaining the concept of pounds per square foot sales targets. Pencil, of course, got the concept the first time it was explained and within ten minutes they had settled on a target that Vicki now needed to merchandise for. With a healthy number of samples stored in her 4x4 Mercedes, the pair found a Pizza Express for an early dinner, Molly as excited as her mother about the launch of Pencil One in just over four weeks' time.

Tears filled the eyes of Malcolm Hillman as he sat alone in his townhouse in St John's Wood later that evening. His trial for the murder of his wife Anna had been underway at the Old

Bailey for four days, and it was due to reconvene on Tuesday, when he and the prosecution barrister were due to commence their summing up in the trial. Convinced by his daughter Julia to plead not guilty, they had built a defence around three key planks. The first was he could not remember what he had done; that what happened was an accident and that he had no intention of harming his wife. Second, that he was provoked by his wife into doing what he did, and third, that he was suffering from diminished responsibility because he was showing early stage signs of Alzheimer's disease.

The prosecution had ripped into his defence and had even produced a video of his speech at his daughter's wedding, which if Hillman was to be honest, did not do his defence any favours. Probably on Tuesday, the jury would find him guilty and a life sentence in prison would follow. That, however, was not the reason for his tears. They were caused by the great sadness he felt for the loss of his wife, a woman he had really loved; a woman whose energy and vitality had brought fresh hope to a tired, late middle-aged man who had been struggling to come to terms with the unhappy end of his first marriage.

In his heart Hillman knew that he should have pleaded guilty, saved the charade and the extravagant cost of the public trial – simply faced his music. But Julia had been at her persistent best. Though not with bad intention, she was just trying to rescue something from the embers of the burnt-out wreckage that he and his life had become.

Alone in the house, he kept going over that morning in July, that moment when he had snapped. He was not a mean man, but her taunts had hurt like no other. Everything he had done had been for his family. Every penny he had earned, every foreign trip, every night away from home, all were geared to provide for them, give them the start in life that he felt they needed.

Standing, he went to the kitchen in search of more whisky. It would be many Saturdays before he could do this again. It was then that it came to him, the blinding realisation that Anna had been right – everything he had done, he had done because he had wanted to do it! *Wrap it up how you like*, he thought to himself, *I have always been a mean and selfish person. She was right, that was why I lost it that morning; that was why I killed her.* Steadying himself against a kitchen unit, his hands shaking, he poured himself a large whisky. It would be okay from now on. He would get what he deserved. Serve his punishment.

CHAPTER 12   SUNDAY
6 NOVEMBER 2005

The Anglican parish church in Petersfield had been on its existing site in the centre of the town since Norman times, and Lucas Hunt's family had been members of the parish there for something approaching three hundred years. So, that cold and damp morning as he led Julia Hillman from the church service, as they bid their farewells to the latest vicar, Lucas was treading well-known footsteps as far as the Hunt family were concerned.

Ironically, given the current situation with his new father-in-law, Hunt's grandfather Christopher Hunt had been a high court judge at the Old Bailey and had earned himself the dubious nomenclature of 'the hanging judge'. Lucas led Julia to Christopher's grave at the side of the church, a once proud monument that was now showing signs of decay and neglect.

'What, I wonder,' began Lucas, 'would the hanging judge have made of Malcolm's plight?'

'I am not sure. He probably would have been looking forward to putting the black cloth on his wig; sentencing him to be taken...' Tears began running down the rustic skin on Julia Hillman's face.

'Stop that,' comforted Hunt, offering his wife a tissue from his grubby pocket.

'Sorry,' she responded, wiping her eyes. 'But I just feel that he's given up the fight; accepted the fact that he's going to be convicted this week.'

'Well, we will see. There's still a fair bit of water to run under the bridge yet.'

'I know, Lucas, but I think that bloody video from our wedding has done real damage. He looked so lucid, so articulate. Why did we let those shit-head cops be there? Why didn't we just get them thrown out of Stoke Park?' She was back to her fuming worst after a slight lull in her venom during the church service.

'We know what happened and what they were threatening, so stop blaming yourself for that.' Lucas tried to calm her down.

'I am not blaming myself, Lucas, I am blaming you!'

'And it's my fault because?'

'Because Father told me that he had called you the day before the wedding to check his bail conditions out, and because you were too fucking quick to capitulate to those bastards that morning.' Lucas was now getting both barrels of her fury.

'I see, and please remember where you are. It's all *my* fault.' Hunt was incredulous and getting angrier by the second with this tirade of abuse. 'It's all my fault – I took the pillow and murdered your stepmother, did I? And then went off to work and acted like it was a freaking normal day?'

'I didn't say that, but if you had been more focused, Father wouldn't have broken his bail conditions and would still have a fifty-fifty chance at least of getting that bloody jury to acquit him this week.' She turned to leave the graveyard; she had got this bail thing off her chest, had confronted the stupid man with his incompetence.

But Lucas was not ready to let the thing drop and strode to catch up with his wife as she left the churchyard and headed for their car. Taking hold of her arm, he pulled her round to face him, noticing the tears still running down her cheeks.

'For God's sake, Julia! Where is this getting us?'

'Take me home, Lucas. I've got a lot of prep to do before Tuesday.' She tried to turn away again but her husband's grip was firm.

'I'll take you home, but not before you apologise for your inappropriate behaviour.' She had never seen Lucas this angry and was taken aback. No one spoke to Julia Hillman like this.

'Get your fucking hands off me,' she commanded, but Lucas held firm. It was time for him to make a stand; he had been too passive for too long. What was the phrase that Gary used at work? Pussy-whipped, that was it. An American expression that was so apt in his relationship with Julia.

'I'll tell you what, take the keys and get yourself home.' And with a final flourish Lucas tossed the keys to their ageing BMW to his wife, released her arm and headed off up the street, leaving Julia Hillman standing there, tears in her eyes, mouth open in total shock.

The shit, she thought. How dare the little shit treat her like this. By now, however, Lucas had turned a corner and was out of sight, leaving Julia Hillman with no option but to walk gingerly to their car and drive back through the town to their cottage. When she got there, she kicked off her shoes and retreated to their bedroom, threw herself onto their bed and began crying, crying like she had never cried before.

Lucas, meanwhile, found a taxi rank near the station and gave the driver his brother's address. Hugo Hunt was Lucas's oldest brother, a retired solicitor who lived alone on the other side of town in a house he had bought after his wife had died five years before. *Yes*, thought Lucas, *that's what I need, an afternoon of brandy and chat with Hugo; let Julia get on with her fucking prep work.*

The Hunts were not the only couple to attend church that morning. In Northwood, Colm Elliot and his long-term partner

Susan Lamont arrived at mass in a quiet and contemplative mood. The thirtieth of October had been the twenty-fourth anniversary of the death of Susan's former lover Sir Peter Piers, who had been assassinated by the IRA outside her home while he was on his way to one of their secret assignations.

Susan had been a young divorcee at the time and her daughter Laura was barely three. Laura was now twenty-seven and lived in Cornwall with her boyfriend Patrick, who she had been with since her days at Plymouth University. Colm had been seconded from Northern Ireland to support the hunt for the assassins and had got to know Sir Peter's son Barry, with whom he was now good friends. It was Barry who had introduced Elliot to Susan and the couple had been together for the last ten years.

During mass, they held hands but did not speak, silent in their respective prayers. Church was not a regular occurrence for them; it tended to be Christmas, Easter and this particular anniversary that brought them to St Matthew's where they knew no one except one of the parish priests, a kind old Glaswegian whose mid-mass sermons were both incoherent and often hilarious.

Elliot had been relieved to get his work at the Hillman trial over with the week before and had spent the weekend speculating if enough had been done to secure a murder conviction from the jury. In truth, Hillman and his unpleasant daughter Julia, who was acting as his legal McKenzie, seemed to have been facing an uphill battle against the prosecution barrister, and the video evidence produced from Hannah Bellamy's phone seemed to damage his defence fairly significantly. But you could never tell what a jury might do, and the Hillmans had been very vigilant in the way that the jury had been structured. That said, Elliot knew that there was nothing else that he could have done, and worst scenario was that Malcolm Hillman would be convicted of manslaughter and sent to prison for a long time. Elliot, of course, wanted a murder conviction and a subsequent mandatory life sentence. Not, he thought, as communion was being taken, that life meant life any more.

After mass, the couple went to their favourite local restaurant for an early lunch and a soothing bottle of Pinot Grigio. It was an Italian place that had been in the town for the best part of thirty years and although not real regulars, the proprietor knew them well enough to find them a good table at the back with views overlooking a neat rear garden. Elliot and Susan did not discuss Piers and her relationship, but she really appreciated his sensitivity at this time of year and as the wine lifted her spirits, she vowed to herself that she would take him home for an afternoon in bed, where she could really show how much she loved him and having him in her life.

In Covent Garden, Pencil Kane was running his undoubted OCD eye over the work that the team creating Pencil One had completed that weekend. Pencil was getting really excited by the look and feel of the place; the new floor of recovered wide plank oak was near complete, and with the grey walls and the chandeliers, the store was taking real shape. The plan was for the product to be displayed on oak tables topped with mirrored glass that would reflect the French lights from the ceiling, and Pencil could now imagine the finished effect.

His store designer let the young man do his inspection without interruption, pen and notepad at the ready, for he was in no doubt that Pencil would have some comment, some things that needed to be put right or altered. His work had introduced him to many people like Pencil, people who had a guru approach to their work, who would not rest until their version of perfection was achieved.

Pencil on this occasion was to surprise him and returned from his perusal with a big smile on his handsome young face.

'Pencil totally adores it,' he began before waving his hands to take in the entire space. 'You guys have done a reem job, thank you.'

'Nothing to change?' queried the store designer cautiously.

'Nothing to change. It's reem and Pencil loves it.'

'Great news. We were pleased too.'

'Cool. Now Pencil needs to get home; big day at the hospital tomorrow.'

'I hope it goes well,' offered the designer.

'It will be as it is,' replied Pencil Kane, walking to the exit of the store before turning back and announcing once again to himself as much as anyone there, 'Reem job, guys. Reem job.' And with that he was out and into his waiting car, leaving the store designer to jot the word 'reem' down in his notepad for checking on the Urban Dictionary when he got home.

CHAPTER 13

MONDAY
7 NOVEMBER 2005

He carefully pushed the product aside before lifting her onto the mirror-topped table; lifted her flimsy dress and began lowering her small panties as she worked desperately to undo his belt and lower his jeans. Seconds later, Pencil Kane was inside her, pumping fast as she lifted his T-shirt to reveal his perfect six-pack, his sculptured young athlete's body. Leaning over her, he pulled her dress down over her shoulder, releasing her left breast from her bra before taking her erect nipple between his teeth. *Please cum*, she whispered to herself. *Please cum before someone arrives and stops this; stops this perfect fuck.*

Vicki Ruthven came awake suddenly in her big bed, her heart pounding, aroused like she had rarely been before. *Jesus*, she thought, *what was all that about?* Reaching for her left nipple, she found it was as erect as it had been in her wet dream, and running her hand down her naked body to her pussy and its Hollywood trim, she could feel her excited dampness. Reaching to her bedside cabinet she pulled out the silver mini-vibrator she had purchased from Ann Summers and placed it gently in Gary's hand.

Taking very little encouragement, he placed his hand with the silver toy now switched on between her legs, rubbing her eager vaginal lips as Vicki worked on his responding cock.

Moments later, Gary was mounting her and encouraged by her gentle cries, began pumping into her as she bit his ear in an attempt to quell the screams she wanted to release, her orgasm having taken her over completely.

A few minutes later, as she sat on the bidet in their en-suite bathroom washing her warm pussy, Vicki was still in shock. *What the fuck was that all about?* She had never considered Pencil in that way; saw him only as a fascinating young man who was trying to overcome his great tragedy. *Shit*, she thought, *that's not quite how I will see him from now on.* Returning to their bed, Gary pulled her to him and cuddled her tight.

'Thanks,' was all he said, his breathing returning to normal.

'My pleasure,' whispered Vicki in reply, still freaked by the last ten minutes.

Jorge the driver had collected the real Pencil Kane from his apartment later that morning and was now waiting for Paul Ruthven to join them for the drive across London to Whitechapel hospital and their latest appointment with Dr Campbell. As part of the documentary filming process, Pencil was keeping a video diary and had just finished filming a short discussion with their driver when Paul entered the car.

'How are we this fine morning?' began Paul cheerfully as he slipped into the back seat beside Pencil. 'And I hope that thing is switched off,' he continued, pointing to Kane's handheld video recorder.

'Pencil is a little nervous, truth be told, man.'

'I am sure, but every day is part of the journey, a day closer to recovery,' consoled Paul.

'True man, very true.'

'Anyway, want some more good news regarding plan Pencil?' asked Ruthven as Jorge drove them expertly through the early morning London traffic.

'Of course, man, fire away.'

'Jonathan Ross wants you on his new series, sometime in the New Year,' began Paul.

'That's cool, man, but Pencil will not go on that show if he's just goin' to take the piss,' reflected Kane.

'We won't let that happen. I was thinking we would do it to celebrate the success of your book. It would be good timing, and can be part of your end of January documentary.'

''Cause if he takes the piss, Pencil might have to smack him in the mouth.' Kane was more than jumpy this morning.

'Okay, Pencil, let's discuss it later. Tell me how things are going at Pencil One.'

'Good, man. That place looks reem,' smiled Pencil at last.

'How're things going with Vicki?'

'Good, really good. That lady sure knows what she's doing. Really gets what Pencil wants in his store.'

'Glad to hear it.'

A typical week for Lucy Campbell at Whitechapel involved her trauma and fracture clinics all day on a Monday, all day operating on Tuesdays, with surgery starting as early as 8am; Thursday morning clinics and her day surgery list in the afternoon, which left Wednesday and Friday free for other professional interests. These included examining, interviewing, committee work, research and teaching, which all ensured that she led a very full working week. In addition, she was expected to be on call at least one day in six, and was also expected to do some administration as well as short ward rounds.

That Monday, she had a very full schedule and was having to be at her professional best to keep anything close to her pre-booked timetable. Scanning her files, with Pencil Kane in next, she knew what had to be done. His screw had to be removed from his right foot and she was going to insist on a brace being fitted on his lower leg for at least six weeks. Pencil, she knew, was not going to be happy with that course of treatment; would feel like he was going back the way. However, it needed to be done. Lucy was no longer concerned with Pencil the high profile young footballer, but more with ensuring that the young man could live as normal a life as possible, his foot as good as she could help it be. She had already slotted him into her surgery list for the following day; felt it could wait no longer.

In St John's Wood, Julia Hillman and her father were rehearsing what would be his closing speech to the jury at the Old Bailey the following day.

'Okay,' she encouraged. 'Go over the three strands of your defence again.'

Malcolm sat and quietly ticked them off on the fingers of his left hand.

'Oh for God's sake, man. Get on your feet and practice like you mean it. Like you really believe that you should be acquitted,' she urged impatiently.

'That's the problem, I don't believe that I should be acquitted.' Malcolm slumped back in his chair, a resigned and worn-out expression on his grey face.

'Shit, Father. How many more times do we need to go over this?'

'Not many more, Julia, thank Christ.'

'Look, the woman is dead and that is bad enough. You going to prison for life is not going to bring Anna back, it's only going to compound the tragedy.'

'Who for, Julia? Who is it going to compound the tragedy for?'

'Well, you for a start. What good is it going to do you being cooped up in some bloody prison?'

'I killed my wife for fuck's sake. What right do I have to anything else?'

'Then there's your family, your grandchildren. What will it mean for them, for us, if you're spending your final years in prison?' continued Julia Hillman, choosing to ignore her father's important personal reflection – his questions.

'You know, I think it might've been better to have just pled guilty. Have got it over and done with, taken my punishment.'

'What a load of piffle, Father. And forgive me for saying this, but if you don't get your shit together, we are both going to look like a couple of shit-heads in court tomorrow.'

'Oh, I am sorry to bring that on you,' exploded Malcolm Hillman in a sudden rage.

Jesus, thought his daughter, *what is it with these angry men?* It was Lucas yesterday, storming off after church only to come home half pissed after spending the day with his stupid brother. And now her father was showing how easy it was for him to lose his temper.

'So, what do you want, Father, a pillow?' she spat back.

'How dare you? How fucking dare you?' Malcolm stood and for a few moments faced his daughter before turning and leaving the room, slamming the door closed as he left.

Julia Hillman sat in shock, shaking from what had just happened. Sure, she had seen her father's temper flare up in the past, particularly with her mother, but never before with her. *Fuck*, she finally thought, *maybe it will be best if the man goes to prison, maybe the world will be a safer place.* Oblivious to her contribution, to her provocative behaviour, she went to the kitchen to make some tea. To wait until her father's anger subsided so that they could get back to his rehearsal; to his plea to the jury for acquittal.

David Lane sat opposite Gary Ruthven in his office and was shaking his head firmly.

'I can't agree to that at the moment,' he reiterated.

'What do you mean, David? We've discussed this and were aligned. We reduce his hours between now and Christmas and let him retire gracefully at the end of March, at the end of our financial year.'

'Not the right time. Lucas brought me into RCS and I feel it would be disloyal of me to agree to what you want to do,' continued Lane to the astonished Ruthven.

'You are kidding me here, David?'

'Not at all, and if you insist, then I will leave as well and then sue RCS for constructive dismissal.'

'What?' Gary stood and walked to look out of his window. This was one of the most amazing turnarounds he had ever experienced in his twenty-odd years in business. Slowly, he returned to his seat, before asking, 'What has happened, David? Why this sudden change of mind?'

'I just think the timing is wrong,' shrugged Lane.

'Help me understand that. Tell me what's different from the last time we talked?'

'I can't, and as I said, if you insist, I will resign with immediate effect and—'

'I heard what you said, David. I asked for an explanation, not a repeat of your stupid threat.'

'Think it's stupid, Gary?'

'I don't know what to think, David. You've certainly taken me by surprise today.'

'So, what do you want to do?' asked Lane quietly, abdicating his senior responsibility.

'I want to stop this discussion and have a private think to myself. Reflect on the fact that I now have two fucking incompetent wankers in my business, when I honestly believed I only had one.' Gary was angry and wanted Lane out of his office. Out of RCS, out of his life.

'I want to see you again at two pm. Now piss off.'

'I am not due to be here this afternoon. I am meeting Karen in Harvey Nichols,' Lane continued, sitting. Karen was Lane's wife.

'Well, change your plans, David. Two pm here for a follow-up.' Ruthven stood and opened his office door, indicating that it was time for Lane to leave.

After he had gone, Gary called Kate Ross and recounted what had just happened in his meeting with Lane. Ross informed him that she would speak to the firm's lawyer and call him back.

An hour later, Gary was informed by Jenny that she had Julia Hillman on the line and that the woman was insisting that she be put through to him. Ruthven reluctantly agreed to take the call and waited for the connection to be made.

'Julia, I hope you are well. What can I do for you?' he began.

'What you can do is listen, Gary, as I will only say what I have to say once,' she hissed down the line.

'I am all ears,' replied Ruthven, suddenly concerned.

'The thing is, I've heard that you are about to can my husband,' she began.

'Where did you hear that?'

'I told you to fucking listen, Gary. I am preparing for tomorrow in court with my father and I have very little time for this, do you understand?'

'I am listening, Julia. Go on.'

'The thing is, if you proceed with your decision, then you will leave Lucas and me with no option but to inform your lovely wife about your trip to a certain abortion clinic a couple of months back.' She was threatening him with something more dangerous than David Lane had done earlier.

'Not sure what you're talking about, Julia,' interrupted Ruthven, his blood pressure pushing boiling point.

'I told you to fucking listen!' she shouted down the phone.

'And I am telling you to go fuck yourself, you stupid woman,' replied Gary, breaking the connection.

Holy fuck, he thought to himself, *how had they found out*? Carole would never have told anyone, and never Lucas and his poisonous wife. Rising from his desk, he left his office, telling Jenny that he would be back for his meeting with Lane. He needed to clear the fog in his brain, get clear about what to do.

Despite the fact that his apartment was probably as clean as your average operating theatre, Pencil needed to meticulously go over the work that his cleaning lady and his mum had completed that morning. In his kitchen, he was systematically removing tins of food and ensuring that they were replaced in both alphabetic and sell-by-date order. He then checked to ensure that his massive fridge had its contents stored just as he liked it, the mental list in his head being ticked off as he progressed. In his bedroom, he checked that all of his twelve pale pink shirts were hanging exactly two inches apart before checking the shelves that he used to store his perfectly lined-up shoes and expensive trainers.

All this activity kept Pencil's mind off his real issue, the fact that he was going back into hospital tomorrow to have the surgical screw removed from his foot and a dreaded brace fitted. Pencil was angry again. Angry at the bastards who had blown him up on the Underground, angry like he had never been before.

Switching on his large flat-screen television, he was in time to hear Sky Sports reporting that Arsenal had just announced that he was to have further treatment on his foot the following day. Outside the club's London Colney training HQ, a small number of fans had gathered carrying a variety of banners wishing Pencil a speedy recovery. Pencil dimmed the TV noise and went to reorder the small number of sports books, mostly biographies, that he had collected and kept on his one bookcase.

Finding a shelf that had not been dusted brought Pencil Kane to a rage once again, taking him back into the kitchen to find a damp cloth to dust with. Why couldn't these people just do their job properly? he fumed to himself, his right foot beginning to ache again, the painkillers beginning once again to lose their effectiveness.

His telephone rang. It was Paul Ruthven whose name flashed on the screen.

'Hey, Mr Ruthven. Checking up on me?'

'Hi, Pencil. No, I just called to see how you are after this morning,' came Ruthven's calm opening.

'Pencil is not too good, man. Pencil has had a massive setback today and is very angry,' replied the young man.

'Anything I can do to help?'

'No, I am just passing the time until tomorrow, tidying things up here.'

'I am sure it's a pretty messy place,' teased Ruthven, aware of Pencil's fastidiousness.

'Pencil likes things tidy. You know how it is.'

'Indeed I do. 7.30 in the morning then, and remember no food allowed after midnight,' concluded Ruthven.

'I've had Julia Hillman on, threatening me about Lucas's time here. How the fuck did she know about our private conversation, David?'

'I tried to warn you, this is not a good moment for me,' replied Lane as they met in Gary's office to reconvene their earlier meeting.

'So, how did they find out, David?' Gary had consulted the company lawyer and was about to sack his head of strategic finance.

'Can I make a suggestion?'

'This should be good,' mocked Gary, who was furious.

'Why don't we postpone this discussion? Give yourself some time to decide what you want to do. Surely you don't need to rush this, bring this crap to your doorstep?'

'You still didn't answer my question,' pushed Ruthven.

'I had a call from Julia a couple of weeks back threatening to destroy you and the firm if Lucas was forced out of RCS in the next year or so,' began Lane calmly.

'And did she indicate how she was planning to do that?' Gary had sat down and was now facing Lane.

'No, but she said she had something on you that you would want suppressed, and that if I wanted to protect RCS, I should let her know if the issue of Lucas being fired or retired came up.' Lane was not enjoying being there.

'Did she tell you what she's supposed to have on me?'

'No, and I didn't push it. Not sure that I want to know, to be honest.'

'Okay, but if that bitch ever shows her face in here, I will not be responsible for my actions.'

'So what she claims to have is true?'

'I need to discuss that with Lucas when he comes back next week, but whatever he says my relationship with him is fatally damaged.'

'So, what are you going to do?'

'Well, there is nothing I can do until he gets back and I can speak to him. Meantime, I suggest that we get on with some work; reconvene again at the end of next week.'

'Do you want me to say anything to Julia?'

'Say what the fuck you like, David. I no longer care. This place has gone to the dogs in the last year and that seems to coincide exactly with the time of your arrival. Pick the bones out of that in any way you like. Something has to change, and maybe that just might need to be me.'

'Nothing drastic for the moment though?'

'I am done, David, fucking done with all this internal shit. It's not what I signed up for when you joined. Not what I imagined happening.'

'It's not what I imagined either – perhaps we need to think about starting again,' responded Lane calmly.

'Perhaps, but I've got a Levi's vintage appointment at BBH at four, so I need to get going.'

'Okay, but can I suggest that we let Lucas get this week's trial out of the way before the three of us sit down to thrash things around?'

'Fine, David. Can you organise that?'

'Leave it with me.'

Before leaving the office for his meeting at BBH's swish offices in nearby Kingly Street, Jenny asked Gary to sign the two share transfer forms relating to the recent sale of more shares to Hunt and Lane. Attached to the Hunt form was a cheque for £50,000 made out to Gary from Julia Hillman's personal account. The share purchase form was in Hunt's name, which was what had been agreed, so he signed it and asked Jenny to get Lucas and David to countersign before they were sent off to HMRC for stamping.

CHAPTER 14

**TUESDAY
8 NOVEMBER 2005**

Just after 11am that morning, the jury in the Malcolm Hillman murder trial were sent out by the presiding judge to consider their verdict. In Hillman's opinion, the judge's summing up had been fairly clear; their verdict was likely to be a guilty one.

Hillman, his daughters Julia and Helen, and Lucas Hunt, left the Old Bailey and walked the short distance to a small coffee house, where they ordered tea and toasted muffins. In truth, their mood was gloomy, their anxiety close to the surface, and as Lucas, who liked muffins with his butter, messed their table, his wife did her best to try and remain calm.

Their tea had just arrived when Hunt's telephone rang. It was the court usher informing him that the jury had reached their verdict and that the court case would reconvene in fifteen minutes.

'That didn't take them long,' muttered Malcolm Hillman, bracing himself.

'Not sure if it's a good sign or a bad one,' offered Lucas calmly, privately glad that the entire thing was about to be settled one way or another.

'Well, we might as well finish our tea,' suggested the normally silent Helen. 'After all, they are not going to start without us.'

'Finish without us,' corrected Julia Hillman.

Slowly and in silence, the four of them made their way back to the courthouse, cleared security and took their places and waited for the judge to reappear. With the jury back, the judge turned to them.

'Members of the jury, have you reached your verdict?'

'Yes, Your Honour, we have,' replied a nervous young man who had been appointed spokesperson.

'And is your verdict unanimous?' checked the judge.

'Yes, Your Honour.'

'In the case Regina versus Malcolm Hillman, is your verdict guilty or not guilty on the charge of murder?'

'Guilty, Your Honour.'

There were gasps around the court, and Julia Hillman cried out, 'No, it can't be.'

The judge then thanked the jury for their time and service and told them that they would now be dismissed from service. Turning back to the court, he informed Malcolm Hillman that, having been convicted by the jury of the murder of his wife Anna Hillman, his sentence would be one of life imprisonment. He also informed Hillman that the Home Secretary would be asked to advise on the tariff that was to be applied to his sentence. This effectively meant that some time would pass before Malcolm Hillman would know what minimum term he would be required to serve in prison. The judge did, however, inform the court that he would be recommending a minimum sentence of ten years.

Julia and Helen Hillman were able to give their father a brief farewell hug, before he was led away by security guards to discover at which of Her Majesty's Prisons he would begin his sentence.

Julia Hillman stormed from the court, leaving her sister and husband to follow meekly in her wake. She was furious. How could this be? How could her father be guilty of murder? Why had he married that bloody woman in the first place? Seeing

Colm Elliot as he made his way from the court, she moved to confront him.

'Think you're fucking smart, I suppose? Conning your way into my wedding. Well, I hope you die of something slow and nasty!' she fumed as she got close to Elliot.

'Threatening a police officer, Julia Hillman?' smiled Elliot calmly.

'Call it what you like. I just hope you can live with yourself, you smug bastard!'

Just then Lucas arrived and began leading his wife, now in tears, away from Elliot.

'Wise decision, Mr Hunt. I suggest you get your wife away from here and calm her down before she gets herself into trouble,' offered Elliot, turning to walk away.

'You've not heard the last of me; that decision will be appealed immediately,' spat Julia Hillman over her shoulder to the departing chief inspector.

'I would think very carefully before you say anything else, Julia Hillman,' replied Elliot, heading for the exit, very happy with the jury's verdict.

Naked, apart from a paper-thin gown, Pencil Kane lay waiting for the porter to collect him and take him into theatre. This was a new experience for Pencil as he had no recollection of his first operation back in July when he had been operated on while still unconscious from the Underground blast, Dr Campbell desperate to save the young man's life. As he lay there, Pencil was worried that the anaesthetic would not work, that somehow he would be awake throughout the operation and would feel everything. A nurse arrived to check that he was okay. There had been a steady stream of such visits, people obviously trying to say they had met the now famous Pencil Kane. As always, Pencil was kind and attentive, despite the fact that he was bricking himself. A few minutes later, the porter arrived to inform him that it was time to take him to theatre.

'I hope it all goes well for you today,' he said, as he pushed Pencil's bed along a corridor towards his operation. 'Even though I'm a Spurs fan.'

'Thanks,' replied Pencil. 'But if they can't fix me, get me fit, I could always get a game for your lot.' Pencil loved football banter.

Arriving in an anteroom outside the theatre, Dr Campbell was there to greet him.

'Hey, Pencil. How are you this morning?'

'Will be better when this is over,' replied the young man honestly.

'When we go in, we will get you comfortable before the anaesthetist gets you to sleep. I am hoping we will be done in less than an hour; have you back in your room in no time.'

'Sounds good, Dr Campbell. Only don't rush on Pencil's account, make a nice tidy job.'

'Don't worry, Pencil. I was given my orders this morning,' smiled the surgeon. Paul Ruthven had been more nervous than she and Pencil were together.

They then wheeled Pencil into the theatre and the porter and another man in a doctor's outfit helped lift him onto the bed. A young black man asked Pencil a few questions before informing him that he was about to put him into a nice sleep. Pencil certainly hoped that was true as a drip was inserted into the back of his hand. The anaesthetist then asked Pencil to begin counting down from ten to one. Pencil did not get beyond seven.

Gary Ruthven was just leaving a frustrating meeting with the UK Marketing Director of Yahoo Europe when he received a text from his PA, Jenny, informing him that Malcolm Hillman had been found guilty and given the mandatory life sentence. Flicking on his telephone, he called Vicki to give her the news.

'Makes you believe in the good old British legal system,' was her succinct response.

'It does. Probably a big mistake to defend himself as well,' mused Gary.

'Especially with the delightful Julia acting as his McKenzie friend,' agreed Vicki. The mere mention of her name brought shivers down Ruthven's spine. She was going to have to be dealt with now that the trial was over.

'Where are you now?'

'I am in Pencil One. The place is coming together nicely.'

'And how is the young genius?'

'He's in hospital for the next few days. Lucy is removing the screw in his foot.'

'Sounds horrible,' reflected Gary.

'It does, but he seems to brush these things off. Focus on his other projects.'

'It's very impressive. He is now one of the most famous and admired people in the country. Must be making a fortune.'

'He must, and remember your little brother will be getting his hefty cut too.'

'Tell me about it. If that guy fell in a bucket of horse shit, he would come out smelling of roses.'

'Ah, well. Not jealous are you?'

'Nah, Paul deserves everything he gets. He works like a bear, always has.'

'What time you expecting to be home this evening?'

'Will aim for seven, see you then.' Gary broke the connection, hailed a taxi and headed back to his office, wondering how Malcolm Hillman was feeling as he was shipped off to prison somewhere.

Colm Elliot stood outside the Old Bailey surrounded by a fairly large group of reporters seeking his response to the jury's verdict in the Hillman trial.

'Obviously,' he began, 'my first thoughts are with the victim and her family. Anna Hillman is the great tragedy here. No matter what was going on between her and her husband, nothing can condone what happened to her.'

'Do you believe justice is really done when only ten years will be served?' It was a common question these days when life tariffs could vary so greatly.

'That is for the judiciary to answer. As a mere policeman, all I can do is try to ensure that all the facts in a case are discovered, all the evidence is presented.'

'And you believe that was the case here?' another journalist queried.

'As far as I can tell, but when only two people are involved and one cannot contribute, one can never be 100% certain of anything.'

'Do you think Hillman made a mistake by defending himself?'

'Not for me to say, although it does suggest that he is a man who likes to get his own way, to be in control. Perhaps that was the root cause of the problem between him and his wife in the first place. Now, if you would excuse me, I need to get back to work.' Elliot closed his mini press conference, pushed his way through the crowd and headed for Marylebone and the privacy of his office.

As he travelled the Underground, he reflected on Julia Hillman's anger and veiled threats. What drove that woman on? he wondered. And how dangerous could she be now that her precious father was behind bars, convicted of murder?

At that same moment, Malcolm Hillman was being processed. Prepared for his lengthy spell in prison. At sixty-six years old, he would be at least seventy-six before he would taste freedom again, and had just been informed that he was being transferred to Belmarsh Prison in Birmingham.

'But that's over a hundred miles away,' he protested to the duty prison officer who was dealing with him.

'Away from where?'

'From my home in London, from my family,' replied Hillman meekly.

'Well, your home is Belmarsh for the next wee while, Hillman, no travelling for you.'

'But my family?'

'Sorry, I am just doing what I've been told to do.'

'Christ, what a nightmare this is.' He was shaking his head wearily.

'I am sure it is, Hillman, but can you please stand still?'

He was being measured for his prison clothes, his personal belongings being checked and put into bags. Next, he would have a brief medical examination before being reclothed and taken to Birmingham.

'So, how do I go about getting this conviction appealed?' he asked quietly, as much to himself as to the prison officer.

'You will be advised of your rights when you get to Belmarsh; all part of your integration,' offered the officer, a burly, overweight Geordie who had seen it all before and would do so again tomorrow and the next day.

His brief preparation complete, Malcolm Hillman was then taken via a side entrance to a waiting prison van where, in handcuffs, he was settled into the back for a journey that would take the best part of two hours.

Coming awake, Pencil had a sudden feeling of euphoria. He felt amazing, then remembered where he was, what he was doing in this room. The anaesthetist asked him if he was okay and Pencil nodded, distracted by two clocks that he could see on the walls of two adjacent rooms.

'Pencil thinks you guys should get your clocks synchronized.' He nodded and the doctor followed his gaze; the times were five minutes apart.

'Never noticed that before,' smiled the doctor.

'Too busy I suppose,' relaxed Pencil. 'Am I all finished with now? Already?'

'You are; you were in theatre for seventy-five minutes and will be taken back to your room and settled into bed. Dr Campbell will call to see you later this afternoon.'

'Pencil is glad it's over.'

'I am sure you are. It's never pleasant to be operated on,' consoled the anaesthetist, double-checking a few things before releasing Pencil to another porter for return to his private bedroom.

Back in his room, Pencil felt sleepy, the post-op euphoria wearing off, replaced by a sudden tiredness. Moments later, the young footballer was fast asleep. When he came to, his mum and his sister were by his bed, both smiling on seeing him open his eyes.

'How are you?' asked his mother quietly.

'Pencil is good. Should we be filming this?' he replied, nodding to his handheld camera that had been left on a spare chair.

'There are two people outside who say they would like some film if you are up for it,' said his mum.

'Get them in. That or we will have to do the whole thing again later,' indicated Pencil, ever sharp to an opportunity.

Moments later, Pencil was pretending to come awake as his mother and sister smiled at him.

'How are you?' asked his mother again, just as quietly as before.

'Pencil is good. Have the doctors said anything? You know, about how Pencil's operation went?'

'We've been told that Dr Campbell will be in to see you shortly,' replied his sister, keen to get in on the act, get on the television.

Julia Hillman was in bits, was inconsolable.

'How can this be?' she asked for the, what seemed to Lucas, hundredth time.

'Well, it's done, so we need to move on, not feel sorry for ourselves.'

'Oh shut up, Lucas. What's it got to do with you?'

'It's got everything to do with me, Julia. My wife's father has just been convicted of murdering my wife's stepmother.'

'Okay, but how could that jury of shit-heads have been so fucking stupid?'

Just then Lucas's telephone rang in his pocket and for a few moments he struggled to locate the device.

'Hello.' He finally took the call. It was Helen to tell them that Malcolm was being taken to Belmarsh Prison in Birmingham.

'That was Helen.' He turned to his wife after concluding the short call. 'Malcolm is being taken to Birmingham.'

'Birmingham? Fucking hell, Lucas, that's bloody miles away!' she screeched.

'It is indeed, but I guess we've no say in that particular matter.'

'Shit, this just goes from bad to worse. Fucking Birmingham! I bet that bastard policeman has had a hand in this.' She was fully wound up now.

'Come on, Julia. I hardly think...'

'Hardly think what? That the nice Irish shit-head wouldn't do something like that?'

'I was going to say I hardly think that even he has that level of influence,' offered Lucas.

'Bollocks, they are all in cahoots, those shit-heads, getting their nasty little revenge.'

'Well, whatever. What happens next?'

'What happens next is that we lodge an appeal and apply for bail pending the hearing. Get Father out of there soonest,' she replied, all businesslike. 'We better get home, Lucas. Get the paperwork ready.'

'Shouldn't you talk to Malcolm first, see what he wants?'

'Sod that. He'll want to appeal, want bail. Anything else is unthinkable.'

'Of course it is, Julia. What was I thinking of?' replied Lucas, realising that the thing was not yet over after all. Realizing that another chapter was about to begin.

CHAPTER 15

WEDNESDAY 9 NOVEMBER 2005

It was a cold and damp morning in London as the 6am Chiltern Line train from Beaconsfield arrived in Marylebone Station. Despite that fact, Gary Ruthven was well wrapped up from the lousy weather and decided to walk to the RCS offices. He had some serious thinking to do and the walk would allow him the perfect time to reflect.

In his mind's eye, he began creating the following list of priorities that required action:

Family finances – no action since the summer. Not good enough.

Lucas Hunt and his bitch of a wife; how to deal with her threat?

David Lane – how to get that relationship on track?

Business performance – expansion not working. What action?

Carole King – the relationship is strained, how to address?

Guilt bag over Tandy and the abortion. Who to talk to?

General sense of being overwhelmed with all of the above.

As he walked, Gary reflected on the fact that despite his seemingly overwhelming list of things requiring action, his actual work with his clients was still going really well. The demand for his time was still growing better than he could ever have imagined. Indeed, when he was with clients and potential customers he seemed able to flick a switch and become a different person. *What*, he thought, *does that say about where my focus should be?* Recalling his conversation with Carole in the late summer, when she had told him that he should find and appoint a high-calibre chief executive to run the business, he now knew that she had been right. So, what had he done? Saddled himself with Lane and Hunt, even sold more shares to them. *Christ, what a jerk I've been*, he muttered to himself as he walked. But who could he turn to; who could give him the advice he needed, lift this burden from him? Next week he was due to fly to Chicago, spend some quality time with a former Levi's client who was now running a medium-sized US fashion brand. He would be there for five days, and would have really good time to get his plans together. First things first, however. Today he was going to throw the cat amongst the proverbial pigeons. Today he was going to resign his position as Chief Executive of RCS with immediate effect. Let the blues brothers deal with that; let them earn their living for a change. From now on, Gary was going to focus on what he was good at, which was being a well-renowned and much sought after brand developer.

Reaching his office, Gary said his usual good mornings to the early arrivers and then went to his desk where he typed his resignation note and sent it to Lucas Hunt, David Lane, Uli Muller, and Carole King. The deed done, Ruthven sat back, a feeling of relief waving over him, counting the seconds before Carole would come to see him.

Indeed, it took her a full minute before she tapped on his door and entered, holding her favourite tea mug.

'Well, well,' she began. 'Looks like someone is taking action at last.'

'Yep. Comments?' he asked his dearest friend as she took the chair opposite him.

'Not what I was expecting you to do, but it puts the issue fully in their laps,' she began, referring to Lane and Hunt.

'That's what I thought, and I need to talk to you. I need you to stop being angry with me and return to being my trusted best friend.'

'I think I am ready for that, but I have to declare that the last couple of months have not been the best between us.'

'I know that, Carole, and I can't say how sorry I am for what happened.'

'Sorry for what happened, or sorry that you got caught?'

'Really sorry for what happened. Really sorry for betraying you, betraying Vicki.'

'Well, it's not the first time. Is it going to be the last?'

'It could well be the end anyway,' he suggested before going on to tell Carole of his threat from Julia Hillman.

'How did they find out?'

'I don't know.'

'You don't think that I had anything to do with it?'

'Of course not, but that shit Lucas found out somehow and I intend to discover how, before I put my fist down his fucking throat.'

'Sure, and that's going to help.'

'It would help me feel better, that's for sure.'

'So is that why you've resigned?'

'No, you were right a while back. We need someone to run the business properly. Someone who can let the rest of us do the great work we are capable of, aspire to. This is one way of forcing that hand. When our senior team meets to discuss, we can outflank them by insisting that we go external for a new chief exec. Muller will support us, although I haven't spoken with him yet.'

'Sounds like a plan,' she agreed, getting to her feet and going to his office door. Before opening it she turned to Gary and smiled. 'Welcome back, Mr Ruthven. It's been a while.'

'Thanks. And again, I am so sorry for the mess I've created.'

'Mmm… I will have to think about what my penalty charge is going to be. Let me know when you want that chat. Dinner would be nice.'

'I will. How does tomorrow evening work?'

'I'll let you know.' As she left, Jenny arrived to inform Gary that Uli Muller was on the line. The flag was up. The new game at RCS was underway.

Carole returned to her own space in the office with a big grin on her face. She and her team of four occupied an open-plan corner of the office and had their various workstations positioned around a large old pine table. This was where the creatives worked; that was the message that the area had been designed to state, and that was how their team was perceived by the others at RCS.

Glad that Ruthven was at last taking some action and pleased with his attempt at an apology, it was time for her to get behind Gary and provide the kind of support that she had always given him. The situation with Tandy had broken her heart, sent her into weeks of self-reflection and regret. Yes, she loved her life with Dan, who in so many ways was a better and more mature mate than Ruthven. However, Gary would always be the love of her life, the one that got away. Sure, they had never been physical lovers, but in so many other ways they were as intimate as two people could be without the sex. With no prospect of children with Dan, Tandy's abortion of Gary's child really hit her hard, surprising her with its intensity and secret longing.

Since then, everything that she had watched Ruthven do in the office, everything that he had failed to act upon, had really irritated her to the point of distraction. So much so that she had even interviewed for a role back at BBH; a role they were keen to give her, but a role that she had eventually turned down just the week before.

Looking up from her Apple screen, she saw David Lane

hovering, unsure whether he could interrupt her or not. She waved him over to her corner of the table.

'Guess you want a chat about Gary's little *billet-doux*?' she opened by way of a welcome.

'Have you got ten minutes?' he replied, nodding towards one of the three meeting rooms.

'Of course.' She stood and followed Lane to the room and closed the door behind her as she entered.

'This is all a bit sudden,' he began, carrying a printed copy of Gary's resignation email.

'Really?'

'You're not surprised?'

'Not particularly. I think Gary is a genius with clients, but I've never been convinced that he was right in the joint role as Chief Exec,' she explained.

'You could be right, but what to do now?'

'Guess we need to get the team together and explore the options,' suggested Carole.

'Technically, Lucas should do that.' Lane was thinking out loud.

'Technically, Lucas should do lots of things. Any idea when he'll be back?'

'No, I spoke with him last night, but could hear Julia giving him grief in the background, so I didn't have his attention.'

'Well, I'll leave that in your hands but we need to be quick. Ruthven is in Chicago next week.'

'Fine, I will get a meeting scheduled for tomorrow.'

'What do you mean you can't go to Birmingham with me?' cried Julia Hillman.

'I'm sorry, Julia, but I need to get back to work. I've had far too much time off as it is and with the Gary situation, I need to be there,' offered Lucas apologetically.

'Sod that, Lucas. I am going to Belmarsh today and you are coming with me, no argument. You can go back to RCS tomorrow.'

'No, Julia. Since July, your father has taken precedence over everything. Now I am going to get my life back. I am going to London to get back to work, full stop.' With that Lucas left their newly built kitchen and headed for their bedroom to ready himself for work.

When they had decided to marry, Lucas had sold his house in Tufnell Park and bought the semi-detached cottage in Petersfield that adjoined the one that Julia had already owned. With the help of cash from Malcolm Hillman, they had knocked the two houses into one to create the substantial home they now shared. That said, Julia was not overly pleased with the finished product and longed for a bigger home with stables, horses and paddocks for when their children arrived.

Standing alone in the kitchen, she was furious. How dare he refuse to go with her to Birmingham. How dare he put RCS or that shit-head Gary Ruthven before her. She was also worried how Lucas would react when he found out that she had called Ruthven the previous day to threaten to expose his grubby affair and its dire consequences to his wife Vicki.

Oh, who gives a shit, she thought to herself as she finished stacking the dishwasher, *all these men are so fucking pathetic. From Father and his piss-poor attempt at defending himself, to Lucas and his weak ways, to Gary Ruthven and his pretend marriage and his seedy abortion. They are all the same, all bloody useless.*

Lucy Campbell also had a big smile on her face as she travelled to Whitechapel that morning on the Underground. She had just had great morning sex with Paul, a session that had lasted a bit longer than they had expected. Consequently, they were both late for work.

First thing, she went to visit Pencil Kane whose operation

had gone well and who would now need a few days' rest before returning home with the brace fitted to help speed the next stages of his recovery.

'Good morning, Pencil,' she began on entering his private room, but Kane did not respond as he was lying with his eyes closed and Apple earphones plugged into his recently acquired replacement iPod. Moving to the side of the bed, she tapped the young footballer's leg and he opened his eyes before pulling the music from his ears.

'Sorry,' he began, trying to sit up in the bed.

'That's okay, it's good to see you relaxing. How are you feeling today?'

'Sleepy, and needing to get out of here.'

'Well, that's not going to happen for a couple of days; you need to rest up before we fit the brace to that foot of yours.' Pencil was okay with the idea of the brace. In truth, they were an occupational hazard and were often used to speed up injury recovery.

'Pencil just hopes that things will improve after this time,' he began, hoping for some form of assurance from Dr Campbell.

'Time will tell, Pencil. One step at a time. Removing the screw should be seen as progress, despite the fact that I am still concerned about the possibility of arthritis and all that comes with it.'

Good news, bad news, thought Pencil Kane. *The story of my life since 7/7.*

The doctor checked some charts attached to the bottom of Pencil's bed and confirmed that it was okay for his diary ghostwriter to visit while he was in Whitechapel, and that seemed to improve Pencil's spirit. The boy always needed to have something on the go.

Having been briefed by David Lane about Ruthven's resignation as Chief Executive, Lucas Hunt was feeling more than a little apprehensive as he sat waiting for Gary to join him in his office shortly before one o'clock that afternoon. Julia had left his ears ringing as she had left to drive to Birmingham and he was in no doubt that he would get another icy blast from her when she got home that evening. *Almost seventy years old and still getting shit from bossy women*, he thought, a ribald smile on his face. Just then Gary strode into the room even more purposefully than he normally did.

'Is this you reporting back for active service, Lucas?' he began, taking his seat behind his desk, a stern look on his handsome face.

'It is,' began Lucas quietly.

'Good. There is lots to get done.' He focused on Lucas, who was not quite sure where to begin.

'David has told me about your resignation,' he dived in, cautiously.

'I am sure he has told you a lot more than that, Lucas,' replied Ruthven.

'About your call with Julia?'

'For starters.'

'I genuinely didn't know that she was going to call, didn't know that she had called until he told me.' Lucas's top lip was shaking with nerves.

'And?' pushed Gary.

'And?'

'And what happens next?'

'I guess that's up to you, Gary.'

'Really? You've got one member of your new family sent down for murder yesterday and you want another charged with blackmail?' Gary was staying incredibly calm as he spoke these pre-rehearsed lines.

'Well, I'd hardly call it blackmail.'

'What is it then? But hey, Lucas, you didn't call "wife killing" murder, did you?'

'Julia has been under a lot of stress,' Lucas tried to explain but Gary was having none of it.

'Don't waste your fucking breath, Lucas, because I am not interested in hearing any of your shit. As far as I am concerned our relationship outside this office is over. We are done.'

'I understand your anger, Gary, I really do, but where does that leave us?'

'For the time being, it leaves us as colleagues in a business that is under performing; it leaves us with a chief executive vacancy to fill, and I expect you, as Chairman, to take responsibility for finding suitable candidates and for doing that as a matter of urgency.'

'I understand we are going to meet with David, Carole and Uli to discuss that tomorrow,' replied Lucas, surprised at Ruthven's calmness despite his obvious fury at what had happened.

'Good. In the meantime, I've got clients to keep happy and new business to develop, so I suggest you get on with it and try adding some fucking value to this company before it's all too late.'

With that, Lucas took his leave and went towards his office thinking that he had got a worse bollocking at home earlier, thankful at least, for that small mercy.

JANUARY 2006

CHAPTER 16   FRIDAY 6 JANUARY 2006

'Ladies and gentlemen, will I bring out my next guest?' asked Jonathan Ross of the noisy audience in Studio TC4 at the BBC Television Centre in London. The crowd cheered the presenter on, willing him to get Pencil Kane out of the green room.

'Okay, my next guest is something of a national hero; survivor of the 7/7 bombings and young master footballer. Ladies and gents, a big Friday Night welcome for the one and only Pencil Kane.' Ross stood and walked round from behind his desk to welcome Pencil as he appeared from behind a screen. The show's resident band Four Poofs and a Piano all wore identical T-shirts with an image of Pencil's handsome face on the front as they sang their own version of Heather Small's best known song 'Proud'.

To a person, the audience were on their feet, tears in their eyes as Pencil, resplendent in vintage Levi's and an immaculate pink shirt, acknowledged their cheers and made his way to sit down on the sofa to the right of Ross's desk.

'Wow, what a reception. They sure love you,' began Ross in his unique fashion.

'Thanks,' replied Pencil quietly, genuinely embarrassed by the strength of his welcome.

'Let me start by getting this out of the way. How is that foot of yours doing?'

'Well,' began Kane, 'it's still here and it's trying its best to recover.' Again the audience went into raptures.

'So, how long until we see you again in an Arsenal shirt?'

'That's still difficult to tell, if it ever happens,' replied Pencil.

'So, a full recovery's not certain?'

'Listen, time will tell. As Pencil often says, Jonathan, fifty-two people died that day. I'm first and foremost just really happy to be here. Playing football again will be the icing on the cake, man.' The audience began applauding once again.

'But you are looking so good, so fit…'

'Pencil is doing great, but getting Premier League fit will take time. I am giving it my best. I've got the best doctor, the best physios, the best coaches… If its possible, Pencil will make it.'

'Delighted to hear that, and you've not been slacking either.' Ross produced a copy of Pencil's *Intimate Diary* from under his desk before continuing. 'This has gone global. It has just reached number one in the *New York Times* bestsellers list.'

'Thanks,' responded Pencil as he waited for the audience to stop their latest round of applause. 'It's been really well received. Thanks to everyone who has bought it.'

'And,' Ross turned to the audience, 'if you haven't got a copy, ladies and gents, go get one. It's a very personal and in some ways harrowing account of that dreadful day.

'And you've had the TV show, and you've opened your new store. Where, in the middle of your recovery, have you had the time for all these amazing things? You must have a terrific team around you. Do you ever sleep?'

Pencil was not sure if there was one question he should answer; it was typical of Ross's style, the multi-question approach.

'Pencil sleeps fine, Jonathan,' was what he finally plumped for.

'And so you should. Does July prey on your mind much? How are you coping with the psychological stuff?'

'I don't remember much about it to be honest, man. One minute Pencil was listening to his music, next I was waking up in hospital.'

'Wow, how do you feel about what happened?'

'Some days very angry if the foot hurts, but most days Pencil is good. Shit happens, man, you know how it is.'

'And have you gone on the Underground since?' asked Ross jokingly.

'What do you think, man? Pencil don't own a pair of brown pants...' The audience burst out again.

'I am sure. Listen, Pencil, it has been a real privilege talking to you. You have really made this nation proud.' Ross was again silenced by the crowd.

'Thanks. And thanks to everyone who has given me their support and backing.'

'Indeed. Ladies and gents, a final round of appreciation for the one and only Pencil Kane!' Ross wrapped up the interview and Pencil stood, embraced the presenter and left waving to the audience as the band reprised 'What have you done today to make you feel proud?' Later, as he travelled back towards his apartment with Paul Ruthven and Jorge the driver, Pencil was really pleased by the way his appearance had gone; pleased that Ross had not tried to be too smart with him; glad that he had not needed to punch the presenter in the mouth.

In Beaconsfield, Vicki Ruthven lay in bed watching as Pencil's TV appearance came to an end. Ever since her erotic dream involving him, she had somehow felt so much closer to Kane. It was as if she was indeed his secret lover, so vivid had that experience been. Indeed just the thought of it made her horny, made her want to have rampant, urgent sex on top of those mirror-topped tables that were now adorned with beautiful vintage product in Pencil One.

Downstairs, Gary was texting his brother saying that he thought Pencil had come across really well on the show. Glad that it was Friday evening and looking forward to a weekend away from RCS followed by a trip to New York on Monday, he was in reasonable spirits despite his continued issues and problems. Finishing his last glass of wine of the evening, he went to their beautifully remodelled kitchen and placed his glass in the top of the dishwasher, before going to say goodnight to Molly, who was watching some American thing in the family room.

Climbing the stairs, conscious of how weary he was feeling, he had a quick shower before joining a very naked and very awake Vicki in their big bed.

'Thought you were never going to get here,' she began as she took his hand and placed it between her legs.

'Blimey, if I had known this was waiting for me, I would've been up hours ago,' he replied, pulling his very wet wife closer.

'Now is just fine,' she whispered, not adding that if he had come to bed earlier, she would have missed Pencil's appearance on the Jonathan Ross show, and might not be quite so eager to fuck her husband.

The gang came just after 11pm, five masked men in two dark blue vans. The first was parked neatly outside the big glass door of the shop next door, the second drove violently through the glass front of Pencil One, destroying the display and coming to rest inside the store. The alarm began immediately, but the gang knew what they were there to do and went about their individual roles with absolute focus and determination.

One began his neat spraying on the meticulously painted grey walls, another took a hammer to the giant chandeliers and another began pouring a large opened tin of white paint over the cashmere displayed on the mirrored table-tops.

A display cabinet was broken open by the fourth gang member and a number of precious exhibits were removed and swiftly transferred to the van that sat with its engine idling outside the neighbouring store.

Three minutes later, the gang were on their way, their destructive mission accomplished as somewhere far off the distant sound of a police siren could be heard. By the time the patrol car reached the devastation that was Pencil One, neither sight nor sound of the other van was in evidence.

Colm Elliot was just about to leave for a leg stretch and a late-night coffee when he took a call from his boss asking him if he would mind having a look at the incident. Not something that would normally require a man of Elliot's seniority and stature was how his boss had put it, but with Pencil Kane's public status being so high at the moment, his boss wanted no fuck-ups.

Hannah Bellamy drove with Elliot across London to the Covent Garden address, enjoying the night-time lights and general buzz in what was Europe's largest city on a Friday night.

'What do you know about Pencil Kane?' asked Elliot as he guided the car through still busy traffic.

'Nothing more than what I've read about him really,' she reflected.

'Seen any of his TV shows?'

'No, you?'

'Yeah, Susan and I have been watching them on BBC2,' replied Elliot.

'And?'

'Impressive young man from what I can make out. Seems to be dealing with what happened to him well; very well balanced and bright guy,' mused Elliot.

'So, he's not just taking advantage?'

'Perceptive question, Sergeant Bellamy.' Elliot's satnav was telling him to go the wrong way up a one-way street.

'And?'

'And, I don't know the answer to that. He comes across as pretty genuine.'

'Take a left, then a right,' suggested Bellamy, helping Colm with his technical dilemma.

Not too proud to accept help, he did as she suggested and they found themselves at the crime scene.

'Christ,' began Elliot. 'What a mess. Easier ways to break into a shop than that,' was his first reaction on seeing the dark blue van protruding from the destroyed windows.

Inside the store, and careful not to interfere with any possible evidence, Elliot and Bellamy took in the scene. Neatly sprayed onto the largest of the grey walls was a simple message that read: 'Where al-Qaeda failed – we will not'.

Bellamy inspected the other damage, which on the face of things, could have been a lot worse.

'What do you think, boss?' she eventually asked.

'A nasty warning of some sort, certainly not a simple robbery,' he replied quietly, as he reflected that his own boss had been wise to ask him to take a look.

'It's kinda scary,' offered Bellamy, a shiver running down her body.

'It's certainly meant to look that way at least,' concluded Elliot, heading outside for another look, another perspective.

CHAPTER 17

**SATURDAY
7 JANUARY 2006**

She sat on the edge of the bath, took a deep breath and then lifted the two test kits that she was holding, one in each hand, and viewed the colour strip on both. Tears welled and then the sobbing started, hard groaning sobs that indicated real pain.

'Shit, shit, shit,' she then began to repeat, mantra-like, as she tried to come to terms with her latest disappointment.

Lucas heard her groans and pushed the door to their en-suite open and entered the small room tentatively.

'Julia?' he began. 'Are you okay?' And then he saw the two white pregnancy tests held in her hands.

'No, Lucas, I am not okay and I am not pregnant either,' she replied through her tears and handed him the test results.

'Oh shit, that's a pity,' he replied, dropping the plastic kits into the sink and leaning over his half-dressed wife to give her a hug; some comfort for her obvious disappointment.

'Is that the best you can say?'

'Well, it's not the end of the world, honey. We can try again this month. The doctor did say that it could take a few months, even longer.'

'I know, but I can't cope with the stress of this every month.

Perhaps there's something wrong with us.' She looked at him through wet eyes.

'Well, the tests suggested we should be alright, so we just need to be patient, enjoy the trying,' suggested Lucas with a gentle smile on his face.

'I think we need to consider having treatment,' she responded quietly.

'What, like IVF?'

'Yes, like IVF or whatever is recommended to us. I want to get help, Lucas. I want to get pregnant and soon.' She was now pleading.

'Okay, honey. Why don't you get dressed and I'll make us a nice cup of tea and we can discuss this properly.'

'Thanks, I'll be down in five minutes,' she managed to reply.

In the kitchen, Lucas Hunt went about making a pot of Twinings and popped a couple of slices of bread in the toaster, an anxiety rising in his gut. Not that he was anxious about the thought of IVF. After all, his tests had suggested that his sperm count was quite good for a man of his age – he was anxious about the cost. Julia would want the best, would want Harley Street, and Lucas was sure that their finances would not stretch to that. The cost of their house rebuild had wiped out their savings and had required a top-up from Malcolm Hillman, while his chairman's salary from RCS all but covered their monthly outgoings.

'I think we should make an appointment for next week,' she began on entering the kitchen, all dressed and business like, the tears now gone.

'We need to talk about this, Julia. It's not going to be easy,' he replied, pouring her a cup of piping-hot tea.

'Of course it's not going to be easy, Lucas, but we can't afford to delay any longer. We are not getting any younger.'

'You mean I am not getting any younger.' Lucas was sensitive on the subject of their age difference.

'Whatever, we've got to get this moving.' She watched as her husband spread copious amounts of butter and marmalade on their toast.

'What about the cost, honey?' he asked gently.

'What about it?'

'Well, IVF is not a cheap option, and I doubt the NHS will help.' He bit into his toast but kept his eyes on his wife, worried how she might react.

'Sod the NHS, we need to go private, get into London.'

'Money, Julia. What about the money?'

'Oh, I am sure that Father will help us out on this. I will talk to him when I visit on Monday,' she smiled, happy with her own solution.

'No!' exclaimed Lucas, banging his teacup down on the granite worktop.

'No what, Lucas?'

'I will not have your father paying to get you pregnant. This is my responsibility and if we agree to go down this route, then I will find the money.'

'Fine, Lucas, but my decision is made. I am not prepared to wait any longer.'

Lucas Hunt looked at his wife for a few moments before finally nodding his agreement. It was no use arguing with Julia when she had her mind set on something. Now he would need to find a way to fund the IVF, to pay to get his wife pregnant.

Sleet was falling in London as Gary Ruthven arrived at the badly damaged windows of Pencil One with Vicki later that morning. The front of the store was blocked off with temporary fencing and a small crowd had gathered to inspect the damage and were hoping for a glimpse of the famous young owner.

'Blimey, what a mess,' began Vicki on first sight.

'Indeed, do you want me to come in with you?' asked Gary,

who had decided to travel with his wife, see if he could be of any use.

'Yes, please,' replied Vicki, pushing through the crowd and the TV film crew to tap on the door and gain entry to the store.

'Pencil has been rinsed, Vicki,' opened Kane as he let the couple into the place that was well on the way to being cleared up.

'I can see that. What's this all about?'

'Pencil is confused too, Vicki. Never experienced anything like this before.' He reached and shook hands with Gary. 'Good to see you, man. Thanks for coming in.'

'Not a problem, Pencil, not a problem,' replied Gary, taking in the scene in general and the writing on the grey wall in particular.

'What are the police saying?' asked Vicki.

'Not much. They seem to think it's some kind of warning; a threat to Pencil for something.' Pencil shrugged his shoulders while looking around again as if for some magic explanation.

'So, what's your plan?'

'Get ready to reopen on Monday. Pencil is not going to be put off by this shit. The police can do their job and we can do ours.'

Just then two young decorators arrived, their van parked outside, ready to receive their instructions from Pencil and the store designer who had just appeared from the staff room. Pencil welcomed the young men, who were staring open-mouthed at the graffiti on the wall, and began telling them what he wanted done and by when.

Meanwhile, Vicki was inspecting the damage caused by the white paint to the mirror-topped tables. The damaged stock was already gone and the paint marking was minimal.

'I think that I'll go get some coffee,' offered Gary, taking a pen and small moleskin notepad from his pocket. 'What would everyone like?'

Ruthven took the order and left the store, which was being marshalled back into shape by the remarkable Pencil Kane, and went out into the cold Covent Garden morning in search of a Starbucks.

Detective Chief Inspector Colm Elliot sat with Hannah Bellamy and viewed the CCTV pictures of the raid on Pencil One. The crime had obviously been planned with great care as there was no obvious communication between any of the five masked men perpetrating the break-in and the damage.

'This was well planned, Hannah,' he began, slowing the replay down to double-check the details.

'But why no robbery?'

'That was not the purpose. They were not frightened away by the alarm or the fear of being caught. No, they came to give Pencil Kane a message, nothing else.'

'But why?' Hannah was really bemused.

'No idea, but we should be taking this seriously until we know more,' replied Elliot.

'The al-Qaeda message?'

'Yep, let's get back there, talk to some of Pencil's people.'

Pencil One was a hive of activity when the two detectives entered thirty minutes later. Pencil greeted them and told them who everyone was and what their respective roles were in his little organization. Elliot thought that he recognized Vicki and Gary Ruthven from some place so gravitated towards them first.

'Have we met before?' he began as they found a quiet corner to talk.

'I don't think so,' replied Gary cautiously. He had never been interviewed by the police before. Vicki was shaking her head, obviously thinking before she answered.

'The Hillman wedding at Stoke Park,' offered Hannah

Bellamy, suddenly recalling where she had seen the good-looking couple before.

'Yes, we were at that,' replied Vicki. 'But I don't recall seeing you guys.'

'That's good,' smiled Elliot. 'We were trying to be discreet.'

'Malcolm Hillman?' guessed Gary.

'Indeed,' replied Elliot.

'It was a bit creepy him being there,' shuddered Vicki. 'Sad and creepy.'

'I am sure,' reflected Elliot. 'Now, to this little mess. Where were you guys last night?'

'At home. Watched the man on Jonathan Ross and then an early night,' replied Gary.

'And where is home?'

'Beaconsfield. It's in south Bucks,' confirmed Vicki. Elliot nodded; he knew where Beaconsfield was.

'And when was the last time you were in the store?' Elliot was looking at Vicki.

'Yesterday afternoon. I was here until about four and then headed home on the train.'

'Thanks. And have you noticed anything sinister, anything suspicious recently?'

'No, nothing. The store is very busy, attracts a lot of people who just come to see if they can meet Pencil, even have their photograph taken with him. We have to limit access when it gets really busy,' offered Vicki, only too happy to help.

'So, people have to queue to get into Pencil One?' Bellamy seemed surprised.

'More often than not. Pencil is a big personality at the moment, he draws a crowd.'

'Must be great for business,' offered Elliot.

'Oh yes, business is very good. Has been since we opened.'

'Thanks. But nothing strange springs to mind?'

'No. As I said, things have been crazy busy, so not a lot of time to notice what might be going on during the day.' Gary was impressed by his wife, the way in which she was handling herself during the interview.

'Thanks. And you, Gary?' Elliot switched his attention.

'I've not been here since the store opening in December. I just came today to chum Vicki, to see if I could help in any way.'

'I see, and what is your occupation?'

'I am the co-owner of a company called RCS. We do brand consulting work,' replied Ruthven.

'Based in London?'

'I am, but we have offices in Hamburg and Barcelona.'

'Thanks. Anything you can add to what your wife has given us?'

'No, but you might like to talk to my brother, Paul. He is Pencil's agent and is as close to him as anyone,' suggested Gary.

'Ah yes, the footballer. He was at Stoke Park as well.'

'He was indeed.'

'Thanks, we'll give him a call. You've both been very helpful, and if you can give Sergeant Bellamy your contact details just in case we need to talk with you again...' Elliot closed the discussion and went in search of the store designer.

An hour later, Paul Ruthven and Lucy Campbell were having a quiet late breakfast in Paul's apartment in Marylebone totally oblivious to the happenings at Pencil One. Having arrived home after the Jonathan Ross Show, they had both agreed to switch their respective phones off and have a Saturday on their own without interruption.

The apartment buzzer brought that plan to a halt and when Paul let Elliot and Bellamy into his home a few minutes later, it was obvious that even spending Saturday together was going to be compromised.

'Lucy, this is Detective Chief Inspector Elliot and Detective

Sergeant Bellamy from the Metropolitan Police. Pencil One was broken into last night and they need to speak to me,' began Ruthven rather formally as he led the two police officers into the sitting room.

'God, how awful,' responded Lucy, standing to shake hands with them both. 'Lucy Campbell,' she introduced herself.

'Pleased to meet you,' replied Elliot, recognizing the very pretty young woman from the Hillman wedding.

'Can I get you a coffee or a cup of tea?'

'No, thanks. We are good and will try not to take up too much of your time.'

'Lucy,' began Paul. 'Would you mind giving Pencil a call? Tell him that we've just heard and that when I am finished with the police I will be over to see him.'

'Will do,' replied Lucy, leaving the three to talk as she went to make the call from the kitchen.

'Lucy happens to be Pencil's surgeon. That's how we met, in the aftermath of the 7/7 bombings,' offered Ruthven awkwardly.

'It's a strange world we live in,' reflected Elliot, thinking of his relationship with Susan.

'It is indeed. So how can I help?'

'Just a few routine questions, and then we would like to discuss the question of personal security. Protection for Pencil Kane,' clarified Elliot.

After going over the details of the previous evening and reassuring Paul that Pencil had come to no harm, the conversation turned to the issue of personal protection.

'Have you and your client discussed protection before?'

'We have, and Pencil has always resisted the idea. He's a very modest young man and has always just laughed off my concerns; said I was being overprotective.'

'But after last night?'

'Well, I am certainly going to insist that we put something in place, at least until you guys have got to the bottom of things.'

'Glad to hear it. I'd be lying if I said I was not concerned for his safety,' continued Elliot.

'What do you suggest?'

'Well, I'd like to see him with a dedicated driver, and Sergeant Bellamy will take a good look at his apartment and make other recommendations. I am sure that his club will be happy to contribute to the cost.'

'The money is not an issue, Inspector. We will do what you suggest. Pencil is a very precious young man, for a whole host of reasons.'

'Glad to hear it, and again, if you think of anything odd or suspicious, don't hesitate to give me a call on that number any time of the day, or night.' Elliot handed his card to Ruthven and made to depart. Before leaving though he turned back to Ruthven and asked, 'Out of curiosity, what was your connection to Malcolm Hillman?'

'Malcolm Hillman?'

'Yes, my colleague and I were at Stoke Park for his daughter's wedding,' explained Elliot.

'Oh, I see,' began Ruthven. 'We've no connection with him, but his daughter was marrying Lucas Hunt, who happens to be the chairman of my brother's company.'

'RCS?'

'Yes, Gary and Lucas go back quite a long way.'

'Okay, thanks for that.' And with that the two police officers were on their way.

'Christ,' reflected Lucy as Paul joined her in the kitchen. 'Poor Pencil, that's all he needs.' She held Paul tight, feeling the need for his strength.

He had been a year ahead of Pencil Kane at school and had even joined Arsenal before his old friend, but these days Delroy Powell plied his football trade in the lower leagues and spent the remainder of his time hustling. Delroy would try his hand at anything as long as it brought him cash, because more than anything he loved money, the feel of it, the freedom it offered, the choices it gave. Sure, he would never be as rich as Pencil, who had always been the sharpest tack in the box, but by most nineteen-year-olds' standards, Delroy Powell was doing very well financially.

Suffering from a mild hamstring pull meant that he was at home that afternoon and not at his club's FA Cup Third Round match at Mansfield when the call came into his phone from his old school friend.

'Pencil, my boy, how are you doin'? he opened.

'Pencil has been rinsed, Delroy, and Pencil is pissed,' replied Kane down the line.

'Yeah, I saw that on the London news. That's well out of order,' sympathised Powell.

'Anyway, I was thinking, man. Would your crew like a job?' asked Pencil.

'What sort of job, my boy?'

'Well, I think Pencil needs a crew to watch his back for a few weeks, until the filth get their shit together and weed these fuckers out,' explained Kane.

'Of course, man. Let me make a few calls and I'll get back to you in twenty.' Delroy broke the connection, smiling, proud that the famous Pencil Kane had made him his first call, had known his old mate Powell was the man he could trust.

CHAPTER 18

Holland Park is without doubt one of London's most affluent locations, with homes in the area costing well in excess of the average jackpot prize on the National Lottery. The house in which Carole King and her husband Dan Jenner lived was probably in the top quartile of expensive homes in the area. Carole could rarely let herself believe her good fortune. Brought up in one of London's less regarded areas, she simply thanked her lucky stars and never took her good fortune for granted.

That cold and frosty Sunday morning, the couple sat in a local coffee shop, their hot drinks on the small table in front of them as they perused the numerous sections that made up the *Sunday Times*. The silence between the couple could not be misconstrued as anything but a very comfortable couple enjoying quiet time together. As they always did on a Sunday, they finished their drinks and made their way to the park, where they would walk and chat about their lives, their business, and the people that they cared about.

'So,' began Dan quietly. 'You and Gary are off to New York tomorrow. How is he doing?'

'Bigger question is, how is the firm doing?' replied Carole reflectively.

'What's the answer to that?'

'Not great. Revenues are flat versus last year, cash is tight and as you know, we have no Chief Executive to drive performance.'

'Are you worried?'

'Worried? I am married to Dan Jenner, why would I be worried?' She smiled and held his arm tightly as they strolled.

'I know, but you put a lot of yourself into that firm, it's not just the money,' explained her husband, loving having his beautiful wife by his side.

'In truth, RCS has lost its way.'

'It's not that unusual you know.'

'What?'

'Well, bright and very able young owner, not able to build an internal organization that can support his talent. The focus gets lost and the internal animal kills the hand that feeds it. I was lucky, I had people who understood that and made it their business to support me, let me play to my strengths.'

'You must've understood that as well, known to let go?'

'Not really, I just had no interest in running the company; the very idea of having an HR department brought me out in spots, gave me palpitations,' explained Dan, smiling ruefully to himself.

'I guess that's what Gary thought he was doing when he hired Hunt and Lane,' suggested Carole. They had reached the Kyoto Garden and stood admiring the calm beauty as they continued to talk.

'Possibly, but it's not worked, so why keep those two twats in their jobs?'

'Ruthven has his reasons.' Carole was feeling uneasy; she had not told Dan about the Tandy abortion, and was reticent about bringing it up now.

'What sort of reasons?' Dan pressed gently, feeling his wife's tension on his arm.

'I promised him total confidentiality. It's very difficult.'

'Listen, you know I can be trusted,' he offered, not looking at his wife.

'Fine, but I will have to tell Ruthven that you know.'

'Okay.'

Carole then told her husband about the situation with Tandy and the subsequent threat of exposure from Julia Hillman. After a few minutes of silent reflection, Dan eventually broke their quiet.

'Blimey, any idea what he's intending to do about it?'

'No, I think we will probably discuss it on the New York trip. What would your advice be?'

'Well, he has to remove the threat, so I would have Julia and Lucas killed. Silence them forever.' Carole stopped and stood in front of her husband.

'Dan?'

'Or, I would tell Vicki, take my medicine, see what happens.' He smiled and hugged his wife.

'It's easy to see why he's done nothing but keep Lucas as Chairman.'

'It is, but that can't last forever. What do you think he should do?'

'Well, he should have kept his cock in his pants for a start.' They were walking arm in arm again.

'Bit late for that, so it's manage the fall-out time.'

'Mmm, you're right of course, but telling Vicki would probably end their marriage.'

'Well, it's kill the fuckers then. That, or pay them off somehow. Glad I am not in his shoes though, his life must be bloody hell at the moment.'

'So, if we do discuss it in New York, what would your advice be?'

'Telling Vicki removes their power; it might end his marriage but it might not. You would know more about that than me. Is their marriage solid?'

'I am not sure that many marriages would survive this, but who really knows but them?'

'True, and then he has the issue of their shareholding. Could he afford to buy them out?'

'I don't know, but if he sold the house in Spain I suppose he could.'

'What a fool he's been. What was he thinking?'

'Your guess is as good as mine, but you are right. He needs to do something.'

'What do you mean? How have you got this sorted, Pencil?'

'Pencil has employed a crew to watch his back, to make sure these fuckers do no more damage,' he explained to Paul Ruthven in Pencil One.

'Okay, so who are these people?'

'A good friend of mine. A former schoolmate, footy buddy. He knows what I need.'

'And how will we pay them?'

'Pencil will pay them cash, man,' replied Kane. He had never seen Paul Ruthven so agitated before, so worked up.

'Pencil, we can't pay them cash. It will need to go through the business. It's too risky for someone with your public image to be trying to dodge tax,' explained Ruthven.

'Okay, but Delroy won't like that, man.'

'Well, it's take it or leave it. If he wants to be paid, he will have to give us an invoice,' Paul stated firmly. It was the only way he would agree with Pencil's plan.

'Fine. Pencil will bell him and let him know.'

'Good. Now tell me how this is going to work.'

Pencil outlined his arrangement as agreed with Delroy Powell. It was well thought through and in some ways it would look better than having a team of heavy security people around him.

'Now,' continued Paul, changing the subject. 'The store will reopen tomorrow?'

'It's all good again, man, all good.'

'Fine, and you are back at Whitechapel to see Lucy on Tuesday, to see how that foot is doing.'

'Pencil is excited, the physio is going well.'

'Sounds good, and the pain?'

'A lot better,' he replied, not being totally honest. His foot still hurt like fuck.

'Good, so it's a busy week and the police will be back to update as well.'

'Pencil hopes that they catch the bastards.'

Extortion, thought Colm Elliot, suddenly. *It has got to be extortion. Why else would there be the threat?* Smiling, he left his kitchen to call Bellamy from the small study that he shared with Susan.

'But what will they be looking for?'

'Money, probably disguised as protection money; if it's not that, what else?'

Bellamy was silent for a moment. Her boss could be right, but something was nagging at the back of her mind.

'Fine, but why go to such great lengths?' she eventually asked.

'You mean the precision of the attack and all that?'

'Yes, why not just make a phone call?'

'Scale, impact. These guys are not after loose change. No, they want some serious cash.' Elliot was developing his thinking as he spoke.

'So, what happens next?'

'That'll depend if they think that they've hit the mark yet. If not, Pencil Kane can expect another surprise. Another bruising closer to home, perhaps.'

'Shit. You think so?'

'Not sure, we should go see him in the morning; share our thoughts and see if he has had any strange contact.' Elliot outlined his plan.

'Okay, sounds good. By the way, where is Susan? Isn't this your day off?'

'Oh, she's gone shopping. Knows what I'm like when I've got something on.'

'Was just wondering,' offered Hannah, before adding, 'Just remind me not to end up like you.'

'There's no chance of that happening, Sergeant Bellamy. Now go back to your Sunday.' Elliot hung up, wondering if he should contact Pencil, give him some form of warning.

In Beaconsfield, Gary Ruthven was packing for his short trip to New York and was planning to take Emma and Molly out for an early dinner. Vicki was at Pencil One finalising the store preparation for the reopening the following day. A minimalist but meticulous packer, he always did his best to ensure that he was not carrying anything but absolute essentials when he travelled. To achieve that aim, though, did require a fair degree of thought and preparation and Gary liked to have his packing done early. A regular traveller, he had learned early in his career that leaving things to the last moment often meant a bad night's sleep on the evening before he left on his journey.

Emma was heading back to Leeds in the morning for her second term, and had not taken too kindly to her Dad's demand that she had her packing done before they went out for food. She was also not best pleased by his hundreds of questions regarding her course progress. Why did parents always want to impart their experience? Could they not just trust that their kids would be sensible enough to knuckle down and take their studies seriously? Smiling, she squeezed her last pair of jeans into her large case and sat on the lid as she tried to zip the thing shut. *Not,* she thought, *that I've been knuckling down very much.*

Molly had finished her homework and was upstairs in her room watching another DVD of *Friends,* hoping that her new hairstyle was beginning to resemble Jennifer Aniston's as it looked in the latest series. Rushing to her en-suite, she double-checked and smiled. It was looking good, although her three pimples were not adding much value.

Bag and his small shoulder case all packed, Gary called his daughters to let them know that they would be leaving for the restaurant in five minutes. He had booked a table at Zizzi's and was keen for them to walk, which was not a suggestion that the girls had been terribly keen on.

'But, Dad, it must be at least a mile away,' Molly had protested.

'Good. A two-mile round trip will work off some of the calories from your dinner,' replied her dad.

'And the point of that is?' continued Molly.

'And, the fresh air will be good for your complexion,' teased Gary.

'Are you calling me spotty?' Molly did not like the way this was going, so went to get her warmest jacket and put on her scruffiest training shoes in mild protest.

Meanwhile, Emma was bumping her outrageously heavy suitcase down the stairs from her bedroom, intending to hide it in the garage before her mum took her to the train in the morning. Her ploy was simple: keep it away from Vicki, who would no doubt want it opened to check the contents and the neatness of her packing; an exercise that Emma was keen to avoid, as well as the argument that would no doubt ensue.

CHAPTER 19

As Pencil One reopened its doors to a very large crowd that frosty morning, most hoping for a glimpse or a word with their young hero, Pencil was in fact at the Arsenal training complex at London Colney, getting himself ready for another day of physio and gentle fitness development.

Popular amongst the other players, Pencil was enjoying the banter, happy to be the brunt of some fairly rude jokes about the break-in and damage a few days earlier.

'You are all just jealous,' he called back to a couple of first team players and headed for the changing room and his personal locker where a small number of other players were already getting into their training kit. Pencil opened his locker and was instantly pushed back as a frighteningly large number of dark grey rats rushed past him and made their escape from his locker and into the changing room.

'What the fuck?' shouted Pencil Kane, his heart beating faster than he had ever known.. Behind him, the other players reacted in a surprising variety of ways at the sight of the rats as rodents scurried about the place in a desperate search for an escape route.

'That's not fucking funny, you cunts,' bawled Pencil as the animals continued their frantic scurrying, but as he turned he noticed that no one was laughing; none of his fellow players had been expecting this to happen.

Turning his attention back to the inside of his locker, Pencil was horrified to see what looked like a severed human foot lying in the bottom on top of his favourite Nike trainers. Panic now sweeping over him, he then saw the note that was pinned to the inside of the wooden locker door. Feeling sick with fear, Pencil pulled the note from the door and read with real dread. The note simply stated: 'Where al-Qaeda failed – we will not'.

Pencil rushed to the shower room and just made it before he threw up what felt like the entire contents of his stomach.

'Fuck me,' he whispered. 'What the fuck is going on in my life?' Finding a sink, Pencil Kane washed his face before returning to the locker room to be greeted by a large man from security who was standing ashen-faced beside the open locker and its shocking contents.

'Are you okay, Pencil?' he asked.

'Pencil is fine, man, but we better get the police.' Kane searched in his pocket and handed the man the card that Elliot had given him on Saturday morning. 'Here, can you please give him a call? Tell him he'd better get over here, that there's been another threat.' The man took the card, nodded, and left to make the call.

David Lane was becoming increasingly frustrated at his failure to find the right person to succeed Gary Ruthven as Chief Executive of RCS. Having just spent the last hour chatting to the latest candidate over breakfast in the Wolseley on Piccadilly, he was doubting if the right applicant would be found. Hailing a cab, he headed towards the office where he was due to discuss the business financials for the period to end December with Rosie Calder and Lucas Hunt. Rosie had emailed her draft numbers to him on Friday and Lane was not feeling terrific about them either.

As always, Rosie was early for the meeting and ready to

begin as soon as Lane arrived. However, also as always, Lucas Hunt was nowhere to be seen.

'Good morning, Rosie,' began Lane in his best charming manner. 'Any sign of Lucas?'

'I am told he is on his way, will be here shortly.'

'Whatever that means,' replied Lane quietly as he poured himself a coffee from a pot on the table.

'Did you manage to have a look at the draft numbers?' asked Rosie, business like. She was not someone who did small talk, certainly not with people she didn't regard. David Lane came into that category, although she was never anything but polite.

'I did. What's your perspective?'

'Well, they're not terrible. Flat on last year and if we took out Hamburg we would be showing a positive eight percent comp,' she offered her summary.

'Absolutely,' replied Lane, wishing that he had a better grasp on things.

Just then Lucas Hunt arrived, apologising profusely for being late.

'Thanks,' replied Rosie Calder. It was a trick she had picked up from Gary and it always had the effect of keeping people on their toes.

'Okay, can we get to our agenda?' began Lane, keen to get the meeting moving.

'How did your interview go?' asked Lucas, totally ignoring Lane's request.

'It didn't; another total waste of time,' he replied, watching his chairman pour coffee and search in his jacket pocket for his copy of the agenda.

'That's a pity, we could do with getting the job filled,' offered Hunt, seemingly ready to get on with their meeting.

Twenty-five minutes later, they reached the final item on the agenda, which was the company application for their Small Company Business Loan from Barclays.

'Everything has now been completed,' began Lane, 'so the funds are available when we need them.'

'That's a relief,' mused Calder. 'Means we can all get paid at the end of the month.'

'It's surely not that bad, Rosie,' suggested Hunt, who had obviously not been keeping track with the previous discussion.

'I didn't say it was bad, Lucas, but if we didn't need the cash, we wouldn't be taking on a two-hundred-grand loan.'

'That's true, I suppose, and well done to you and David for putting this in place.'

'So, any other business?' asked Lane.

'Yes,' stated Hunt. 'Share certificates for the money that Julia and I invested a couple of months ago.'

'What about them?' asked Lane, who had received his certificates weeks earlier..

'Well, Julia asked me to remind you that she has not received her certificates.' Calder looked at Lane expecting him to reply and when he didn't she decided to attempt to clarify.

'Julia is not due any certificates, Lucas, you are. My understanding is that you refused to accept them when they were offered to you at the same time as David was given his,' she began, hoping that she had her facts straight.

'Yes, but Julia signed the cheque, so the shares should be in her name.' Hunt was going red as he stood his ground.

'Not possible.' Lane at last joined the discussion.

'What do you mean?' asked Hunt.

'We've had this discussion before. The rules of the government-backed Small Company Business Loan scheme means that it is not possible to have married shareholders; if we did then those shareholders would have to guarantee the loan. And, as nobody here was willing to provide such security, we can't have married shareholders. Which, as I am sure you will recall, Lucas, is why Vicki Ruthven had to transfer her shares to Gary before we made the application to Barclays.'

Lucas would not make eye contact before continuing, 'That is not my understanding.'

'Well, that's a pity. Do I need to go and get the minutes from our meeting when this was all agreed?'

'No, David, I don't want you to do that.'

'Good. So can you please collect your share certificates from Jenny? She has been holding them for you,' asked Rosie, keen to get on with her day.

'Okay, I will do that before I leave today. Julia is not going to be too happy though.'

'Ah, well,' smiled Lane. 'I am sure you will make it up to her.'

Bellamy had cordoned the locker room off by the time that Elliot arrived at London Colney to inspect the scene of Pencil Kane's latest, somewhat gruesome message. The rats had all made their escape and a SOCO officer was busy photographing the inside of Pencil's locker.

'Is that what I think it is?' asked Elliot, nodding towards the severed right foot.

'It certainly looks like it, although no one has touched it yet,' replied Bellamy, who was feeling very concerned by this latest turn of events.

'Okay. Have you spoken with Kane yet?'

'Only briefly, he is with the club's physio at the moment.'

'How did he seem?'

'Pretty shaken I'd say, but you know how he is, trying to be cool.'

Elliot began a cursory inspection of the locker room. No expense had been spared in the construction of the place, all in keeping with the money in modern-day football. He had read in the press that morning that Arsenal had agreed to pay £10 million for a sixteen-year-old player from Southampton. What was the world coming to?

'So, what happened to the rats?' he asked, eventually returning to Bellamy.

'Escaped apparently. Out into the training ground I suppose,' she replied.

'Numbers?'

'Various guesses, from twelve to twenty-five.'

'Christ,' reflected Elliot, just as another specialist arrived to examine the foot in Pencil's locker.

Getting into the visitor centre at Birmingham's Belmarsh Prison was something of a lengthy process and Julia Hillman was less than happy to be taking her shoes off and having to have her body scanned. *People like me*, she thought, *should not have to go through this crap every time they visit.* The system had obviously been designed for the plebs and the shit-heads who tried to smuggle drugs and weapons and other shit into their loser friends and partners.

Her father greeted her as always with a very gentle hug and one peck on her cheek.

'How are you today?' she asked, genuinely worried by Malcolm Hillman's appearance. He looked like he was not sleeping and his skin had sagged significantly since he had first been arrested for Anna's killing. For a man who had looked much younger than his age, he now was looking a great deal older.

'Oh, you know. I am as good as can be expected in the circumstances I suppose,' replied Hillman quietly. He was delighted to see Julia, the one person he could always rely on, the one person who had not given up on him.

'I've brought the books that you asked me to get,' fussed Julia, as she handed him the two legal volumes that he wanted to read as he worked on his preparation for his appeal against his ten-year minimum sentence. Hillman removed both books from the plastic bag and flicked the pages gently as if keen to start reading.

'Thanks, these should give me all I need to finalise my position.'

'Good, and if you need anything else, just email me when you can.'

'So, how are things with Lucas?'

'Well, I am not pregnant yet, if that's what you mean,' smiled Julia, who had decided that she was going to ignore her husband and ask her father for the money to cover the likely cost of her IVF treatment if the subject came up.

'That's not what I was asking, but now I know, how are you feeling about that?'

'Frustrated. We've decided to go down the IVF route; we have an appointment in London tomorrow to explore that option.'

'Do you think that's necessary?'

'I do. Lucas is less sure but it's a cost issue with him.' She had guided the conversation to the money.

'Ah well, let me know how it goes and if I can help with that I will.'

'Thank you, we'll be clearer after tomorrow.'

They then spent time updating on other family members and how Malcolm was passing his time in prison. With his appeal pending, there was enough to keep him busy and he was building a bit of a reputation as an adviser to other inmates who found him both approachable and wise.

'You should be charging a consulting fee,' suggested Julia, half in jest, the very thought of him mixing with such people making her feel angry inside. Her beloved father should not have to be going through this torture, should never have married that bloody woman!

Elliot and Bellamy met with Pencil Kane, and his agent, Paul Ruthven, in Ruthven's offices in Fitzroy Square later that afternoon. The place was modest in size, consisting of a reception area and a meeting room-come-office, a small kitchen area and a washroom. That said, it was well decorated and furnished and gave the sense of calm control and professionalism. Just the effect that Paul had tried to create, the impression he wanted his clients to have when they walked through his door.

The pretty receptionist, who was also office manager, led the two detectives into the room for their meeting and after brief welcomes they got down to business.

'So, Pencil, how are you after your latest ordeal?' Elliot began.

'Pencil is fine thanks, although I did get a bloody fright when I opened that door,' replied Kane, a large grin on his face.

'I can only imagine,' empathised Elliot, 'but the good news is that we believe that giving you a bloody fright was the main aim of the exercise.'

'What do you mean?' asked Ruthven.

'Well, we are of the view that this morning and the raid on Pencil One are the first stages of an extortion plan designed to get money.'

'What about the al-Qaeda message?' continued Ruthven, somewhat relieved by this news.

'Just part of the game. Believe me, if their intention had been to kill Pencil, then he would be dead already.' Elliot hesitated; he was not sure if he had crossed the line with that remark.

'I see, but what about the foot in the locker?'

'Stolen from a freezer at the University of London four days ago. The person whose foot it was died a few years ago in a motorcycle accident,' clarified Bellamy, who had been watching Pencil's reaction to the news.

'So,' began Pencil eventually. 'These people will be getting in touch, to demand a big bag of wonga?'

'That's what we expect to happen,' replied Elliot. Pencil was sharp.

'And what do we do then?'

'That's for us to discuss now, to prepare and plan for.'

'So, Pencil should be relieved?' asked the young footballer.

'In some ways, but until we catch these people we need to be taking every precaution possible. They are smart and well organised and we think they will be looking for a large amount,' replied Elliot.

'Okay, let's get to the plan,' proposed Ruthven, quietly impressed by the two police officers.

At the age of fifty-seven, Dan Jenner still considered himself to be at his peak. Healthy, very wealthy, and still handsome, Dan was no doubt one of the lucky ones, one of those people for whom life just seemed to work out. His marriage to Carole had been the icing on the cake, the final piece of his perfect jigsaw, a puzzle with a picture postcard image on its box.

Dan had left school at seventeen, much to the annoyance of his parents who had expected the bright and talented public schoolboy to go to university. Their son had other ideas and was desperate to get into business, to make some money. His awareness of business opportunities and his willingness to work hard and learn saw him become a young and valuable asset to a local businessman in his home town of Reading, and by the time most kids his age were entering university, Dan was already area sales manager for a firm that sold electronic equipment. The development of television and video recording led Dan to his first business, when he set up Jenner Electronics and quickly established his retail outlet as the destination store for people wanting leading-edge advice and equipment. Taking the gamble to back VHS technology over the better designed but poorly marketed Betamax system gave him a big lift and by the time he was twenty-four he owned twelve stores in the south-east of England and his business turnover was exceeding a million pound per annum. By thirty, Dan was done with that business and sold the company in 1985 for a healthy £10 million, of which Dan pocketed just under 80%.

After a three-month sabbatical, Jenner, now considered to be one of England's most eligible bachelors, was on the hunt for his next project. His model was simple – find leading-edge technology before it becomes mainstream and build an outstanding retail and customer service regime to take advantage when Joe Public caught up and began demanding that technology. Fascinated by the leaps taking place in computing, Dan spent six months on research before making a swift move into the fast-developing mobile telephone industry. Indeed, it was when attending an innovation workshop run by BT in London that Jenner saw the future, and for him, the future was mobile telephony for the masses. Using the same delivery model as before, but with his learned lessons applied, he set up the Mobile Phone Company and within a year of opening had seventeen stores in London and the south-east. By employing bright young telephone geeks and focusing on finding the right mobile for each individual customer, the Mobile Phone Company became a darling of the British High Street and once again for Dan Jenner, business boomed. For Dan, however, the excitement he got from business was not in the running of his organisations, but in their creation; and so, with the MPC now established as the UK market leader, Dan Jenner sold the company for just short of £250 million and announced his retirement from business at the age of just thirty-nine.

What followed were what Dan refers to as his dark years, years in which he dated a string of young supermodels and relatively famous actresses and aspiring pop stars. He would spend his summer on holiday aboard his yacht in the south of France, his winters holidaying in the Caribbean and his spring in and around the nightclubs of London. Jenner discovered that with wise and careful investment, he could do nothing in the way of work and his fortune would still grow, and for a number of years he enjoyed doing just that. However, with the millennium fast approaching, Dan Jenner was getting restless with his sterile and hedonistic lifestyle and began looking for his next big idea. What he landed on, however, was a surprise to him as much as it was to those who watched and followed him. He saw a gap on the high street market for branded coffee shops; places where people could meet, talk, email, search the Internet and be charged premium prices for exotic-sounding drinks and pastries. By the end of 2001, Caffe Bianco had twenty stores in London all turning over in excess of £1 million per year and was considered to be the coolest new addition to UK popular culture. Three years later, Jenner sold his latest business with its 250 stores across the UK to global hotel giant Hilton for another £96 million, and stepped away happy with what he had achieved.

By now afforded business guru status, Dan was much in demand as a non-executive director and public speaker and it was on such an engagement in 2004 that he was introduced to the very beautiful Carole King. After a whirlwind romance, the couple married the following year and moved into the house in Holland Park after the couple had overseen a significantly expensive refurbishment. For Dan, life with Carole was almost perfect; she was independent, easy to live with and their sex life was as good as any man of fifty-seven could hope for.

As he strode back to their home that Monday afternoon, Dan Jenner had two things on his active mind. First was the conversation that he and Carole had held during their walk in Holland Park the previous day about the situation at RCS. Dan liked Gary Ruthven, and knew how close and important he was to his wife; what was wrong at RCS, however, was nothing to do with Lane and Hunt but to do with Gary's basic failure to understand that his business was fundamentally not scalable. It was built around one man and his close team, and Ruthven was not able to be cloned – the product was too complicated to replicate, the expansion plan wrong. The second thing on his mind was his private investment in Pencil Kane's store project; now that was scalable, replicable, and if all the data coming out of Pencil One was correct, then the quicker they could open new stores the better. Pencil Two was scheduled for opening in Knightsbridge in April, and Pencil Three in September, but Dan would like thirty 'Pencils' opened within twelve months and that was not in the plan. A quiet call to Paul Ruthven was called for that evening; the younger Ruthven who was also a private investor in the project knew to trust Dan and would heed his advice.

'As Chairman of the company, I am telling you to replace this share certificate with a new one in the name of Julia Hillman,' instructed Lucas Hunt to Gary Ruthven's PA, Jenny, as he stood over her at her desk that evening.

'I am sorry, Lucas. I can't do that unless either Gary or Rosie Calder confirm that it's okay for me to do so.' Jenny stood her ground.

'You are not listening to me. If you do not do as asked, then I will have no option other than to dismiss you with immediate effect.'

'Yeah right, Lucas,' Jenny smiled, and turned her attention back to her computer screen, leaving Hunt holding the certificate that she had just given to him.

'You have not heard the end of this,' he finally conceded, and stormed to a small anteroom that was used for storing stationery and the like. There, he angrily fed the share certificate into a small paper shredder and watched as the strips fell into the Perspex box below.

At her desk, Jenny was typing an email to Gary and Rosie Calder, explaining what had just happened and asking them for their advice on how she should deal with the matter. Before sending the note, she decided to copy it to Lucas and David Lane for their information. As was her style, she then calmly cleared her desk for the night and locked the share certificate folder in a drawer, happy that she had a copy of the certificate that Lucas Hunt had just signed for, and left the office for her evening at home.

The call that came to Pencil Kane's mobile phone later that evening was pretty much as had been predicted by Detective Chief Inspector Elliot.

'This is Pencil,' opened the young footballer.

'We know who you are, Pencil, so do not say another word,' it began.

'Okay,' replied Pencil calmly.

'That's a fucking word, Kane. No more, just listen,' the quietly spoken male voice on the line demanded. 'If you want your recent troubles to stop, you are going to have to pay. The amount that you are going to pay for that is five hundred thousand pounds cash, and it will need to be paid by mid-day on Wednesday, and we will call you back at 10am tomorrow with further instructions. Involve the filth on this and where al-Qaeda failed, we will not.'

Pencil listened but the connection had been cut, the caller gone.

CHAPTER 20
TUESDAY 10 JANUARY 2006

A very frustrating weather-related delay to their train journey meant that Julia Hillman and Lucas Hunt arrived ten minutes late for their appointment in Harley Street that morning. Their names taken, the couple were then led to a private waiting room and asked to complete a series of forms before their consultant meeting.

'Jesus, Lucas. How many forms do you think we have to complete during a lifetime in this bloody country?' ranted Julia, who seemed to have no problem in finding something to complain about.

'It must be a few honey,' replied her husband absent-mindedly, as he tried to focus on completing his details in his neat handwriting. In truth, he was also a little nervous as he was still very worried about how much all this was going to cost them, and when that hurdle was overcome, he was also anxious about the true state of his sperm count. His GP had told him previously that he was pretty good for a man of his age, but what did that really mean? This laboratory process was very likely to be considerably more specific than that and who could tell what the impact of that would be? Sure, he could still ejaculate, he had always kept himself active on that front, often with the aid of a decent porn site on the Internet, but could the little blighters still deliver? Could they still achieve breakthrough when needed?

'Lucas?' Julia brought him back to the present.

'Yes, honey?'

'When did we begin having unprotected sex?'

'Sorry, I've not got to that question yet,' he flustered his reply.

'I have, so when?'

'I am not sure, honey. Sometime before our wedding if I remember right.'

'Okay, I am going to say July 2005. Make sure that you state the same,' commanded Julia Hillman as she returned to her form.

The administration complete, they were then led to a consulting room on the first floor of the building where they were introduced to their baby-faced young doctor who looked like he had just returned from a month in the sun somewhere. The man smiled, welcomed the couple and began by asking them a number of intimate and somewhat personal questions that seemed to throw Julia off her usual guard. This session complete to the doctor's satisfaction, he then began giving them an introduction to IVF.

'In vitro fertilisation is a process by which an egg is fertilised by sperm outside the body. In vitro from the Latin meaning "in glass", hence the rather ugly term "test tube baby",' he began slowly but clearly. 'The process involves monitoring a woman's ovulatory process, removing ovum from the woman's ovaries and letting sperm fertilise them in a fluid medium in a lab. The fertilised egg is then transferred into the patient's uterus with the intention of establishing a successful pregnancy.'

Julia, who had done her homework, then embarked on a rigorous questioning regime, aimed at covering as much ground with the doctor as practically possible. She wanted to leave no stone unturned, wanted him clear that she wanted to be pregnant and as quickly as possible. They explored medical history of both and soon focused on the thorny issue of Lucas's age.

'One approach that we might want to consider in this case is ICSI,' suggested the young doctor eventually.

'ICSI?' asked Julia.

'Intracytoplasmic sperm injection, known as ICSI, can be used as part of an IVF treatment to help you and Lucas conceive a child. ICSI is the most successful form of treatment for men who are infertile and is used in almost half of all IVF treatments.'

'Nobody is saying I am infertile here, doctor.' Lucas was suddenly listening.

'Indeed, but where a sperm is not naturally able to penetrate the egg, a little help can get the job done,' offered the doctor gently.

'Say more please,' requested Julia.

'ICSI only requires one sperm, which is injected directly into the egg and the fertilised egg; the embryo is then transferred into the womb.'

'Sounds less dependent on nature,' reflected Lucas.

'Indeed. Leaves less to chance,' agreed the doctor.

'How long would a treatment take?' asked Julia again.

'One cycle of ICSI takes between four to six weeks to complete. You and Lucas would come to the clinic for a full day for the egg and sperm retrieval procedures and then return between two and six days later for the embryo transfer procedure.'

'Any downsides?' It was Lucas who spoke this time.

'ICSI is a newer procedure, so specialists are still learning about it, but the same risks that I mentioned regarding IVF, such as multiple births and ectopic pregnancy, apply to ICSI. And ICSI is a more expensive option when it comes to cost.'

'But you think it might be a better procedure for Lucas and me?'

'Obviously, we would need to have you both in for examination before we begin, but in all likelihood, I do, yes.'

'Okay, that is very helpful. When can we get going?' Julia,

irrespective of what Lucas might be thinking, had made up her mind.

'Well, my assistant can help get you scheduled for the examination stage. But before we go there, any more questions?'

'Cost,' asked Lucas. 'Any indication of cost?'

'Again, my assistant can help with detail, but for one ICSI cycle, you will be looking at something in the region of twelve to fifteen thousand.'

'Okay, thanks,' replied Lucas, sounding a hell of a lot calmer than he was feeling.

Elliot and Bellamy, keen to be as discreet as possible, met with Pencil Kane, Paul Ruthven, and the Arsenal head of security at the London Colney training complex just after eleven that morning. Pencil had received his promised call an hour earlier and now had his instructions regarding the payment of the half million pounds that was being demanded.

'They seem to know what they are doing,' began Elliot, as they all settled around a table in a small team room.

'No shit, Sherlock,' commented Pencil, who was obviously feeling the strain.

'So, we need to align on what we are going to do, how we respond to their demands,' continued Elliot, choosing to ignore Kane's sarcastic remark.

'Pencil ain't got half a million in cash, that's for sure, so an electronic transfer is out of the question.' The instruction had been for Pencil to have an electronic transfer ready to be made at midday tomorrow; bank transfer details would be texted to his phone at 11.55, giving him five minutes to make the transfer. It was certainly changed days from the old bag of cash drop, and Elliot knew that what would follow would be a series of electronic transfers that would be very difficult to trace quickly.

'No, we can't risk transferring the money.'

'Pencil is glad to hear it, so what do you suggest?'

Elliot looked at the others before replying, 'Call their bluff.'

'What?' asked Kane, his eyes almost popping from their sockets.

'Call their bluff,' repeated Elliot. 'Tell them to piss off and that if they come near you again, you will have them shot.'

'You are fucking kidding me here, Mr Elliot. Tell me you're kidding?'

'I don't do kidding, Pencil. Never have and never will.'

Pencil Kane sat back in his chair and looked at Paul Ruthven and the others in the room.

'Let me explain,' began Elliot. 'These people have organised themselves planfully and professionally in order to extort money from you. They have shown themselves capable of being smart and clever and they believe their two stunts will have put you on the edge, made you willing to pay to stop their shit. If they didn't believe that, they would have tried another stunt, but they think you are ready to give in.'

'Pencil is focused,' smiled Kane.

'So, you just tell them to fuck off. See what happens.'

'Shit, that just might make them kill me,' laughed Pencil nervously.

'Not sure what good that would do them – they need you alive and we need them to make a mistake. So, we tell the class bully to go pick on someone else.'

'You are serious?' asked Ruthven finally, surprised by this proposal.

'We are. You see Sergeant Bellamy and I think these people know you, are familiar enough to think that they can predict what you will do. Perhaps they're even close enough to be able to watch what's going on, probably aware of this meeting this morning.'

'What makes you say that?' asked the Arsenal security man.

'Can't share that at the moment. We are just pretty confident that we're correct.'

'Okay, so what next?'

Elliot then outlined the plan and after a few minutes' discussion it was agreed to proceed with the police proposal, although Pencil did leave the meeting no less anxious than when he had arrived.

It was well below freezing when Gary Ruthven and Carole King exited the offices of The Phi Collections in New York's trendy Meatpacking District just after two o'clock eastern time. Carole was in awe of what Gary had just achieved, a six-figure brand development project fee requiring four quarterly visits to the USA with all expenses paid. In truth, she was also inspired by what The Phi Collections were producing: high end and very dramatic women's clothing that was causing a real buzz among the fashionista and global magazines, with *Vogue* running a special feature on the burgeoning brand in February. The global development of the brand was going to require careful handling and the people at Phi were more than happy to place their trust in the hands of Gary, Carole, and their team at RCS.

Deciding to walk a few blocks before catching a taxi back to their hotel, they set off in silence, both reflecting quietly on the meeting and the prospects for this new and very exciting project. Their return flight to Heathrow was scheduled to depart JFK at 8.20pm that evening and it was their intention to visit ground zero, pay their private respects, before having a late lunch and beginning their thinking regarding The Phi Collections. As they walked the four or five blocks to Fifth Avenue, Gary reflected on the fact that this was how he enjoyed spending his time; winning and developing new client projects, travelling to fascinating places to work with talented and driven people, all of which was in stark contrast to the laboured atmosphere and culture that existed within his own business.

They had arrived late last night and been driven in their

hired limo to the Hudson Hotel with its trendy decor and frenetic energy, and had taken a quick supper before an early night in their respective, very small New York hotel rooms.

'Don't you just love this city?' It was Carole who broke their reflective silence.

'I do. Wish I had discovered it twenty years ago, had come to work here,' replied Gary as they crossed at a junction.

'Really, you wish you had come here to work? More so than London?'

'I guess I am just a bit jaundiced by RCS at the moment. I still love the smoke.'

'Glad to hear it, we've got a business to sort out back home.' Carole linked an arm with Ruthven's and they walked again in silence like two lovers out for an afternoon stroll.

'Why don't we go direct to ground zero, then back to the hotel?' suggested Gary suddenly.

'That makes sense. Let's look for a taxi.'

Moments later the pair were crushed in the back of one of New York's uncomfortable yellow cabs as the driver who informed them that he was from Bulgaria, steered them through the traffic towards the site of the tragic 9/11 attack on the World Trade Center by al-Qaeda. As they approached the place, they fell silent again, both wondering how they would feel, how they would react to be at the actual site of such an atrocity. After paying their Bulgarian taxi-driver, they walked somewhat tentatively down a street at the right of what just looked like any other major construction site. Signs directed them to the makeshift visitors centre and again they made their way in silence.

Carole felt shivery, a combination of the freezing temperature and the thought of people jumping to the ground to escape incineration, the TV shots of the collapsing towers vivid in her mind. Ruthven was lost in his own thoughts; the plans for the re-build were yet to be finalised but a tall replacement was expected. That decision, in Gary's mind, was what made the

USA the world power that it was; by putting a memorial and building an equally high tower, the country was saying that it would not be bullied, would not give in to terrorists. London had reacted in a similar way after last year's 7/7 attack. Perhaps there was no alternative. Life simply had to go on.

Twenty minutes later, they were once again crushed into the back of another yellow taxi as they made their way back to the Hudson.

'Do you think they will ever catch him?' ' asked Carole quietly.

'Bin Laden?'

'Yeah. Do you?'

'We might never know. What would they do with him if they did get him? Public trial? Death penalty?'

'Who knows, he deserves something.'

'Probably just shoot the bastard and not tell the world,' speculated Ruthven.

'Wouldn't that make his captors as bad as him?'

'Stick to the rules, you mean? Human rights and all that crap?'

'You sound pretty angry about it.'

'I guess knowing what happened to Pencil in London has put me in a hard place,' he replied honestly.

'I suppose, but it would be good to know that he was not out there anymore.'

'I agree with that.'

They had reached their hotel and agreed to freshen up and meet in the restaurant for a quick late lunch and do some work on the Phi project.

'There's not a lot more to say I am afraid, Pencil. Your foot is as well recovered medically as it's going to be, but you are going to suffer from life-long chronic arthritis.'

'What do you mean by chronic?' asked Pencil, who was feeling totally deflated. What a day it had been.

'Chronic is simply a term that we use for something that is not going to go away. It does not necessarily mean that your life is going to be ruined by it. On bad days, for example, you will need heavy painkillers and on good days you may need to take nothing,' explained Lucy Campbell.

'Okay, so what about the football?'

'That's something we can't answer. There's nothing to stop you from stepping up your fitness programme; my guess, however, is that it is going to be painful but not impossible.'

'So, if Pencil gets fit and has painkilling injections, a comeback is possible?' This was the most important question that Kane had ever asked anyone in his young life.

'I would say so, but it's going to be very tough,' replied Lucy carefully.

'But you're giving Pencil the go ahead to resume training at Arsenal?' Kane asked. He was ecstatic with this news, despite the chronic arthritis issue.

'I am, Pencil. There is nothing more I can do. I would, however, like to see you again in six months.'

'Of course, Pencil will be delighted to see you again then.' The boy smiled his biggest, most attractive smile and reached out to hug his doctor tight. Paul joined them in a threesome, tears in his eyes and unable to speak with the emotion of the moment.

During the drive back to Pencil's apartment, with Delroy Powell's man now driving, Paul Ruthven called Arsenal's French head coach with the news that Pencil had been given the go ahead to resume full training. The coach was delighted and asked if it was okay to make an announcement on the club's website. After referring the point to Kane, Paul confirmed that it was indeed okay.

Delroy had two of his team deployed on night duty at Pencil's home and as agreed with Elliot earlier, Kane informed them that he had lost his telephone and gave them his new temporary number.

'Now I can say that I've slept with you,' joked Carole King as she and Gary took their flat-bed seats on the British Airways flight at New York's JFK airport later that evening.

'Tell whoever you like. It won't do my street cred any harm,' replied Gary, getting rid of the various additional items that were being passed to him by the over-attentive air hostess.

'Before you crash out, I do need to chat to you about Julia Hillman and what you intend to do about her threat,' added Carole, as they buckled their seat belts in readiness for the taxi to the runway and take-off.

'That sounds ominous,' said Ruthven, surprised that it had taken so long for this little item to enter their trip agenda. Looking at his phone before switching it off for the flight, Gary picked up a text from Paul informing him that Pencil had been given the all clear to resume training at Arsenal. Smiling, he turned his attention to Carole.

'Okay, tell me what I need to do with Julia Hillman.'

CHAPTER 21   WEDNESDAY 11 JANUARY 2006

'That really is pathetic pillow plumping,' laughed Lucy Campbell.

'Pathetic pillow plumping?' replied Paul Ruthven, lifting his pillow and tossing it across the bed to where Lucy was making her side of the large bed in his Marylebone apartment.

'And that helps how?' she responded, ducking to let the object fly over her head to land in a far corner of the bedroom.

They stopped laughing and made their peace, before finishing the task and heading for work, both conscious that being late had become a bit of a naughty habit since they had started spending nights together.

'First home can make the bed properly,' offered Paul as he hugged Lucy and headed off on foot to his office in Fitzroy Square. Lucy headed in the other direction, needing to catch the Underground to Whitechapel.

As he walked, Paul reflected on the week so far, the endless drama around Pencil Kane and the business discussion he had held with Dan Jenner the night before. Dan, he knew, was a business genius capable of driving the Pencil store project to massive success; all Paul had to do was persuade the young Kane to heed Dan's advice and plan a quicker expansion. Pencil liked to be in control, to oversee all the fine detail, but with his football training about to step up a gear and with his next TV documentary due soon, he was going to have to learn to let go and trust his team.

Reaching his office, a coffee already in hand, he went through his appointments for the day. January was a traditionally crazy month for players' agents as it was the only month where players were allowed to transfer clubs during the actual football season in Europe. Paul did not like the transfer window period, a time when ruthless agents and their cohorts tried to make money by engineering deals that often disrupted player and club form. That said, he now had twelve players on his books and four would soon be reaching the stage where early negotiations would begin on new contracts with their clubs. One, a young Scot at Everton, was unhappy with his progress and was already making noises about getting a transfer. Paul knew the Everton manager and had already had a private chat about the situation; the club wanted to keep the player but were not able or willing to guarantee how many first team matches the young man could expect if he extended his deal.

Ruthven was a wise agent, had built himself a great career by working hard and being a top team contributor, and tried to advise his clients that it was rare for the grass to be greener at another top club. Having chosen his clients sensibly, Paul knew that they all had the raw ingredients to become regular Premier League players and hence build highly secure futures for themselves. That said, he had no control over how a young man would react when the high levels of earnings started to burn holes in their pockets. For every shrewd business mind like Pencil Kane, he would predict another four or five would at some point go astray. Doing a quick calculation, he reckoned that of the twelve young players on his books, ten were now earning in excess of £1 million a year excluding boot and equipment deals and other add-ons such as image rights. With his fee of 12.5%, his turnover that year alone was going to exceed the million mark just on player wages. Smiling, he realised that that was more than he had ever earned in a year as a top player at Liverpool, and with TV rights continuously rising, top division players would soon be earning significantly more. How long such salary levels would last was anyone's guess but Paul Ruthven felt that unless something significant happened, another decade of astronomical wages could be expected by the top players. When Ruthven added transfer fees, signing on fees, and all commercial deals, his business could provide him with years of sterling growth.

His office manager/receptionist and only employee informed him that Kate Ross was on the line and wanted a quick word. She would be confirming his recent purchase of Apple stock, a six-figure purchase that had surprised her, and no doubt updating him on his relentless quest for an investment in Facebook. He sure as hell hoped that Gary had got it right and Apple would move into the mobile telephone world; Dan Jenner had also believed that it would happen at some point, so Paul had been happy to take the plunge.

The small but highly efficient police raid on the new location for Pencil Two in Knightsbridge took place shortly after midday. And, after a brief skirmish in the store, a twenty-five-year-old man employed as an assistant to the store's designer was arrested and taken in a police car with its siren blaring to Marylebone Police Station for questioning in connection with the raid on Pencil One.

Elliot and Bellamy were waiting to question the man as soon as the police car arrived at the garage entrance at the back of the station. A duty solicitor was on hand to sit in on the interview and Elliot hoped that the matter would be wrapped up pretty quickly now that they had their breakthrough.

As per their agreed plan, Pencil had given three different new mobile phone numbers to a variety of people close to him with the story that he had lost his phone. The call that he had received just before 11.55 to instruct the transfer of the half million pounds that was being demanded had come to the phone that Pencil Kane had only given the number of to two people. With police teams waiting in close proximity to all the potential suspects, the store designer's assistant was the first to be arrested and two hours later, six other suspects, all unknown to Kane, were under arrest and awaiting questioning by Elliot and Bellamy.

Gary Ruthven and Carole King arrived in the RCS offices direct from Heathrow later that afternoon. Both had demanded an urgent meeting of the senior team but had to wait until 3pm when Lucas Hunt eventually returned to the office from a lunch engagement.

'This shouldn't take long. I just want us to clear up the situation regarding Lucas's share certificate and his request to Jenny that she make out the shares to his wife,' began Gary in a clear, focused and calm manner.

'I think it's all a bit of fuss about nothing,' responded Lucas, who had obviously had a fair amount of liquid with his lunch.

'So,' continued Ruthven, referring to a copy of Jenny's email that lay on the table in front of him. 'You did not demand that she reproduce the share certificate in Julia Hillman's name? You did not threaten to dismiss her from the firm?'

'I think she got the wrong end of the stick, got a bit flustered,' continued Lucas, looking at David Lane for support but not getting any.

'To be clear then, you have signed and received your share certificate?'

'I did indeed, and have it safely locked away at home,' lied Hunt.

'And we will hear no more of this nonsense about Julia being a shareholder in this firm?'

'You will not hear another word on the matter again from me,' replied Hunt, now very red in the face.

'Good. Now I would like Jenny to come in to receive your apology for this unfortunate incident,' pushed Ruthven, keen to cover all angles.

'Before we do that,' interjected Carole, 'can I ask what you mean when you say "from me", Lucas? Can you confirm that Julia is completely aligned with what you have just confirmed to us?'

'What's it got to do with Julia?' asked Hunt defensively.

'I just want to know that your wife's understanding on this matter is aligned with your own,' she continued.

'It is,' stated Lucas firmly.

'Good. And for clarity, I will draft a note of this meeting for future reference.'

'Thanks, Carole,' smiled Ruthven. 'Now let's get Jenny in for that apology.'

With that matter dealt with, Gary went to his office and worked for the remainder of the afternoon on the draft contract agreed with The Phi Collections in New York, before having it checked by Carole and Rosie Calder and emailing it to his client in the USA for perusal and comment.

Just after 6pm, he left the office to catch the train home to Beaconsfield and a conversation with his wife that just might end his marriage.

Vicki Ruthven had spent the afternoon going over the latest numbers coming out of Pencil One when she had received a call from the store designer in Knightsbridge updating her on the police raid and the arrest of his assistant.

'The little fucker,' she exclaimed in response to the news.

'You're not wrong. I would like to kick the little shit in the balls. You think you know people, but what do we really know?'

'I hope they lock the bastard up and throw away the key.'

'So do I, and I hope they catch all the fuckers involved with him.'

Vicki tried calling Gary with the news but his phone went to voicemail. He was no doubt up to his neck after New York; she would update him later. Molly was staying at a school friend's house that evening, had an early morning trip to the Tate Modern with school, so she and Gary would be home alone and able to have a good catch-up.

Pencil Kane was very relieved, very relieved indeed. Indeed, Pencil was so relieved he almost committed what would be his worst cardinal sin by having a glass of beer, a glass of anything alcoholic to celebrate his return to training that morning and the arrest of the fucking bastards who had tried to extort half a million from him. At eighteen years of age, the young footballer had never so much as had a sip of an alcoholic drink, such was his passion for his sport, his desire to be a great success. He had joined Paul Ruthven and Lucy Campbell in their local Italian for dinner and his arrival had caused the usual stir among the other patrons, all delighted to see the young heroic survivor of the 7/7 bombings sitting in their midst.

Sticking to fizzy water, he ordered a chilli-based pizza and sat back, relaxing for the first time in some considerable time.

'So,' began Lucy. 'How was your first day back in proper training?'

'It was cool, Dr Campbell, really cool. But Pencil has got a big hill to climb before I'd say I was back in proper training.'

'I know, but you know what I'm getting at?'

'Yeah, of course Pencil does, and it's all down to you.' Pencil raised his water glass in a toast to the young surgeon.

'Thanks, Pencil, but I've had the easy job. How was the pain today?'

'Pencil was cool. Had an injection, so it was okay.'

'Glad to hear it, and remember to take your time, recuperate properly.'

'Pencil will, and with these scumbags that were tryin' to rob me now banged up by the filth, my day could not have been better.'

'The police did a grand job, didn't they?' reflected Paul, joining the conversation.

'Pencil thinks that Elliot geezer is a top bloke, top top bloke,' agreed Pencil.

'Your face when he suggested that you tell them to fuck off,' laughed Ruthven. 'I thought your eyes were going to pop out.'

'Pencil thought he was taking the piss, man, thought he was joking.'

'What was it he said?'

'"I don't do kidding, Pencil",' replied Kane, trying and failing badly to imitate Elliot's Northern Ireland accent.

'That was it. Precious,' smiled Ruthven at Lucy, who was watching Paul, realising how much she was in love with the man.

'Fuckin' precious, man. "I don't do kidding."'

Their food began arriving and Paul made a mental note to have a chat with his client about his use of bad language when out in public. All they needed was some jerk with a phone recording something inappropriate and a chunk of Pencil's great reputation could be damaged badly.

There had been no furious outburst, no smashed wine glasses, tantrums or tears. Vicki had simply sat in relative silence as her husband had told her the full and honest story of his short-lived affair with Tandy and its horribly gruesome consequence. He had then, without interruption, proceeded to tell her about the threat of exposure by Julia Hillman and her husband, Lucas Hunt. Gary had been broken-hearted when he was telling the tale to his wife, the wife that he now risked losing and whom he now realised he loved more than ever. When he had finished, Vicki stood and went to the kitchen, returning moments later with a fresh bottle of wine. She looked pale and drawn as she poured herself a full glass and offered some to Gary, who was happy to accept.

'I suppose it could be worse,' she began quietly.

'In what way?'

'Well, you could be telling me that you had another kid somewhere, or that you were leaving me and the girls to go off and start another happy family.' She looked at Ruthven and took a deep drink of the wine.

'I would never have done that,' replied Gary very quietly, wondering where this was going.

'Tell me something,' she continued.

'Everything, anything,' conceded her husband.

'Would you be telling me all this if Julia fucking Hillman was not threatening you?'

'I don't know, Vicki. What I do know is that this horrible thing had made me promise to myself that nothing like it would ever happen again,' he replied honestly.

'Have there been others? Is this Tandy person just the last in a long line of Gary Ruthven conquests?'

'There's been no long line,' said Gary cautiously, not wanting to lie but seeing no benefit in dragging the far past into this confession.

'So, you and Carole have never nipped up an alleyway for a quick fucking knee-trembler?' Vicki was in tears now, really afraid of what her husband was about to say next.

'Vicki, on the girls' lives, there has never been anything intimate or physical between Carole and me. Yes, we are close, but we are friends and she is your friend. Nothing has ever happened between us.'

'Well, that's something I suppose.' Vicki gulped more wine.

'So, what happens now?'

'What do you mean?'

'For fuck's sake, Gary. What do you want to happen next?'

'Surely that's up to you,' replied Gary, more frightened than he had ever been.

'Well, I can't say I am totally surprised. I've seen you around women when you've had too much to drink; watched you feeling people's arses when you were dancing at parties. Sometimes wondered what you were whispering in their fucking ears like some slimy kid in a cheap porn movie.'

'I am so sorry, Vicki. So ashamed.'

'Stop it. You're not the only prick who fancied a quick bunk up; been a few blokes that have stuck their hard cocks against me on a drunken night out or ten, left me wondering what a fresh cock would feel like.' Vicki poured them both more wine.

'I am sure,' replied her husband finally.

'The only difference is that I kept mine as silly little fantasies, while you went out and got some tart up the fucking duff and then had to fork out our cash to get rid of your unwanted foetus!' She was raising her voice for the first time, her anger beginning to bubble to the surface.

'Like I said, I couldn't be more sorry. More ashamed.'

'That's alright then. Made your little Catholic boy confession; say three Hail Marys and all will be forgiven. You are such a fucking twat, Gary. A twat for doing it, a twat for getting caught, and a twat for having to tell me about it.'

'Like I said—'

'Yeah, yeah, like you fucking said,' she cut him off, obviously getting a little tipsy from the wine. Gary reached out and tried to take her hand but she pulled away from him before saying, 'Don't try to touch me. I am not sure that I ever want you to touch me again, you fucking stupid prick!' And with that she stood to leave the room.

'I am going to have a bath. I feel filthy. Suggest the spare room is best for you, unless you have someplace better to go.'

'Of course I don't.'

'Not this week at any rate, you fucking prick!' she screamed, before climbing the stairs and banging shut the door to their bedroom.

CHAPTER 22

THURSDAY
12 JANUARY 2006

The luminous display on the bedside clock told Vicki Ruthven that it was eleven minutes after three and she felt that she had been crying for hours. This was not how it was supposed to be, lying there with her dreams in ruins, her lovely husband having just taken a proverbial sledgehammer to her life and smashed it to pieces. And a lovely husband was how she still considered Gary. Yes, he had his weaknesses, who didn't? But despite all of that, she still liked him, still loved the bastard with all her heart. But, could she ever bring herself to move on from this place with him? Could things ever get back to normal? That was something she couldn't answer. To Vicki, marriage was for life, was something you committed to and stuck to; that was how she had been brought up to think and now her silly little dream world of a marriage was in ruins. It was over, and she was really frightened about what would now happen to her and her girls, when Gary no longer lived with them, no longer cared for them, no longer looked after them.

In the spare room, Gary Ruthven lay awake too. Mild jetlag had seen him drift momentarily into light sleep, but he soon was awake again; tense, worried, but at the same time relieved that he had told Vicki before some other fucker did. She deserved that, didn't need to hear it from anyone else, least of all that bitch Julia

Hillman. Reflecting on the fact that tonight had been his most honest, most adult act of tough love, Gary vowed to continue this journey by removing Hunt and Lane from RCS that very day. His die was cast and he was totally intent on putting right the wrongs he had colluded with over the last months, if not year. Hoping Vicki was okay, he went quietly to their bedroom door and could hear her weeping and more tears welled in his own eyes. Returning to his bed, he lay on top of the duvet and wept deeply.

Just after four, the bedroom door opened and Vicki joined him on the bed and Gary pulled her to him and enveloped his distraught wife in his arms. Vicki cried salty tears onto his chest before finally being able to speak.

'What is going to happen to me?' she cried weakly.

'Whatever you decide, I will always care for you, always look after you, do what I can to protect you. Please know that,' he replied, wiping her tears with the palms of his hands.

'I don't know what to do, who to talk to about this,' continued Vicki, sobbing.

'I am good with you talking to anyone who might help,' he offered.

'That's big of you, you wanker,' she replied, and began banging his chest viciously with her fists, her elbows.

'I didn't mean it like that,' he tried to explain, not attempting to stop her blows, which he felt he more than deserved.

'Good, because your days of telling me what to do are over.' She stopped hitting her husband and sat up on the bed in front of him.

'Have I been that shit?' he asked, sitting to face her.

'Not until tonight, Gary, not until tonight.' She looked away from him and stared out of the window into the cold, dark country night.

'Well, at least that's something,' reflected Ruthven, exhausted by trauma and travel.

'But is it enough?'

'For what?'

'To enable me to forgive you, to enable us to move on, put this shit behind us.'

'Not for me to say, Vicki. I hope and pray that we can. But I have lost any say in that, blown it with my stupid selfish behaviour.'

Suddenly, she was on top of him, kissing him, pulling his boxer shorts from him and getting herself naked.

'Fuck me, Gary. Fuck me like you fucked her! Fuck me like you love me more than any other person in the world.' Naked now, she opened herself to her husband and for the next twenty minutes they made love with a combined violence and tenderness like they had never had sex before, culminating in a massive joint orgasm that left them both breathless and spent.

'Did that help anything?' asked Gary eventually.

'Not sure,' replied Vicki, thinking that if it was to be their final marital fuck, at least it had been a good one.

They made tea in the kitchen and drank from their cups in silence before heading back upstairs where they spent the rest of the night together in their big bed, holding each other tight, waiting for the morning to come, waiting for some solution to this horrible thing that had come between them.

And when they woke, just before seven, Vicki Ruthven told her husband that she wanted him to pack a bag and find himself someplace else to live for the foreseeable future, until she had time to get her head together.

'What will you tell the girls?' asked Gary quietly, accepting his wife's decision.

'The truth I suppose,' replied Vicki, knowing that she would not do that, could not do that to Gary.

'Okay. Can you let me know when you've spoken to them. I owe them a big apology too.'

'You do, Gary, you really do. And, do one other thing for me,' she asked.

'Of course, what?'

'Get rid of that cunt Hunt from your business – from our business.'

'Consider it done,' replied Ruthven, before he hugged his lovely wife for perhaps the last time as a married couple.

Carole King sat opposite Gary in his office reflecting on what he had just told her. Sipping her herbal tea, she finally began to respond.

'So, where are you going to live?'

'I've booked into a hotel in town for the next week; will get a search on after that. Frankly, I am not sure what I am going to do, Carole. I've really fucked things up.'

'You have, Gary, but I believe it's for the best that Vicki knows the truth. After all, if we all knew, it was not fair that Vicki didn't.'

'I know, and in many ways I am really relieved. Carrying that Julia Hillman threat had me scared shitless and it was not a good place to be,' agreed Ruthven quietly.

'So, what are you going to do about Hunt and all that shit?'

'Well, I am going to ask you, Lane and Uli Muller if you will back my decision to remove him from his job *quam primum*,' began Gary, his mind totally firm on that decision.

'Well, you have won that battle before it starts. None of us will disagree.'

'Good. So I think that we should get on with it.' Ruthven pushed back his chair and went to his office door. 'Let me speak with the others and get it done. I can't stand being in the same room as that man anymore.'

Lucas arrived in Gary's office twenty minutes later, and was not sure why Ruthven had asked to see him as they so rarely spoke these days.

'What can I do for you?' he began, a small notebook and pen in his hands.

'Nothing,' replied Gary. 'The purpose of this meeting is simply for me to inform you that you are being relieved of your Chairman duties at RCS with immediate effect.'

'You can't do that, Gary. You need approval from our Board.'

'Oh, I've got that, Lucas. You are sacked, old mate; the decision was agreed this morning.'

'You might want to think about this. There will be consequences for you and your family,' stuttered Hunt, his heart pounding, his position of relative safety being totally dismantled.

'Is that a threat, Lucas?'

'I guess it is,' replied Hunt firmly.

'Fine. Do your worst, mate. However, David Lane and Carole are waiting in meeting room two to take you through your severance details. After that, I don't want to see you in these offices again. It's sad that it has come to this, but in my view you became a different person when you hooked up with that poisonous shit that you're now married to and, in truth, I really fear for you, Lucas.'

'That's all a matter of opinion,' countered Hunt.

'It is, and it no longer matters. The only opinion I am concerned with is mine, and you are gone.' Gary Ruthven stood and walked to open his office door, not even taking the opportunity to shake his former friend's proffered hand.

With Hunt gone, Gary slammed his door shut and returned to his desk, clicked on his Apple and began checking his emails, smiling as he did so

Hearing a car pull up outside her house, Julia Hillman walked purposely to her front door and opened it to be faced by her returning husband.

'Lucas, I thought you were expecting to be in London all day,' she began, surprised to see him there.

'I did, but we need to talk.'

'Why, what's happened?' she replied, leading Lucas into the kitchen.

'I've been fired,' offered Hunt sheepishly, lifting the kettle to check if there was enough water for a pot of tea.

'Fired?' repeated Julia, sure that she had misheard.

'Yep. Fired with immediate effect.'

'Who is behind this? I will have the shit-heads for this!'

'Gary told me, then David and Carole confirmed that it had been a unanimous decision. I will be paid my three months' notice period, but I am gone.'

'I am going to call Ruthven now, tell him he's made the biggest mistake of his fucking life. Who does he think he is dealing with?' Julia stood and crossed the room to pick up her telephone.

'You are wasting your time. It's done, there is no way back.'

'Fuck that, I am going to destroy that shit-head!' Hillman was shouting now, her face red with anger.

'Let's discuss this first, Julia. We have other things to worry about, to organise,' requested Hunt, pouring boiling water into the teapot.

'Like what?'

'Like our finances. I've got three months' salary and nothing else. We need to think about the mortgage, the IVF money.'

'We will sue RCS for unfair dismissal; sue Ruthven for everything we can think of, breach of promise. Shit, I am so angry. What about David Lane? He is your friend, you brought him into the company, what did he say?'

'Tea?' asked Lucas, recognising the need to calm his wife down.

Pencil Kane was on a football pitch for the first time in over six months, but was finding the experience a strange mix of agony and ecstasy. He had been told to take things easy, was only going to get ten minutes of practice game time, but his right foot would not do what his brain was telling it to do; it felt totally alien to him. Having worked solely on his fitness, he was good with the running, was aware of what was going on, but his God-given talent was nowhere to be found.

On the sidelines a camera and sound crew were filming his miraculous return to the field of play, while a number of the club's coaches were keeping a watchful eye on the return of the club's most famous player. Despite the painkillers, Pencil's right foot was still very painful, sending streaks of pain up his calf muscles every time he suddenly changed direction. For Pencil, however, that did not matter. What mattered was that he was back on the pitch, back where he believed he belonged.

The ten minutes over, Pencil jogged back to the locker room; had a quick shower before heading for the physio and an end-of-session massage. The banter amongst the players was in full flow and Kane received his fair share of abuse and piss-taking, but was happy to take it, happy to be back in the thick of things despite the fact that he knew he was still months away from fitness, months away from playing a proper match at Premier League level.

Lying on the bed receiving his massage, he recalled the words of Dr Campbell, the wise words that suggested he treat each day as a step on his journey. Today had been a big step, a major step, and Pencil Kane was on the way back.

Two of Delroy Powell's people were waiting to drive him to Knightsbridge and the Pencil Two store after training, and on the way, Pencil ate a sandwich that his mum had prepared for him that morning. His appetite was back to normal. He was eating like the young sportsman he was and with the stress of the extortion now lifted from his young shoulders, Pencil Kane was happy again.

'Is that Vicki?'
'Yes,' she replied.

'Good. It's Julia Hillman here.'

'Hi Julia, what can I do for you?'

'Well, if you're not sitting down, I suggest that you do so.'

'Really? And why would I need to do that?'

'Well, what I've got to tell you might come as a bit of a shock.'

'Oh, I doubt that, Julia, and before you say any more, I might warn you to be careful what you do say as I am now recording this conversation.'

'That's good, because you can play it back to your shit-head husband.'

'I suggest you get on with it then, Julia. Hold on, before you do, how is your murderer of a father enjoying life in prison?'

'Fuck you. You won't be so smug once you hear what your delightful husband has been getting up to behind your pretty little back.'

'Blimey, you're not going to tell me about the lovely Tandy and her sad abortion are you?'

'You know about that?'

'Of course I know about that. My husband made a mistake, has apologised and we're getting on with our lives, Julia. Suggest you do the same now that your husband has retired and your killer dad is banged up for life.'

'You fucking bitch!'

'Takes one to know one, as my dear old gran used to say. Have a nice life, Julia.'

Vicki cut the connection and sat down, shaking with a mixture of fury and perverse satisfaction. Oddly, she felt the need to call Gary and tell him about the call, but that was no longer the right thing to do. She had to deal with this on her own for now, while she decided what she was going to do with her husband, with her marriage. Meantime, Julia Hillman had been brought down to size and would no doubt be plotting what to do next. *Let her try*, she thought as she picked up her car keys to go to the supermarket and get some dinner for herself and

Molly, who would be home from school soon and no doubt be wondering what time her dad would be coming home from London.

Paul Ruthven sat in stunned silence as his older brother completed the details on his latest life chapter. Having always looked up to Gary and admired him for the way he ran his life, Paul was experiencing an odd mix of concern and downright anger at his brother for his foolishness. But then again, who was he to judge anyone? What right did he have to be angry?

'Okay, so what happens next?' he finally asked, sitting back in his chair and taking a sip of the beer in front of him. Gary had called and asked to see him urgently and they were in a small pub that was located roughly midway between their respective offices in central London.

'Well, I've booked myself into a hotel for the next week, while I look to find something more appropriate, somewhere more appropriate to live.'

'So, Beaconsfield is out of the question?'

'For now, yes.'

'And how is Vicki? Would it be okay for me to call her?'

'Of course you can call her. Christ, you've known her for as long as I have. It would be very odd if you didn't.'

'I'll call her later, but how was she?'

'Difficult to say really; an odd mix of calm, angry and calm again. Says she needs time to think things through, to talk to someone.' Gary gulped his beer deep, enjoying the soothing feeling that it was giving him.

'What about the girls? What are you doing about them?'

'Vicki says she is going to tell them the truth, and will let me know when she has done so,' replied Gary.

'Do you think she will?'

'Not sure. She might, she might not.'

'Oh well, time will tell.'

'So, is this when you tell me what a fucking twat I've been?'

'Is that what you want me to say? Then tell you to say an Our Father and ten Hail Marys?'

Gary smiled at his exceptionally rational brother before answering, 'Probably.'

'Not going to happen. My guess is that you don't need me to say anything, that you will be more than capable of beating yourself up over this.'

'So, no judgement? No telling me off?'

'Nope, but I am worried about you all. What can I do to help?'

'Check Vicki out for me. I've promised not to contact her until she tells me it's okay.'

'And what do you want to happen?'

'That's out of my hands right now. And, just maybe, the separation is the right thing. Maybe our marriage has run its course; after all, if we'd been happy and all that.'

'Do you believe that?'

'Not sure, Paul, I am not sure. Yes, I love Vicki and adore our daughters, but something has not been right, couldn't have been right, or I wouldn't have been out getting another woman pregnant, would I?'

'When you put it like that, but what do you want to happen?'

'I'd like to turn back the clock, but as we all know, that ain't possible. So I guess I just have to wait and see how she wants to take things forward.'

'Well, if there is anything I can do, let me know.'

Gary thanked his brother and stood to leave, tears once again welling in his eyes.

'What a fucking mess. Bet you're glad you didn't get married?'

'Oh well, you never know. Maybe one day.' And with that the

Ruthven brothers parted and headed back to their work, both lost in their individual thoughts.

Just before 9pm that evening, Detective Chief Inspector Colm Elliot, in the company of Detective Sergeant Hannah Bellamy, formally charged the six young men arrested in connection with the attempted extortion from Pencil Kane. The six were then taken to a variety of police prison cells after being informed that they would be appearing before a magistrate in the morning.

Elliot, delighted by how quickly things had progressed following their initial breakthrough, invited Bellamy to join him for a celebratory drink. In their time working together, it was the first time that she had received such an invitation from her boss and was happy to accept.

In their beautiful home in Holland Park, Dan Jenner and Carole King spent much of the evening discussing the situation regarding Gary Ruthven and his marriage as well as the sacking of Lucas Hunt.

'By the time he arrived for the meeting with Lane and me, the wind had been well and truly taken out of his incompetent sails,' smiled Carole, not overtly smugly, but something pretty close to it.

'He's married to a bully, and was probably a bit worried about how to break the news to his bride,' reflected Dan, relieved that RCS was at last taking some action.

'You think?'

'Probably went home to a bruising,' laughed Dan, who had no sympathy for the man.

'She will be as angry as a cut snake; will be plotting revenge on someone, no doubt as we speak.'

'Changing tack, did Gary say how Vicki was?'

'Not really, he's moving into a hotel in town tonight. Letting her have some thinking time I guess.'

'Do you need to give her a call?'

'What do you think?'

'Well, she is a long-time friend. If it were you, would you expect people to call?'

'I guess so. Not sure I would like to find out, Mr Jenner, so please note.'

'My days of indiscriminate shagging are long gone,' replied Dan sheepishly.

'I should hope so. Let me go call her.' Carole stood to leave the room but before she had left Dan added, 'And when you come back, I'll share my thinking, my plans on what I believe we should do with RuthvenCampbellStuart.'

'Will you indeed?' replied his wife. 'That should be good!'

At that precise moment, Gary Ruthven was lying fully clothed on his small hotel room bed feeling sad, lonely and utterly distraught. In his mind he was tallying up all of his recent fuck-ups. One fuck-up after another. What on earth had possessed him to suddenly become so utterly fucking useless?

Washed up arsehole at forty-two, he was telling himself; angry at himself, angry at Lucas Hunt and David Lane, and murderous at the very thought of Julia fucking Hillman.

Yes, he finally concluded, *if I can't put things right, at least I will save the planet from that monstrous bitch!*

Gary Ruthven then spent the next hour planning how he was going to have Julia fucking Hillman killed. Slaughtered, wiped off the face of the planet; crushed to a pulp, destroyed like you would destroy a rabid dog, for that's what the bitch was: a mad, out of control, rabid dog!

Despite the fact that he was sure he would never go

through with this plan, just the very thought of it cheered him, and that, at least for the moment, made him feel a hell of a lot better.

FEBRUARY 2006

CHAPTER 23

SUNDAY
12 FEBRUARY 2006

The Greater City of New York was being deluged with perhaps its worst snow blizzard since records began. In Manhattan, snow depths were already being reported to be in excess of twenty inches in Central Park and the city's main airports were all closed for the first time since the period immediately after the 9/11 attacks on the World Trade Center.

On the television news, it was being reported that the storm system had begun its development on the 11th of February as a relatively minor event, bringing snow along the southern Appalachian range. The area affected was relatively small but its scale had taken many forecasters by surprise. During the height of the storm that morning, thunder and lightning occurred as the snow fell and for Gary Ruthven, the idea of being able to go out in this unique thundersnow was just too tempting to miss.

So, standing in his heavy coat, scarf and ridiculous beanie hat, he felt incredibly lucky to be experiencing nature in the raw. America was a big country and on occasions like this one, the country tended to get big weather.

He had travelled to New York for two reasons on the previous Thursday, and had decided to stay for the weekend. After all, he might as well be alone in this amazing city as alone in his tiny furnished apartment in London. His separation from Vicki and the kids was still being described as temporary but in his mind, the longer it lasted, the less he was able to imagine any outcome other than divorce.

His meeting at The Phi Collections had gone well, and his second at Levi's USA had proved more lucrative than he had hoped for. The second project would provide a much needed top-up to his private account on the Isle of Man.

As Gary absorbed the scene, he was stunned by both how quiet the city had become and how efficiently the place was going about clearing sidewalks and the wide roads. If something like this had ever happened in London, the city would be brought to a standstill for weeks!

Making his way back to his hotel, he reflected on the last few weeks at RCS. With Hunt gone and Lane scheduled to leave at the end of their financial year in March, some form of rational normality was replacing the maelstrom of the crazy growth strategy proposed by Lane and Hunt, and followed sheepishly by himself. Dan Jenner and Carole King were now proposing to purchase a 50% stake in the firm, buying out Hunt and Lane and a further chunk of equity from Gary. No doubt there would be some haggling over the price, but he trusted Dan to do the right thing and quite frankly was too tired to even argue his corner. No, the way he felt now, they could have the entire company for free if they wanted it.

Just then, another sharp lightning bolt lit up the grey skies and was followed by crashing thunder the likes of which Ruthven had never heard before. The snow was falling in flakes the size of Gary's hands and he decided that it was probably prudent to hurry his retreat to the safe haven of his hotel.

Upstairs in their converted cottage in Petersfield, Julia Hillman lay face down on a plump pillow while Lucas took her energetically from behind. Naked, her huge bosom bounced to the pounding she was receiving from Lucas who now seemed to be more relaxed since he was no longer under the previous pressure of getting his wife pregnant. The IVF would take care of that, leaving him to live out his sexual fantasies with Julia, even with the much needed assistance of his little blue tablets.

'Oh fuck, oh fuck, oh fuck,' repeated Julia Hillman, as her arousal began to peak.

'How good is this?' reflected Hunt, to nobody in particular.

'Oh fuck, Lucas. I am going to cum, please cum soon. Oh fuck, cum now!' she demanded.

'Almost ready, honey. Two more minutes,' replied Lucas breathlessly.

'Cum in me now, Lucas. Fill me up now, please.'

'One more minute, honey. I am almost there.'

'Thank fuck for that, cum now.'

And with that Lucas Hunt ejaculated deep into his wife before collapsing in a sweaty heap beside her on the bed.

'Christ, that was good,' smiled Julia Hillman, her mind already turning to the hearing at the High Court in the morning, the hearing that would determine if her father's appeal against his minimum ten-year life sentence would be successful.

Rising slowly from the bed, a towel held between her legs to prevent seepage, she entered their bathroom and began running a bath.

Lucas rose and pulled on his old dressing gown and plodded wearily downstairs to the kitchen to get them both a drink. A nice glass of Merlot was called for and as he searched for a bottle in their recently installed wine cooler, he smiled to himself, a self-satisfied smile of someone who could not quite believe his luck. Yes, Julia was a difficult and challenging woman to live with; yes, she drove him to despair with her rages and tempers and mini-vendettas, but by Christ, she was a great fuck. Not that they got round to it much these days, but when they did, boy it was good.

Climbing the stairs, he re-entered their bedroom to find his wife making the bed and tidying the room. The sex over, it was time to get back to work.

'I've been thinking, Lucas. I think we should sue Gary Ruthven for his failure to provide me with my share certificates. What do you think?'

Lucas handed his wife her wine glass and sat on the edge of the bed.

'With Dan Jenner buying us out, why would we do that, honey?'

'Because we can, and because I really want to fuck that bastard's life up as much as I can,' she replied, taking a sip of the Merlot.

'Yes, but what would we gain? We are going to get our money back.'

'Pleasure, Lucas, that's what I would gain. Pleasure at fucking him over.'

'Tell me one thing, honey?'

'What is that, Lucas?'

'Tell me why you hate him so much. After all, how many times have you met him? Three, four, including the wedding?'

'I don't know, Lucas. I just do and for me right now, that is more than enough.'

Malcolm Hillman lay on his prison bed and reflected on the fact that the outcome of the next day's hearing would make little to no difference to his life. He had been given a minimum life tariff of ten years and even if successful, the best he could hope for was that sentence being reduced to eight years.

That said, his reading and research had given him a new interest in all things to do with criminal law and its associated appeals process. This new knowledge had made him a popular inmate at Belmarsh and many of his fellow prisoners now sought his advice. In turn, this had brought a new charitable perspective to Hillman's life. After decades of chasing the capitalist dream, he now wondered if he could turn the remainder of his life to better causes. A conversation with his difficult but loyal daughter Julia had got him thinking about setting up a charity to help newly released prisoners start their own businesses. After all, what employer in their right mind would want or need to give a job to an ex-con with no track record of sticking to anything other than what they knew, and what most of them knew was crime.

Julia had been quite taken by the idea and had gone away to develop what she referred to as a charity business plan. Malcolm Hillman was in no doubt that she would be poring over the figures so readily available in government reports relating to the incidence of reoffending and the cost to Britain's already hard-pressed taxpayer.

In all probability, he reflected, he would have more than nine years left for the murder of his lovely wife, and short of killing himself (the thought had crossed his mind on numerous occasions), what harm could there be in turning his mind and financial resources to the good purpose of rehabilitating offenders? Offenders who had been far less fortunate than he himself had been. Indeed, some of the stories he had heard from people who had come to him for advice were enough to bring tears to his weary and sad eyes. One young hard man who he now knew as Jynx had grown up in a two-bedroom Glasgow tenement, with five siblings and a father who spent the majority of his time in the city's Barlinnie Prison, and a mother who earned her money through prostitution. A bright boy, Jynx had soon been put to work shoplifting for food for the rest of his family and by the age of twenty had already spent seven years in one institution or another. What chance had he ever had? What hope did young men and women like him have when born into situations of abject helplessness?

With Julia's help, a new project in his life was formulating.

A charity through which bright young men like Jynx would be given funds and mentoring to start their own businesses, learn to fend for themselves, build self-respect and lives away from their criminal upbringing.

And, it would give Julia something to put all her bright and boundless energy into. He would incentivise her by creating a trust through which she could earn her living and keep her and Lucas in the manner to which they aspired. But first, he would have to lay down some ground rules, try and defuse the anger she was carrying against the world. An anger that he had only managed to make considerably worse by the situation he had got himself into.

Pencil Kane was frustrated and just a little angry. In the morning, the Arsenal first team would be boarding the team's luxurious coach and heading north to prepare for their Tuesday evening Premier League match against Liverpool. Pencil would not be travelling with them, would be back at London Colney doing more physio and gym and ball work. He was working harder than he had ever worked, training like his very life depended on it, and yet was making very little real progress, no nearer the first team than he had been a month ago. Indeed, he had only had a total of forty-five minutes on the field with the reserve team in that time and his form remained poor. Adding that to the fact that his right foot was still agonizingly painful without the daily injections meant that his normally high personal spirit was as low as he could remember.

Despite his football woes, Pencil One and the newly opened Pencil Two in Knightsbridge were doing even better than he had hoped for. Revenues were ahead of plan, and the margin they were making was off the scale. Jenner and Ruthven were delighted and proposing that he should step up the speed on new store openings, but Pencil lived in fear of losing control of his baby, of the business getting too big too fast; that he would no longer feel like the project belonged to him.

Checking his phone, he had a text from Vicki Ruthven that contained the trading figures from yesterday, Saturday always being their busiest day of the week. Vicki was putting more hours in than she was paid to do and Pencil put that down to the fact that she was living apart from her husband. Delroy Powell's boys reckoned she was a right MILF, and Pencil had to admit that he had spent more than a few minutes wondering what she would be like in bed; had even had a wank or two thinking about it. But Vicki was Gary's wife and Paul's sister-in-law and Pencil would never allow himself to think that Vicki might be available to him. For shit sake, the woman was older than his mother!

Thinking a little porn might take his mind off his football and his sore foot, Pencil flicked through the Sky adult channels before settling on an old movie he had seen before. Just what Pencil needed: enough nudity and soft porn shagging to help him forget about the coach that would leave for Liverpool without him in the morning.

With her business text gone to Pencil, Vicki suggested that she and Molly get a bath ready and take a DVD, the first series of *Desperate Housewives*, up to her room and watch it together before they crashed out for the night.

Twenty minutes later, snuggled in their dressing gowns and with a large bowl of popcorn and a glass of wine each, they settled on Vicki's bed and switched the TV on in preparation for an episode or two of 'Desperates', as the American series had become known to them.

The news on ITV was reporting the shocking blizzard that had been battering the east coast of the USA in general and New York in particular.

'I hope Dad's going to be okay,' mused Molly, tucking large handfuls of popcorn into her mouth.

'God, I forgot he was staying there for the weekend,' replied Vicki honestly.

'You seem to be finding it easy to forget him all the time now, Mum,' suggested Molly, her eyes firmly on the screen.

'I think that's a little bit unfair. There is not an hour of the day that goes by without me thinking about your father, without me thinking how all of this is going to end up.' Vicki waved her wine glass in a sweeping action as if to take in the room, the house.

'Okay, I'm sorry, but do you think I should call him, see if he is okay?'

'What time is it?' asked Vicki.

'Ten fifteen, what will that be in New York?'

'There's a five-hour time difference, so five fifteen,' replied Vicki.

'In the morning?'

'No, early evening, silly. Go give him a call. I promise not to start the DVD until you get back.'

'Okay,' replied Molly, getting up from the bed to go and call her dad on the landline from the kitchen.

'Just don't be all night. Calls to a mobile will cost a fortune.'

Vicki was annoyed with herself for saying that; the girls adored their father and she never wanted to say or do anything that might compromise the relative peace that had descended on the family since Gary had moved out in January. Waiting for Molly to return, she wondered for the millionth time what was going to happen, whether or not they would ever be a couple, a family again. She had taken legal advice and knew her rights, her entitlements, and knew that Gary would give her anything that she demanded if divorce was how things ended. But Vicki was not totally sure that divorce was what she wanted; she missed Gary a lot but had not yet found it in her heart to forgive him. One person she would never forgive, however, was Julia Hillman. Why that bitch had felt it was her right to become involved in their private life, she would never understand. God how she hated and wished nothing but harm on that fucking woman.

Just then, Molly arrived back in the room to announce that Gary was fine, that the idiot had been out in Central Park to watch the thundersnow firsthand and was claiming that the snow in the park was close to two-feet deep. Vicki smiled at her daughter and wished more than anything that she had been in that deep snow with her husband, and at that moment she knew she would not be asking Gary Ruthven for a divorce any time soon.

CHAPTER 24   MONDAY
13 FEBRUARY 2006

Since the 7/7 bombings in London, Colm Elliot had been carrying a secret fascination with all things related to the idea of suicide killing. To his surprise, he discovered that the concept could be traced back as far as nihilists in Russia in the late 19th Century. The modern version of the concept dated back only thirty years to the Tamil Tigers in Sri Lanka, who were followed by the Palestinian group Hamas. To Elliot, this modern form of terrorism presented a significantly greater threat and challenge than anything he had become used to in his dealings with the Provisional IRA in Northern Ireland and on mainland Britain.

Yes, the Provisionals were capable of significant and often bloody mayhem, but in those days the terrorists planting their explosives in pubs, cars and shopping centres always determined to leave themselves with an escape route. As a result a large number of proposed attacks failed. For the life of him, Elliot could not get his head around the concept of suicide terrorism, and he believed that a greater understanding was needed if the threat was to be marginalised. Were people really prepared to commit such atrocity in the name of martyrdom and religious zeal? Elliot was not convinced that this was the case and intended to pull together a paper that challenged such thinking. Sure, terrorist organisations would want people to believe that was the case. After all, what could be more frightening to ordinary citizens?

Intuitively, Elliot wondered whether or not the fact that many of those who carried out the 7/7 bombings and those who failed during the 21/7 attempt had come from depressed and socially deprived areas of the UK. What if terrorist organisations simply targeted people who were suicidal in the first place? In many ways, this mirrored what the IRA did when recruiting young people who were often family members or relatives of people who had themselves been victims of terrorism.

Elliot knew that his theory would need proper research if he was to present something substantial to his bosses in the Met or the latest version of his old haunt the Anti-Terrorist Squad. So, as he closed his computer at 5.30am and headed for his bathroom for a shave and a shower, he did so with a new spring in his step.

As he readied himself for his day, he began to formulate a plan for pulling together a small research team. He would draft Bellamy in and get a couple of the Met's new graduate entrants assigned to his project and charge them with looking into the backgrounds and mental stability of those who had recently been guilty of suicide killings. His thoughts turned to the 9/11 attacks in the USA. There was bound to be significant material available on that group and other such acts in Palestine, Pakistan and Afghanistan. For the first time in a long while, Elliot felt inspired by his work and that made him feel a lot better than he had for a year or so.

Malcolm Hillman had been up very early that day as well, but was certainly not feeling inspired as he was driven in the back of a very uncomfortable G4S prison van to London for the hearing on his appeal against his minimum ten-year life sentence.

'What a fucking waste of time,' he murmured to himself, as

the van approached a gated side entrance to the Royal Courts of Justice in central London, where his hearing was scheduled to be presided over by the Lord Chief Justice and two other high court judges.

Once again, Malcolm Hillman was representing himself with the assistance of his daughter Julia, who was there to meet her father when he was shown into a small consulting room at the side of the court his case was to be heard in.

'It's really nice to see you away from that dreadful Belmarsh,' began Julia, giving her father a big hug.

'Feel like I am on a day trip. My bed will still be warm when I get back.'

'I know, but if we can get any reduction, it will all be worth it.'

'I suppose so,' replied Malcolm with little enthusiasm.

'Right, are you properly prepared for this?'

'As prepared as I'll ever be.'

They were eventually asked to take their place in court just after 11am, and the entire hearing lasted no more than twenty-five minutes, after which the father and daughter were returned to a small waiting room whilst the three senior judges considered their decision.

'Months of preparation for less than half an hour in court. What a travesty,' moaned Julia as she and her father sat waiting to be called back to court.

'We will see shortly,' sighed Hillman, who in all honesty just wanted to be back in Belmarsh getting his time served.

'I've been doing some work on your charity idea, and should have a draft proposal for you by the end of next week.' Julia changed the subject; she didn't like to see her father when he was displaying pessimism.

'Sounds good, Julia, just don't go getting all grand and ambitious. We should start the thing quietly and in a low key way, prove the idea works first.'

'I get that, but if we're going to do something, we should do it properly,' replied Julia, who had plans to launch the thing in a grand manner, attract as much publicity as possible. She was thinking big.

'Well, if you want my financial backing, Julia, you need to listen to my needs too.'

'Of course, Father. Let me get my proposal finished and we can discuss things in more detail then.'

Just then, a court usher advised them that they were required back in court. The appeal judges were ready to return with their decision.

The 9.35am train from London King's Cross had been due to arrive in Leeds twenty minutes ago, but was still at a standstill just south of the city. The train manager was doing his best to keep customers informed of the reason for the hold-up, but Lucy Campbell was not paying a lot of attention to his announcements, happy that the train would start moving when the problem, whatever it was, was resolved.

Other passengers in the fairly quiet First Class carriage also seemed happy to get on with their laptop work or their reading or their never-ending mobile phone calls, as Lucy reread an interesting article about the long-term damage of fad dieting in the Times2 section of her newspaper.

She was on her way to Harrogate to visit her parents and her sisters and their families. It had been three months since she had been home, and she loved going back to her pretty Yorkshire town. Outside, in the fields south of Leeds, she could see the remnants of recent snowfall and wondered at the vast openness of the land, with fields of farmland stretching away as far as her eyes could see. From Leeds, she would need to catch the slow-moving train north to Harrogate, a journey that she always enjoyed as the beauty increased as she headed north through the Dales.

At last the train shuddered forward and began picking up

speed as it headed towards Leeds, and as Lucy began packing her things into her jumbo handbag, she was conscious of a nervous tingle in her belly. She was going home to inform her family that she and her former football star boyfriend were to be married. The discussion with Paul had not taken her by surprise when she considered how they seemed to feel about one another, but had surprised her in that she didn't think that Paul Ruthven was the marrying type. The conversation had covered a number of topics, from money – she was shocked by how wealthy Paul actually was – to children, with neither of them sure if they wanted to become parents. They had left that question unanswered, happy to wait and see how things turned out, let the decision be made if and when the right time came. Paul was also a little sensitive regarding an announcement, conscious of the fact that Gary and Vicki had recently separated and were seemingly no closer to a reconciliation than when the whole Tandy matter had come to light.

Changing platforms in the cold and breezy Leeds station, Lucy found herself a seat on the local Metro train for Harrogate. A journey she was well familiar with from her youth, she knew the stations of Burley Park, Headingly, Horsforth, Weeton, Pannal and Hornbeam Park off by heart, excited to get to Harrogate and see her mum and dad.

The late winter sun was low in the sky, and up here the snow was in greater evidence, lying in the fields and on the rolling hillside and looking as pretty as any countryside picture could be. As the female conductor checked tickets after every stop, Lucy smiled to herself, wondering if the happiness she felt could possibly last. At Harrogate, she left the train to its meandering journey east through Knaresborough and places like Poppleton and onto York, and was greeted by the smiling face of her mother, who told her she looked tired and fussed as they headed out of the station and into her immaculately clean old Volvo.

In New York, Gary Ruthven was up early and working at his laptop in his hotel room, not yet clear when he would be able to get on a flight back to London. With so many flights cancelled because of the blizzard, British Airways were being appropriately careful about making any promises that they might not be able to deliver. What Gary did know was that as a Gold Card holder on the BA Executive Club, he would be given a high priority seat.

Ruthven was calm; he could deal with his emails and make calls from here as well as he could from anywhere, and the view from his bedroom window was breathtaking, as way below him New York gradually began to get back to some form of normality. The other thing he was grateful for was the chance to do some serious thinking about his life and the current predicaments that he had found himself in.

With Hunt gone and the Lane matter all but resolved, he knew RCS was going to be fine although he did long for an extended break from the place, to recharge his depleted batteries and get his mojo back. The situation with Vicki was another matter altogether. Yes, he missed his wife, his girls, and his lovely home, but was beginning to enjoy living alone and the freedom that afforded.

That said, there were serious financial issues still to address despite the fact that his sale to Dan and Carole could well solve his problems, especially if he sold their Spanish home as well. If he escaped with so little damage he vowed to himself that he would ensure that a proper financial structure would be applied and adhered to in the future. He never wanted to expose his family again, and with his intuitive belief that the global economy was in an unhealthy state, he wanted to be immune from anything that might happen on that front.

Just then a text arrived on his phone from Vicki, suggesting that she would like to get together for dinner and a chat later in the week. There was nothing particularly surprising in that, they had met on a few occasions recently, but what was surprising was that she had ended her message with two kiss symbols.

'What the fuck is that all about?' he asked out loud as he headed for the bathroom and to get ready to go in search of a much-needed hearty New York breakfast.

'Well, at least it didn't get any worse,' offered Lucas Hunt to his wife Julia as they sat in a Starbucks not far from the Royal Courts of Justice.

'Lucas, if you can't say anything useful about this, please keep your shit-head mouth shut!' demanded Julia Hillman, who could be best described as being incandescent with rage at the Appeal Court's decision to reject Malcolm Hillman's appeal against his minimum ten-year life sentence.

'I know you are upset, honey, but Malcolm is no worse off than he was before the hearing,' persisted Lucas bravely.

'As I said, shut the fuck up, Lucas.' Julia Hillman was using her phone to text her sister and her mother with the outcome of the hearing.

'If you're not careful you'll be travelling home alone, Julia. Don't talk to me like that.'

'I am sorry, Lucas. I am just so bloody angry.'

'I understand, but nevertheless, please watch your tone.'

Her text messages complete, she turned her attention back to her husband, who had gone red in the face as a result of their angry exchange.

'Now, do you have Gary Ruthven's home address in Beaconsfield?'

'I have it in my desk diary at home. Why?'

'Well, I've been looking at the County Court website and I will need his address to have my claim against him served there,' she explained.

'Can we talk about this, Julia?'

'Nothing to talk about. I paid him fifty grand for shares and he has not issued them to me. So, having not had the benefit of the shares I intend to sue him for £100,000 damages.'

'Yes, but we've had an opening offer for all our shares from Dan Jenner and Carole King and that offer includes the shares you are referring to. Surely that is enough?' proposed Hunt, who was now terrified at the thought of getting stuck in the middle of a legal dispute that he knew his wife had no hope of winning.

'Why are you protecting that shit-head, Lucas? After all, the bastard fired you just over a month ago. Surely revenge would be sweet?'

'Oh sure, revenge would be sweet, Julia, but we are talking about money here and if we get our cash back from Jenner and King, we have done okay. Or am I missing something?'

'You're missing a big something, Lucas,' smiled Julia Hillman.

'And what is that, Julia?'

'That it's not about the money, you dopey fuck; it's about giving that shit-head who got his tart pregnant and who fired my husband a fucking hard time!'

'Julia, do we need this in our lives? Your IVF starts next week, we're in negotiations with Dan and Carole. Do we really need to start another fight with Gary Ruthven?'

'Unless there is something you're not telling me, Lucas, my answer to your question is a resounding yes. Now, let's get out of this quasi-American shit-hole and get things moving,' she stated as she pushed her chair back and reached for her coat.

'Okay, Julia, but we need to discuss this properly.'

Hannah Bellamy was not too sure if she should interrupt her boss with the news, but decided to do so anyway. And besides, she also had a couple of suggestions to make about the terrorist research project that Elliot had briefed her on earlier in the day.

Knocking on his office door, she opened it by no more than a foot and spoke quietly.

'Boss, could I have five minutes on a couple of things?'

'You can. I am almost done here today anyway, come in,' invited Elliot.

'Thanks. I promise I'll be gone in five, max.'

'No worries, grab yourself a chair.' Bellamy pulled a chair in front of his desk and sat down.

'So, what can I do you for?' It was a phrase Elliot used that Hannah didn't understand.

'Well, the good news is that our old mate Malcolm Hillman had his appeal against his sentence rejected in the Royal Courts of Justice this morning.'

'Very good. So ten years it is then,' reflected Elliot, who stared momentarily out of his office window, wondering what he would be doing in 2015 when Hillman was eventually released. That is, of course, if Hillman survived that long, reached his mid-seventies.

'So, what else brings you here?' He suddenly turned his attention back to his sergeant.

'Well, I've been thinking about your new suicide terrorist research project,' she began.

'Glad to hear it, Sergeant Bellamy. And?'

'Well, I know a couple of young Asian officers who are stationed up north; one in Bradford and one in Leicester.'

'Leicester is not up north, Bellamy, Leicester is in the midlands. You of all people should know that.' The news of Hillman's rejected appeal, coupled with his new project, had really improved Elliot's mood.

'I've been south of Watford too long. I am beginning to go native,' replied Bellamy.

'Anyway, you were saying before I so rudely interrupted?'

'Well, what I was going to suggest is that we invite them to join our little part-time team. All strictly confidential, of course. What do you think?'

'Sounds like a good idea, why don't you sound them out? See what sort of response you get and if I need to talk to their seniors, let me know.'

'Okay, will do,' replied Bellamy as she stood to leave.

'Thanks, Hannah. It's been a good day today. Get home and enjoy the rest of it.'

'I will. You should do the same, boss.'

The Old Swan had stood in the centre of Harrogate for 200 years and yet it was perhaps most famous for being the tranquil setting chosen by the renowned crime writer Agatha Christie when she famously disappeared for eleven days after discovering her husband's infidelity in 1926. A nationwide search and much speculation had followed her disappearance before she had reappeared in Harrogate having taken in the town's recuperative spas and bathing houses.

It was to the Wedgewood Restaurant in the Old Swan with its amazing glass ceiling and Victorian surroundings that Lucy Campbell invited her parents for dinner later that evening to break the news of her impending engagement to Paul Ruthven. As they settled at their table, her dad, who was now fifty-eight and semi-retired, did what he had always done and fussed over his wife of thirty-four years.

'Well, I must say, Lucy, you are looking really well. That London pollution must suit you,' he began as he settled in his chair and pulled a napkin onto his lap, ready for his dinner.

'That's odd, Mum said I was looking tired,' replied Lucy, who loved her parents dearly, but preferred her time with them to be in small doses. They had never quite got to the place of appreciating that she was a grown-up thirty-plus-year-old woman.

'Oh, you know what your mum's like, Lucy, speaks before she thinks; always has and no doubt always will,' replied Jim

Campbell, a Scot who had come south to Yorkshire back in the days when that was considered a major move.

'I am here you know,' interjected Liz Campbell as she accepted the menu from a waiter and passed the wine list to her husband.

They fussed for another five or so minutes, until their food was ordered and their wine chosen and Lucy felt that now was as good a time as any to inform them of her good news.

'So,' she began, suddenly hesitant. 'I've got a little bit of news to share with you both.'

'Good news, I hope,' replied Jim Campbell.

'That depends,' smiled Lucy, knowing that she was teasing.

'Come on, hurry up,' pleaded her mother.

'Okay. Paul and I have decided that we are going to get married.'

'Lucy, that is wonderful,' began her mum, who went to her daughter, and they both stood to embrace.

'Congratulations, but shouldn't he be here with you, to ask for your hand?' smiled her dad as he joined their group hug.

'If it was still 1926, Dad. These days I decide if he can have my hand.'

'I know, I am just pulling your leg, but when do we get the pleasure?'

'Of meeting Paul?'

'Yes, we'd love to meet the man you are going to spend the rest of your life with.'

'Steady on, I am not committing to that,' Lucy continued to tease.

'You know what your dad means, Lucy.'

'Of course I do, and he is driving up tomorrow evening to meet you. Then we'll head up to Scotland to meet his parents,' clarified Lucy finally.

CHAPTER 25

**TUESDAY
14 FEBRUARY 2006**

A weary Gary Ruthven arrived back in his small temporary apartment in London just after nine that morning. Flights from New York had eventually been returned to some degree of normality just after lunchtime and he had managed to get himself listed on the first British Airways flight to Heathrow.

After a quick shave and a shower, he dressed, checked his voicemail and emails, before heading for the RCS offices in a taxi. He was scheduled to meet the new brand president of Levi's Europe in the early afternoon at BBH's trendy offices behind Regent Street and wanted to be as well prepared for that as possible.

Carole King was first to see him after his arrival and she had prepared a really impressive update on the vintage Levi's launch they had been working on and Gary felt that their work would go a long way to keeping his relationship with BBH, who were Levi's main agency, in a good and healthy state. He was also aware that they had been a bit pissed that Carole had turned down their job offer, so she would not be joining him at the meeting.

Gary then met with Rosie Calder, who wanted to go through their latest figures for the year, and from the expression on her face as she entered his office, he was not expecting to be thrilled by what she had to offer him.

'How was New York?' she asked, pulling a chair for herself at the round meeting table in her boss's office.

'A winter wonderland,' replied Ruthven. 'Quite the most amazing snowstorm I have ever experienced.'

'It looked amazing on the television; they were saying that Central Park had two feet of snow.' Rosie's husband Stuart was a logistics guy at British Airways.

'It was indeed. I took myself into the park on Sunday; there was actual thundersnow. Amazing to stand in it really.'

'I am surprised that you made it back today. BA work their magic?'

'Yep, they were great. They might not be as sexy as Virgin Atlantic, but they always seem to deliver to a high standard; are always reliable.'

'Glad to hear it,' replied Calder, keen to get on with her update.

'Okay, Rosie. What have you got for me?' Gary sensed her need; she was not a small talk person.

Rosie Calder then distributed a short four-page financial update and waited as Ruthven gave it his usual quick perusal.

'How is February looking thus far?' he asked eventually. The firm was well behind on its annual revenue plan and despite the fact that costs were well under budget too, it was obviously not going to be a great year. With two months to go, he was hoping for some miracle from early February.

'Slightly ahead of plan, but Germany is still the laggard.'

'Well, that's something. How confident are you with your year-end forecast?'

'I think I would put it at 95%,' she offered.

'So, we will miss plan by 15-17%?'

'That sort of number, but cost reduction is kicking in; that will help with final profit numbers.'

'And cash?'

'All on plan. Better than plan, actually. David Lane has finally added some value on that front.'

'Better late than never I suppose.'

'Any update on the Jenner purchase?'

'No, I am due to meet Dan and Carole for dinner tonight to discuss and agree their final offer. These figures should help a bit, if not a lot.'

'That's good, and how are you feeling about the situation?'

'Okay. No, better than that, I feel really positive about it. The big issue for me will be about who gets appointed as Chief Executive. Dan has got a few people in mind, so we'll see.'

'Glad to hear it. Are we done?' Calder was already pushing her chair back, ready to make her exit.

'Yes, but before you go, what about Germany?'

'You know where I've always stood on that. I think you should close it down, pay the overdraft off and put it behind you.'

'What's the current number?'

'Not too bad. Sixty thousand euros, give or take.'

'And the office lease?'

'There is a break-clause in June, penalties attached, but all in all a hundred thousand would cover the closure.'

'Mmm, I'll discuss that with Dan and Carole tonight. Thanks, Rosie.'

With Calder gone, Gary realised that he was feeling a lot better about his business. Maybe, just maybe, they had started to turn a corner. Just then, he received a text from his wife who was saying that she would like to have dinner with him soon.

Pencil Kane was not too sure where the saying had originally come from, but as he dressed after training in London Colney, he believed that he was having a 'road to Damascus' moment.

That was not to say that the very sharp Pencil Kane was happy with this moment, it just felt momentous and in the same breath devastating. His insight was that his talent had gone; his unique Pencil Kane soccer ability had been blown from his body that fateful July day in London.

Feeling the blood drain from his face, he needed to get out of the training ground, get home and consider this possibility; privately reflect on what the fuck he was going to do if he was right. Paul Ruthven would help, would be honest with Pencil, would not give him any fucking bullshit.

Flicking open his new Nokia, he found and pressed his agent's number as he headed for the exit and his driver, who was scheduled to take him to a possible site for Pencil Four in Fulham. Unusually, Ruthven's phone went straight to voicemail, which took Pencil by surprise and caused him to cut the connection as he hadn't prepared a message in his head. Thinking as he walked, he then called the estate agent who was due to meet him in Fulham and cancelled, explaining that something had come up and that Pencil would need to reschedule for later in the week. He then dialled Ruthven's number again and was surprised when Paul answered this time.

'Hey, Paul Ruthven. How are you this fine day?' he began, a whole lot more bouncy than he felt.

'I am okay, Pencil. I am on my way to Harrogate to pick up Dr Campbell and drive up to Scotland to see my parents,' came Ruthven's unhelpful reply.

'Why you drivin', man? Haven't you heard of planes and trains?'

'I was just wondering about that very point when you called. What can I do for you?'

'Pencil was hoping to have a chat with you later, face-to-face like.'

'I'm sorry, Pencil. Can it wait until Friday?'

'Pencil can survive until then,' offered Kane, somewhat subdued.

'You don't sound so sure. Do you want me to pull over and we can have a chat now?'

'Nah, Pencil is fine. Let's meet on Friday after training.'

'If you're sure. Think the Gunners will beat my old team tonight?'

'Pencil hopes so, but is not too sure; it should be a close match.'

'No chance, the Reds will coast it. Two-nil is my prediction.'

'Nobody beats the Arsenal two-nil. What's your bet?'

'You know me, Pencil, I don't gamble. Only on dead certs.' Ruthven felt Pencil was sounding better.

'What about the Pencil stores then?'

'As I said, Pencil, only on dead certs.'

They arranged to meet at Paul's office at 2pm on Friday and Pencil changed his mind, deciding to go and see the site in Fulham after all. The estate agent would think him a twat, but that was his problem, not Pencil Kane's.

Delroy Powell was quite pleased with himself; he was now making four times more money from looking after Pencil Kane and two other recently acquired clients than he was from playing football. Sure, there was always the ever dwindling chance that he would get snapped up by a Premier League or Championship club where the football money would be much better, but this driving and bodyguarding lark was proving to be pretty easy money.

What he now needed to do was branch out, get more clients; get a few more big guys on his team, smarten them up and become the elite in this service provision. Selecting more recruits was going to need care and attention. He needed people who were polite and respectful and not too handy with their fists or boots or knives or guns even. No, what he needed was the right type; the tall, silent, respectful type who could be well trained and who could be trusted not to try and stitch him up. The DP Crew, that's what he would call his new venture, and they would be the best and most respected in the business. The other thing that the DP Crew would do was protect all the Pencil stores, make sure that none of those extortion fuckers ever reappeared and threatened his great bud, Pencil Kane. He jotted a note to himself to talk to the man about it, to get Kane on board.

The County Court in Slough had been fairly easy to find, and as she parked outside the small-looking building, Julia Hillman rummaged in her purse for change for the parking meter. Inside the seedy entrance, a quietly spoken black man asked her to empty her small handbag and remove her heavy coat before she could pass through the security screen.

At that time of day, the public counter was deserted and she had to ring a bell before someone came to attend to her.

'Hi, how can I help?' asked the friendly, fresh-faced, young Asian assistant.

'I am here to lodge a claim. I've brought three copies as your website requests.' Julia handed over the neatly typed and well prepared, even if she said so herself, claim for £100,000 in damages against one Gary Ruthven.

The assistant took the document and gave it a cursory perusal before telling Hillman that she would go and get a court clerk to scrutinize her claim, leaving Julia to stand and scan the ugly surroundings that was the public area of the County Court.

Ten minutes later the assistant returned to confirm that her claim could be lodged and asked her for the relatively modest court fee.

'You do understand that I am not trained to give you procedural advice?' continued the assistant as she prepared a handwritten receipt for the fee.

'Of course, but what happens next?'

'Well, your claim will be sent by first-class post to the person named and he will have twenty-eight days from the date of the claim to respond to the court. There are a number of options open at that stage and what happens after that will be dependent on that response. Do you have a solicitor?'

'No, I don't need one of those useless shit-heads. I'll be representing myself when this case reaches hearing stage.'

'Okay, that's your decision, but we are a fairly long way from the hearing stage.'

'We are indeed. When will the claim be sent to the defendant?' Julia Hillman was impatient to be away from this place and this low-level civil servant.

'Most likely, it will be posted tomorrow, possibly Thursday,' replied the assistant, who was well used to dealing with abusive people at her desk.

'Can you ensure that it goes out tomorrow?'

'Not my decision, but it will be no later than Thursday.'

'Fine, but it better not be Friday or you'll be hearing from me,' stated Julia Hillman.

'Can I help with anything else?' responded the assistant, keen to be rid of this terrible woman.

'Not for the moment,' replied Hillman, who had already turned away and was headed for the exit.

Sitting for a moment in her aging BMW, Julia Hillman smiled a nasty, self-satisfied smile. *That will teach that Ruthven bastard to fire my husband.* Starting the car, she headed back through Slough for the M4, the M25, and the tedious drive home to Hampshire.

They had agreed to meet on the steps in front of St Marylebone Parish Church at 5pm and as Gary waited on his estranged wife's arrival, he had the feeling that the place had been chosen as a symbol of peace. Not because of the holy place that the site was, but due to the fact that the small park in front of the church faced the Conran Shop on Marylebone High Street, and that particular store was their favourite furniture shop that had expensively fitted out their Beaconsfield home.

In direct contrast to NYC and its blizzard, London that early evening was experiencing the first and much wanted signs of an extremely welcome spring and Gary was regretting wearing the light Barbour jacket that Vicki had bought for him a couple of Christmases past. He saw her before she saw him and admired her good looks, figure and great dress sense as she entered the park and walked towards him. His meeting with Levi's at BBH had gone well, and he was due for dinner with Dan and Carole at eight, so he hoped what Vicki needed from him was in fact urgent. They kissed cheeks like two old friends and agreed to walk along Marylebone High Street to a coffee shop they had often frequented during their furniture expeditions to Conran. There, they found a corner table and ordered two pots of mint tea, removed their coats and jackets and settled down for their chat.

'So, what's so urgent, Mrs Ruthven?' enquired Gary, getting to the point.

'No small talk? No how are you?'

'We can get to that in a minute. You've just got me anxious,' he offered.

'Okay, your daughter wants to quit university, wants to pack it in straight away,' explained Vicki, heeding her husband's request.

'What's brought all this on? She's not said anything to me.'

'That would've been a bit of a challenge given your recent missing persons act,' replied Vicki, a bit too aggressively for Gary's liking.

'Of course, it's all going to be my fault; most things are these days.'

'Mmm, well you are the doting father who went off and got

his bit on the side up the duff before paying to have the thing knifed,' shot Vicki, obviously on edge over this latest storm to batter her family shore.

'Okay, but all that's going to help this situation in what way?' Ruthven was breathing softly as he tried to tell himself to act 'adult' and not let Vicki's reaction draw the worst from him.

'Sorry, I just can't believe that this shit keeps happening to me. Why can't things just be back to where they were before?'

'I get that, but let's focus on Emma for now. When did you last talk with her?'

'A couple of hours ago. There is no reasoning with her; she says that her mind is made up; she hates the fucking programme, she hates fucking Leeds and she hates her fucking life,' replied Vicki, indicating with her fingers that she was quoting their daughter verbatim.

'Right, so something has happened and we need to get sat down with her, get to the bottom of this,' offered Gary calmly.

'And how and when do you suppose we do that, Dr Phil?'

'Who the fuck is Dr Phil?'

'Some twat problem-solver on American TV. Surely you've heard of Dr Phil?'

'Nope, but back to your question.'

'What question was that?' Vicki was laughing and crying at the same time.

'How and when we get together with Emma,' reminded Gary.

'Oh yes, that question.' Vicki poured them both some mint tea before opening the teapot to examine the contents.

'Tomorrow is Wednesday, so let's get her home on Friday and we can get this on the table, put the little brat right.'

'If that's the plan, whose home are you intending to use for this little gathering?'

'Now you're being a twat. Do you want me to call her, tell her to get her ass home on Friday afternoon?'

'Good luck with that. Her mobile seems permanently on voicemail these days.'

'Ah well, I'll try. Now, Vicki, how are you doing?' Ruthven smiled at his wife and they both laughed together, which was something at least.

'We've had an email from Carole King,' opened Lucas Hunt as he entered their remodelled kitchen holding a printout of the share purchase offer.

'What about?' asked Julia Hillman, as she placed a tray containing their dinner into the preheated oven.

'Making their final offer on our RCS shares,' replied Hunt, annoyed by his wife's stupid little games. Why else would they be receiving an email from Carole?

'And?' she asked, still distracted by her food preparation.

'They've offered the original purchase price plus five percent.'

'Fuck that. Original plus fifty percent and they've got a deal. Five percent my ass.'

'Come on, Julia. You know that ain't going to happen. I think getting our original investment back is a small miracle as it is; now is not the time to screw around.'

'You're too soft, Lucas. Tell the shit-head bimbo to go fuck herself. It's fifty percent or it's no sale.' Julia Hillman was now standing in front of her husband, hands on hips, giving her final say on the matter.

'I will not do that, Julia, and whose decision is this anyway?'

'It's our decision, Lucas, so off you go and send that reply.'

'As I said, I will not do that. I believe the offer to be a fair one and I am minded to accept; get the entire RCS shit over and done with.'

'Oh, really? And what will Father say when I tell him he only got a five percent return on the money he loaned to us to make the investment in the first place?'

'Well, half the money was mine, and I am going to accept the offer.' And with that Lucas turned to leave the kitchen, to go to their small office and type his reply to Carole.

'No, Lucas, you'll not do that until I've discussed the matter with Father.'

'It's not his decision, Julia, it's mine and my mind is made up.'

'Fuck that! Over my dead body,' screamed Julia Hillman, rushing across the kitchen to block her husband's exit.

'Jesus, Julia. What's got into you?' asked Lucas calmly.

'Gary fucking Ruthven, that's what. He is not getting away with this without a proper fight. He is going to pay one way or another for the shit he has brought on us.'

'Now you are just being silly,' laughed Hunt.

'Fucking silly am I? Fucking silly? That's it, Lucas. You will not reply to that email until I've spoken to my father later in the week, end of!'

'I'll tell you what I'll do, I will sleep on it and we can discuss it in the morning. In the meantime, get out of my way before I do something that I know I'll regret.' They stood face-to-face for a good few seconds before Julia Hillman stepped aside and let her husband, her very angry husband, leave the kitchen.

Pencil Kane was feeling cool, cooler than he had been in a long time. The site for Pencil Four was perfect and when the designers got to work on it, he was excited by how the place was going to look. Pencil was also cool now that he had worked out that his football career was over. His stellar career as one of the great English Premier League players was going to be over before it had really got started, blown apart by those four bastards who had done for him and so many others last July. Now Pencil had to make sure that he got the most out of this, that he planned with Paul Ruthven the perfect way to announce Pencil's retirement from the game at the heartbreakingly young age of eighteen.

The next television show was a few weeks away, and with official viewing figures showing some signs of dropping off, Pencil was going to do what was needed to grab the nation's attention again, to get the good people of Blighty right back on Pencil's side. It was going to be spectacular. Pencil was not sure what was going to be spectacular, he just knew that it would be.

His apartment buzzer sounded. Pencil was expecting Delroy Powell, who had stuff he wanted to explore with him. It would no doubt be another of Delroy's ideas for his business; hoping to get the famous Pencil Kane on board, hoping to build his own success, his own career in parallel to Pencil's. *What the shit*, thought Pencil as he pushed the button to let his old schoolmate into his building. *Success breeds success and if Pencil can help Delroy, then that's just what needs to happen.* Not that Pencil would ever be putting any of his hard-earned wonga into any of Delroy's schemes. No, Pencil was too sharp to invest in anything that was not true blue chip.

Checking her image in the full-length mirror, Carole King thought she looked just right if a little anxious about the meeting that she and Dan were about to have with Gary Ruthven in their beautiful Holland Park home. They were going to propose that they buy a 51% stake in RuthvenCampbellStuart, which involved buying Lane and Hunt out, plus 19% of the stake owned by Gary. It was then their intention to appoint an old colleague of Dan's as Chief Executive and begin the process of maximizing the long-term potential of the agency.

For Carole this was a massive step. She had always wanted to keep her career separate from her marriage, had always imagined keeping Gary and Dan and her complicated relationship with both men apart. But Dan had been persuasive, getting her to believe that this was the ideal solution to the mess that Ruthven had created at RCS when he had introduced Lucas Hunt and then David Lane into the business.

Dan had arranged for a local catering firm to prepare a simple dinner for the evening and he was finalising the setup in the large open-plan kitchen when Carole entered, needing a glass of something to settle her nerves.

'How are you now?' asked Dan, kissing his wife's cheek and offering her a glass of champagne.

'I am a little better. It's the first time that I've bought controlling interest in a company. Old hat to you, new to me.'

'Not that old hat to me, actually. I am more used to setting up and selling than buying. You look lovely by the way.'

'Thank you. You look quite tasty yourself.' She smiled at Dan and sipped at her drink and just then their doorbell sounded. Gary liked to be punctual.

They had decided that it would be best to get the business concluded and then have dinner, celebrate their new partnership over food, so Dan led them into a large sitting room at the front of the house, got them comfortable with a drink and got straight down to business. The deal was simple. Gary's shares were going to be valued at £380,000 and since he had held the shares for a long time, his Captal Gains Tax liability would be modest, leaving him with well over 350k net. Dan and Carole would pay another £500k to Lane and Hunt, and both deals would give the couple a controlling 51% stake in RCS. In addition, it was agreed that working capital of a million would be put into the business by way of a long-term loan from the Jenners, thus enabling repayment of the German overdraft and the director's loans that Gary had given the company up to the end of 2005. For Ruthven, the £520k net he would get from the deal would fix his own financials in a way that they had needed for a number of years, so he was more than happy to sign the paperwork, get the deal done.

'Great,' said Carole. 'Now the only fly in the ointment is Lucas Hunt and his delightful wife. They've yet to accept our offer; Lucas has just emailed me to say that he'll get back to me in the next couple of days.'

'Well, let's see what they say. Their decision will not affect what we plan to do, although their twelve and a half percent needs to get settled at some point.'

Gary considered what Dan had just said and hoped that that matter would be simpler than he feared it might be.

They then topped up their champagne glasses, did a toast to partnership success and went through to dinner, with a jet-lagged Gary Ruthven feeling that a major load had just been lifted from his shoulders.

CHAPTER 26

WEDNESDAY
15 FEBRUARY 2006

From experience, Vicki Ruthven knew that it was not a good thing to get close to men at work. Gentle flirting was probably natural but all it took was for the signals to get picked up wrongly and on a boozy work night out, mistakes could be made. On the few occasions that it had happened to her, she had been able to extricate herself from an unwanted grope or an attempted snog in the back of a taxi on the way home.

With her and Pencil, things were a bit different. After all, he was only a boy and if it hadn't been for her very erotic dream about them fucking on the mirrored tables in Pencil One, she would probably have no fears that they could get themselves compromised. That said, she did consider him to be extremely attractive and knew that if he did make a move on her, then she was very likely to succumb to his advances; see if the reality was half as good as her wet dream fantasy. The nature of their work meant that they were often alone together and that evening she was due to meet him at his apartment for the first time to go over the merchandising detail for the summer season at the Pencil stores. Naturally, her thoughts went to Gary and their current mess and in a strange way she believed that an illicit shag with someone else would bring an equilibrium back to their relationship; balance the books that he had so recklessly disturbed with his affair with the beautiful Tandy.

So, with Molly off to school, she prepared for her day, ensuring she was smooth where she needed to be, before choosing a sexy Karen Millen navy dress to put on top of her expensive underwear and carefully chosen stockings. Yes, if Pencil Kane felt the need to take her clothes off after their meeting in his home, then the young man would not be disappointed, would have the MILF story of all MILF stories to tell his mates if that was the kind of thing that Pencil did.

On the train into London, she felt a nice mixture of being beautiful and sexually excited and had to remind herself that it would have to be Pencil who made the first move – it was up to him whether they became lovers or not. Reflecting on that, she considered what she might do if nothing happened that evening. It was not something she was too keen to consider; the gap between fucking Pencil or getting home to her Ann Summers toys was too great to contemplate.

Since he had lived in central London, he had not really seen the point of owning a car. When he needed one, as a member of a prestige owners club, he was able to hire the vehicle of his choice by the day. For his trip to Harrogate and then to Scotland, Paul Ruthven had taken an Aston Martin 4.3 litre titanium silver Vantage and was more than enjoying the drive with Lucy by his side as they headed for the east coast of Scotland town of Dirleton, and their meeting with his mum and dad.

He had really liked Lucy's parents and had enjoyed meeting her lovely sisters, Lesley and Lyndsay, although he felt that he was getting the pick of the Campbell crop when he married his delicious fiancée later in the year.

'I think that they all really liked you,' said Lucy for the

umpteenth time as he guided the car onto the A1 motorway and pressed the accelerator, forcing the vehicle up to a respectable 80mph in no time at all.

'Do you think?'

'I do, especially Lyndsay, who I think would like to have you for herself.' She smiled at Paul and secretly wished he would slow down a little.

'What makes you say that?'

'Just sisterly instinct, you know how it is.'

'Not really, but I would be open to a threesome, if you thought it might help.'

'You're incorrigible, you do know that?' Lucy leaned over and slapped Paul's thigh just above his knee.

'Not sure that I know what that means,' replied Ruthven, enjoying the tease.

'It means impervious to correction by punishment,' offered Lucy.

'Thanks, but what does impervious mean? I'm a simple old footballer, you know.'

'Not capable of being affected, I think you'll find.'

'Blimey, Dr Campbell. How do you know all that shit?'

'I just love the English language. Loved studying Latin and identifying all the connections.'

Paul took his eyes off the road and looked at her with real affection, before continuing. 'But back to the idea of a threesome,' he smiled, and refocused on his driving.

'In your dreams, cretin. Just be thankful for getting your messy paws on one Campbell girl. You've lucked out, Sunny Jim, pure and simple.'

'Ah well, maybe after we get divorced.'

'How long to East Lothian?' asked Lucy, changing the subject, while realizing that although Paul had been teasing, the silly exchange had stirred jealous feelings deep within her.

'The satnav is saying two and a bit hours,' replied Paul as he pulled out into the fast lane and gave the beautiful car another blast of acceleration.

The mood at the Arsenal training complex in London Colney that morning was not great. The first team had lost 2-0 to Liverpool the night before, so it was a weary bunch of players who prepared with Pencil in the locker room, tired from the defeat and the long drive back from the north-west after the game.

From Pencil's perspective, he was at best ambivalent about the result; he had enough going on in his mind about how he was going to deal with the inevitable end of his career at the club and how he was going to exploit the situation to his advantage. Paul Ruthven was back in a couple of days, so the planning could begin then. Meantime, he needed to go through the motions of training as positively as possible. A TV crew was at the ground that morning and would be filming background shots for the next instalment of the BBC2 documentary. The crew would then be with him all day until he arrived home for his meeting with Vicki Ruthven to go over her merch plan for the early summer season. It was a busy schedule as he also had a meeting with his lawyer to discuss his statements for the trial of the bastards who had tried to extort his money from him. They had not been given a trial date yet, but Pencil hoped that it would come in time to be included in the TV show and get him more brownie points from the great British public.

Walking out for his warm up, Pencil was conscious of how sore his right foot was; he had good days and bad days with the pain and today was obviously going to be one of the bad days and Pencil cursed the fact that he had not taken a double dose of his painkiller earlier that morning. Training would be light after last night's match, so at least that was something. Pencil would just have to grin and bear his pain for the cameras as he did not want to give his public any cause for concern until he had agreed his plan with his agent on Friday.

During training, he reflected on his meeting with Delroy Powell the night before, not because he had been surprised in any way by the discussion but because he had been impressed by Delroy's business thinking. With so many black players coming into the game, there was a really strong argument for the DP Crew concept, although Pencil was committed to sticking to his guns regarding investing in the fledgling business. It was blue chip only. Christ, man, he had not even put five bucks of his own money into the Pencil stores, happy to let others take the risk while he reaped max rewards.

When the tackle from behind hit him, everyone on the pitch at that moment heard the crack and Pencil fell to the ground as if he had been shot by a cannon to the chest. The pain was excruciating and he knew at once that his right foot had gone again, most likely broken where the screws had been used by Dr Lucy Campbell to pin the bomb-damaged foot together. Then Pencil Kane lost consciousness, hoping as he did so that the fucking camera crew had got everything on tape.

The pretty golf-centric east coast town of Gullane was looking at its pristine best, and Paul was just telling Lucy that they were five minutes from his home when her phone rang and she was informed by a member of her team in Whitechapel that her most famous patient was at that very moment being rushed by ambulance from the Arsenal training complex. Cutting the connection, she turned ashen-faced to Ruthven, who already knew that something major was up in London.

'Did you get that?'

'Not really, something up back at the ranch?' he guessed.

'It's Pencil,' she sighed. 'He's had an accident in training and is being rushed to Whitechapel as we speak.'

'How bad?' quizzed Paul as he slowed the Aston Martin to a crawl. This was not the homecoming he had imagined.

'Not sure yet, but the club doctor is convinced that his foot is broken, and felt it best that he gets his care with us.'

'Oh shit. Could be the shortest visit home in history. What do you want to do?'

'Let's meet your parents and wait to see what the initial examination and X-rays tell us. We can decide from there.'

'Okay, we will be there shortly. What a bugger. I pray to God that he is okay.'

'He's not going to be okay, Paul. This is going to be an abrupt end of the road for our boy, let's be under no illusions about that.'

Paul's mum and dad were out of the house to greet them as he guided the throbbing car onto the driveway of their modest home that stood in the immediate shadow of the historic Dirleton Castle less than a hundred yards to the south-east of the Ruthven house.

'God, Paul, this is a beautiful place to have grown up,' began Lucy as she unstrapped herself, opened the door and began clambering from the black leather of the car's interior.

'It's not too shabby, is it?' smiled Paul as he shook his dad's hand and gave his mum a quick hug. Lucy almost felt like she was intruding as she came round the back of the car to be introduced to Ruthven's parents.

'Mum, Dad, this is Dr Lucy Campbell. Dr Lucy Campbell this is Peter and Catherine Ruthven.' Lucy shook their hands formally, noticing how like his father Paul was and the somewhat stand-offish greeting from his mum. *This*, she thought to herself, *is going to be very interesting,* and just then her telephone rang, and she excused herself to take the call from the hospital while Paul explained the situation to his parents.

Opening his dreaded spreadsheet, Gary Ruthven began to peruse the summary of the assets and liabilities that he and

Vicki had accumulated during their married life. He had already added his anticipated receipts from his share sale to Dan and Carole and run his eye over the figures:

Assets

Beaconsfield Home	*1,650,000*
San Roque House	*575,000*
Cash at bank	*520,000*
Pension	*315,000*
49% Stake in RCS	*980,000*
Total Assets	*4,040,000*

Liabilities

Mortgages

i) Beaconsfield	*780,000*
ii) San Roque	*245,000*

Loans/Credit Cards

i) Cars	*48,000*
ii) Cards	*65,000*
Total Liabilities	*1,138,000*
Net Assets	*2,902,000*

There was no denying that this now made better reading than before. That said, he knew that he really needed to discount his pension and RCS stake and focus on what was actually liquid, available to him now as he attempted to address the current situation. So, he reasoned, if he sold the San Roque house, they could clear the mortgages on Beaconsfield and San Roque and still have £70k cash to clear his credit card debts, leaving net cash of just £5k plus his secret stash on the Isle of Man. If he forgot the secret money, then their net asset with no debt would ironically be the same but a much more secure £2.9million.

Switching off his computer, he sat in reflection for a few minutes, wondering how Vicki would react to his proposal to sell their much loved house in Spain. That could prove tricky, but if they wanted to protect their family from the mess the world economy was threatening, then he could see no alternative. Just then, Jenny entered his office and told him that he needed to come and see the breaking news appearing on the television screen in the RCS reception.

The Six O'Clock News on the BBC started with the dramatic story of Pencil Kane's rush to hospital from the Arsenal training complex in London Colney. Press and TV crews were gathered outside Whitechapel Hospital and from there a report was made following a hospital statement that had simply confirmed that the young footballer had regained consciousness and was awaiting examination and X-ray results.

The next four minutes of that evening's news bulletin was then taken up by a reprise of all things Pencil Kane since his tragic injuries sustained during the al-Qaeda bombings on the London Underground on 7 July 2005.

Lucy Campbell watched the programme with Paul Ruthven and his parents as she awaited an update from her team in London. Paul had asked his office to enquire about flights from Edinburgh to Heathrow for her later that evening and now she could only wait to hear from Whitechapel before making the decision to get back down to the capital.

'What's he like, this young man?' asked Catherine Ruthven,

who was quietly impressed by Paul's new girlfriend and her obviously high-powered job.

'Paul knows him a lot better than I do,' replied Lucy, her eyes still on the television.

'Very impressive young man. Has coped with this trauma in his life better than most would have,' offered Ruthven, accepting a mug of tea from his dad.

'Guess he must come from a pretty poor background,' suggested Catherine.

'Why? Because he's a black guy?' Paul tried to keep any tone from his voice; he was well used to the fact that his mum was to all intents and purposes an out and out racist.

'No, not because he is black, Paul, because he's...'

'A footballer?' interjected her son, smiling sarcastically as he spoke.

'No, of course not, and you're just trying to trick me.' Catherine left the room and headed for the kitchen, feeling slighted by her son in front of his new girlfriend. Paul knew the situation and followed his mother, knowing that she would need a hug and a gentle apology.

'Those two have always been like that,' offered Peter Ruthven to Lucy when they were alone in front of the television.

'Families, eh?' smiled Lucy, not letting the tension get to her.

'Aye, you could put it like that. How long have you two been going out now?'

'Six months, I first met Paul on 7/7 when he came to my hospital to check up on his client, Pencil. We started dating in August.'

'That's a long time for Paul, he must be very fond of you,' smiled Peter Ruthven.

'I hope so, he has asked me to marry him,' whispered Lucy with a big smile on her very happy face.

'Has he indeed? Well, that is bonny news. His mother will be delighted when she hears.'

Just then Paul and Catherine returned to the room arm in arm, his mother wiping her eyes with a tissue, to confirm that she too had been told the news. However, before anything more could be said, Lucy's phone went and she went out into the hallway to take the call. The other three waited in silence for her return.

'His foot is broken and very badly swollen,' Lucy began on re-entering the room. 'There is little for me to do down there tonight, so I've told them that I'll get an early flight in the morning, be back at the hospital by midday.'

'Did they say how his spirit was?' asked Paul.

'Oh, he's sitting up and giving them the usual Pencil banter; seems okay.'

'Great. I'll give him a call shortly. Now, I think that it's time for a wee toast, what do you say, Mum and Dad?'

'Perfect,' replied Peter Ruthven, going off to find a bottle of something suitable and four glasses.

CHAPTER 27

THURSDAY
16 FEBRUARY 2006

Despite the fact that Amanda Patel had felt like leaping the public counter and pulling the hair of Julia Hillman, wrestling her to the ground and gouging her eyes out, she had instead decided that it was perhaps best to simply process the obnoxious cow's claim as efficiently as possible and prevent any further unwanted contact from her. To that end, she had ensured that the claim was appropriately processed and numbered and posted to the defendant by end of play on Wednesday.

On leaving the County Court in Slough, she had even then taken a detour to ensure that the brown envelope containing the claim for £100,000 against Gary Ruthven, whoever he may be of Beaconsfield, was delivered to the local sorting office well in time to make the last post that evening. The Royal Mail, to their credit, then played their particular part in the drama by ensuring that the claim was delivered through the door and onto Vicki Ruthven's expensive hall rug just after 9am next morning.

Vicki, still reeling from Pencil's latest injury, an injury that had robbed her of her potential and eagerly anticipated sexual shenanigans, handled the envelope carefully, wondering just why Gary was receiving correspondence from the County Court as indicated by a stamp on the front of the envelope.

Placing it on a kitchen counter, she went about her routines, tidying after her breakfast and pulling together the ingredients for her dinner with Molly that evening. Her chores complete, she then sat absentmindedly watching breakfast television as she considered whether or not to open the envelope. In truth, her heart was racing above its normal calm level as she had no idea what the County Court was responsible for and somewhere in her brain the possibility of divorce proceedings or the like was flashing in neon. 'Sod it,' she mumbled as she crossed the kitchen and switched on the kettle. She remembered seeing someone in a movie or TV thriller steaming open an envelope and decided to give the technique a try. Four minutes later, she was rereading the contents of the claim, not very sure what the thing was about but never the less pretty sure that Gary was going to be pretty pissed off at this latest attempt by the delightful Julia Hillman to do him damage.

Reaching for her phone, she tried to remain calm as she dialled Gary's number only to be disappointed for it to go straight to voicemail. She decided against a message; she would call him again after she got to London, might even drop the offending item into RCS on her way to Pencil Two. *What next?* she thought as she climbed the stairs to get ready for her day.

'Tell me that you're kidding me,' pleaded Dan Jenner ten minutes later down his phone to Carole, who was already two hours into her busy day at RCS.

'Nope. He says, and I quote, that after careful consideration he cannot accept an offer for his shares of anything less than fifty percent above the price paid.'

'The little shit. Where on earth did Gary find these people?' replied Dan quietly, despite clearly being annoyed.

'Well, we know who is behind this little scheme. Lucas would've bitten our hand off at the plus five percent offer.'

'Christ, she really is a nasty piece of work.'

'And that's being kind, Dan. So how do you want me to respond?' Carole just needed to be told what to do; she had a busy schedule and did not need her day being derailed by the Hunts.

'Just tell him thanks for the reply and confirm that our full and final offer has now been withdrawn,' proposed Dan clinically. 'Let them put that in their pipe for a smoke.'

'Okay, consider it done. We can discuss this later. Meantime, I need to get going.'

'No worries. Have a great day and I'll see you this evening.'

With Dan gone to do whatever it was that Dan did with his day, Carole rushed towards meeting room two for a gathering with Ruthven and the team to update on the latest thinking for The Phi Collections.

Pencil Kane had slept like a baby and was feeling surprisingly bullish about this latest injury setback. Sure, Pencil did not need the hassle of having his foot in a plaster cast for another six or so weeks, but Pencil was sharp enough to already be formulating his plan to exploit the scenario to best advantage. Yes, Pencil had known his talent had already been blown away, but this injury, happening as it had on the Arsenal training ground, would enable the famous Pencil Kane to exit the club on his terms; to exploit it to his maximum benefit.

Flicking television channels, he was pleased to see that he was still a hot topic of concern with reporters now camped outside Whitechapel Hospital to wait for news of his wellbeing or otherwise.

The medic who had looked after him on his arrival had told him that Dr Campbell was returning from Scotland on an early flight in order to be able to perform any necessary surgery on the damaged foot and for that Pencil was really grateful. Privately, he just hoped that he had not ruined Lucy's break with Paul Ruthven and lay back to await her arrival, plotting his campaign of exploitation.

His mind then went to a question he had not been able to answer: which player had tackled him and broken his foot? Pencil would have to find that out; would have to get the TV crew in when he met whoever it was so that they could capture the moment when Pencil Kane forgave him, the moment they shook hands confirming their friendship. Pencil would have no hard feelings, would be the good guy and leave his fans in awe at his magnanimity, although Pencil was not 100% sure if that was the right word for it.

Just then Dr Lucy Campbell knocked on his private room door and breezed in without waiting for an invite, all full of healthy energy.

'Pencil Kane, and here was me thinking that we had got rid of you,' she opened, smiling at her favourite patient.

'I know, Doc, but Pencil has just been missing you so much he had to do somethin' drastic to get your attention away from Pencil's agent,' retorted Kane.

'I can fully understand that, Pencil, but next time how about you just send me a text?' Lucy was by his bedside reading his charts.

'Next time, Doc, that's exactly what Pencil is going to do.'

'Glad to hear it, Pencil, glad to hear it. But first we're going to get you glued back together.'

The trick with the envelope had worked really well, so when Vicki Ruthven arrived in the RCS reception area later that afternoon, she was working on her approach with Gary. After all, what was her justification for dropping the thing off in person?

Jenny was delighted to see her and told her that Ruthven was just finishing off a call to the USA and was free for thirty minutes after that. She hovered in the small kitchen while Jenny made her a coffee from a fancy new bit of kit that had been bought since the last time that she had been in the office.

'That looks an expensive item, and I thought business was tough,' she observed jokingly to Jenny, who had been working with Gary for ten years and was like one of the family.

'I know,' replied the PA conspiratorially. 'It was the last thing that Lucas Hunt did before he left, said our clients deserved a good coffee when they were here.'

'Some logic in that I suppose. Pity the wanker didn't come up with more value add,' conceded Vicki. Jenny smiled, not sure if she should really contribute to the naughty tone of their chat.

'Ah well,' she eventually replied. 'All water under the bridge now, I guess.'

'Indeed it is,' concluded Vicki.

'So, any news on young Pencil?' asked Jenny, guiding the talk to safer ground.

'Not much. Seems his foot is broken, but I've heard nothing more than that,' replied Vicki, just hoping that she was not blushing at the mention of her young fantasy.

Just then Gary popped his head round the kitchen door and interrupted them.

'You two putting the world to rights?' he began before entering and kissing his wife on the cheek.

'No, I was just admiring your new and very expensive coffee machine,' said his wife, before thanking Jenny and following her husband through to his office.

'So, what brings you up here this fine day?'

'I brought a letter that arrived at home this morning; it looks official and serious,' she replied, fishing the County Court stamped envelope from her expensive Mulberry handbag. Ruthven fidgeted with the thing for a few moments before picking up a letter opener and slitting the envelope. He then carefully withdrew the contents and perused the claim.

'Well?' prompted his wife, feigning curiosity.

'Mmm, it looks like our old friend Julia Hillman wants another fight,' replied Gary distractedly. He passed the claim to Vicki and sat down at his round table, the blood having drained from his face.

'Is there any merit in this?' asked Vicki, holding the two-page document in front of her.

'Absolutely not. Firstly, as you know, she has never been a shareholder and the shares that the claim refers to are in Lucas's name. Secondly, we have formal records of Lucas having accepted the share certificates, all appropriately witnessed. The woman is really beginning to get on my fucking tits; this will just be more hassle and cost.'

'Why does she hate you so much, Gary? What have you ever done to her?'

'Two really good questions, although I'm afraid I don't have any answers.' Gary took the claim from Vicki, carefully folded it and put it back in its envelope. He crossed to his glass-topped desk, pulled open a drawer and dropped the thing in before slamming it shut.

'One for the lawyers in the morning. Meanwhile, how is that young boss of yours?'

'Let's come back to that. Firstly, did you get hold of our daughter yet?'

'Oh yes, and she will be home tomorrow afternoon as we discussed. I should be there by six. Perhaps we can have dinner and put her right then.'

'Good luck with that, but six is fine. Do you want to stay the night?'

'That would be great. It's been a long week.'

'Cool, I will get Jay to make up the spare room.' Their cleaner came on a Friday.

'So, no estranged shagging then?' Ruthven smiled, breaking the tension.

'As that little brown envelope suggests, you're out of luck at the moment, Mr Ruthven,' she replied, not altogether sure that she was being honest.

'It was worth a try; so back to your boss. What's the latest?'

Vicki then updated him on the little she knew and Gary led her to the reception, kissed her goodbye, before returning to his office to call his brother who was apparently driving back to London on his own.

Later that evening as Lucy Campbell was in surgery operating on the badly broken foot of Pencil Kane, Colm Elliot and his long-term partner Susan Lamont were just arriving at the grand front entrance to Piers House in Berkshire. They had been invited for drinks and dinner by their old friends Ann Stuart-Piers and Barry Piers. To give their hosts their proper titles, Lady Piers and Sir Bartholomew Piers were well-known writers who had built very successful careers since they had first met at Oxford some thirty years earlier. Barry had inherited his father's baronetcy following Sir Peter's assassination by the Provisional IRA in 1981, and the couple had moved to their handsome Palladian home following the death of his stepmother Elizabeth in 1999.

Colm had become friends with the young author when he was part of the Anti-Terrorist Squad team searching for the killers of Barry's father, who had been one of two members of Margaret Thatcher's Cabinet assassinated by a team of hitmen hired to bring down the Tory government. Susan had formed an unlikely alliance with Ann and Barry who had discovered that she had been having an affair with his father at the time of his death. Elliot and Piers played the occasional round of golf, and Ann was perhaps Susan's best friend.

'So, how are those two boys of yours?' asked Elliot as they were led into a massive kitchen at the back of the house.

'Doing well, we think, not that we see them that often these days,' replied Ann. She and her husband had twin sons who were now twenty-two and away from home studying architecture at Oxford. Before becoming a politician, Sir Peter Piers had been a highly successful architect and Barry was delighted that the boys had chosen to follow in his father's footsteps.

'And how is Laura getting on in Cornwall?'

'Good, we think,' replied Susan honestly, as she was still not convinced that her daughter was doing as good as she had always hoped.

'So, Detective Chief Inspector, what's keeping you awake at night?' asked Barry, handing Elliot an opened bottle of his favourite beer.

'Nothing in particular, although I've got an interesting research project on the go and I'd like to pick your brains on it when we get a minute to do so.'

'Sounds intriguing. I am sure the ladies wouldn't mind us tootling off to the snooker room for a frame and a chat.'

Elliot and his old friend then made their way out of the kitchen, Colm delighted to get the chance for his renowned friend's input on his suicidal suicide bomber theory.

302

APRIL 2006

CHAPTER 28   MONDAY 24 APRIL 2006

Perusing the legal documents with meticulous care, Julia Hillman could feel her blood beginning to boil. Incandescent with rage did not do real justice to how she was suddenly feeling. Dropping the papers onto her kitchen counter, she went in search of Lucas, who had gone down the garden to chop some logs and had therefore been out of the house when the courier had arrived with the package from Gary Ruthven's lawyer.

'Lucas,' she called as she opened the door that led to their rear garden.

'I'll be there shortly, honey, just tidying up,' came Hunt's sheepish reply.

'Fuck the tidying up and get your shit-head arse in here now,' demanded Julia Hillman at the top of her voice as she returned to the kitchen after slamming the door shut in a way that left her husband in no doubt that this was urgent.

Moments later, Lucas arrived, removing the gloves he had been wearing during his log chopping. Seeing the papers now opened again in front of his red-faced wife, Hunt knew that this was not going to be the highlight of his day.

'What is it this time?' he opened more calmly than he was feeling.

'I've just had this shit couriered over from Gary fucking

Ruthven's solicitor, and they seem to be showing that you have in fact received the share certificates for the last batch of money I paid.'

Hunt had pulled off his gloves and was standing washing his hands at the sink, not too sure how to respond to this information, genuinely fearing that this thing could end his marriage. Keen not to make matters any worse, he decided that honesty was the only policy that he could deploy at this particular moment.

'Let me read the papers and we can discuss this calmly,' he began as he hurriedly dried his hands before turning back to face his furious wife.

'Calmly? You think we can discuss this shit calmly?' she responded as she pushed the papers along the counter to Lucas, who picked them up and went to find his reading glasses.

'Where the fuck are you going?'

'To get my glasses. I need to read this with care.'

'Too right you do, and there had better be a great explanation for this. Otherwise, you and I could be heading for a major fall-out!'

Less than a minute later, Lucas returned to the kitchen and settled himself down at the table, intending to take as much time as possible to read the papers, despite the fact that he knew full well what they contained.

'Well?' urged Julia Hillman.

'Well, the papers do seem to confirm what you thought, although I should point out that I am not in possession of the share certificates and never have been.'

'So this is a fabrication?'

'Well, I wouldn't go that far,' replied Lucas, aware that this game was up.

'Well, Lucas, how far would you care to go?'

'Fundamentally, what they claim is correct. The shares were issued in my name; it was the only way that we could get the Small Companies Loan Scheme from Barclays.'

'So, my own husband lied to me? Told me that the share certificates had not been issued? Let me go to Slough and the County Court and start a claim for a hundred grand when I had no chance of winning?' Hillman's neck was red with fury and sweat was gathering in small droplets in the fine hair above her top lip.

'I think you'll recall that I said we needed to talk about suing Gary, that we should consider the offer from Carole and Dan. But no, you headed off to Slough and as always did what you wanted to do.'

'And made myself a fucking shit-head laughing stock in the process, is that what you are saying, Lucas?'

'No, Julia, that's what you are saying.'

'What? Are you saying this mess is all my fault?'

'If that's what you want to hear, then yes, that's what I'm saying.'

'So, I need to apologize and withdraw my claim? Make myself look like a total tool, when my husband could have stopped this shit weeks, months ago?'

'Not sure you were listening, Julia,' replied Lucas, hoping that his wife's storm had blown itself out.

'Fucking great, and now Carole and her hippy husband have withdrawn their offer we are stuck with what, twelve and a half percent of that bloody company? Jesus, what am I going to tell my father?' And with that Julia Hillman burst into tears and barged from the kitchen. Hunt then heard the front door being pulled shut before moments later, their aging BMW was driven at great speed away from their house.

At least that is out in the open, thought Hunt as he filled the kettle, having decided that a nice pot of tea and a couple of Hobnobs were called for.

Delroy Powell had a dilemma and was not too certain about how to go about dealing with it. One of his newest clients, a young player at West Ham, had got himself in deep with a black market bookmaker and had managed to run up losses of almost thirty grand. That in itself was no big deal, the player was on 15k a week, so with a bit of sensible budgeting the money could have been paid back. But no, the prick had gone to a loan shark and borrowed the thirty grand and was now being leaned on to pay back the new balance of sixty-five grand by end of play on Wednesday.

Delroy knew of the loan shark's reputation and from what he had managed to gather from his sources, an amicable midway compromise was highly unlikely. So, the sixty-five grand needed paying, which for Delroy Powell was the main dilemma. He did not need it getting out that one of his DP Crew clients had got rinsed by some loan shark; that would do his reputation no good. So, the man and his people would need to be confronted; a way would need to be found for both parties to save face; a win-win solution was needed. That, he knew, was not going to be a walk in the park.

Picking up his mobile, he dialled the loan shark's number and waited patiently for his call to be answered. No such luck, the thing went straight to voicemail. Letting the drivel of the man's message play itself out, Delroy left a simple request for a call back, gave his spare mobile number and disconnected. Starting his black Audi with its blacked-out windows he headed for Pencil One in Covent Garden, deciding to get together with his two right-hand men first thing in the morning and hatch a plan aimed at saving face.

A small party was taking place at Pencil One that evening and a fifty-inch television had been set up to ensure that the gathering would able to spend an hour from 9pm watching the latest instalment of *Pencil's 7/7 Recovery: An Intimate Portrait* as it was broadcast on BBC2. Insiders at the television company were predicting their largest audience so far as carefully planned media leaks had hinted at some earth-shattering news on Pencil Kane's future.

That very morning, Pencil had been to Whitechapel where Dr Lucy Campbell had overseen the removal of his latest plaster cast, all discreetly filmed and rushed to Television Centre for inclusion in that night's broadcast. Pencil had also been filmed speaking with Arsenal's head coach and both men had left that session with tears in their eyes.

Pencil had invited forty guests to his party and valuable cashmere had been removed from one of the mirror-topped tables and replaced with champagne flutes and copious amounts of Moët & Chandon. Food had been delivered from Fortnum & Mason and a small team of beautiful waitresses in short skirts and see-through tops had been briefed on their role for the evening. A DJ and sound system had been provided by the Ministry of Sound and the club's eccentric owner James Palumbo was expected to attend.

Outside Pencil One, a security cordon had been erected and Delroy Powell was ensuring that his team of eight were totally clear on expectations. A crowd was beginning to gather, word having got out that some sort of party was taking place in Pencil Kane's now iconic first store. Pre-booked paparazzi were already on duty and the place was now beginning to buzz nicely as early guests began to arrive and squeeze past the growing crowd and into the store.

Vicki Ruthven had spent her afternoon at Pencil Four and had then gone to Gary's small apartment to get ready for the party. Her estranged husband was having a short sabbatical from RCS and was now spending time playing golf and catching up on his reading at their house in San Roque. She knew that Pencil was planning some sort of announcement that evening but was not privy to what it was. Since Kane had broken his foot, she had been able to back away from her desire for the young man and was now hoping that she and her husband would be fully reconciled when he returned from his break. Indeed, Vicki was planning to join him in Spain in a couple of weeks for a full review of their situation. Dressed in a simple but very sexy little black dress, her taxi dropped her across the street from the store and she made her way through the gathering throng, past the DP Crew guys and into Pencil One, feeling a lot more confident about her future than she had done in a long time. The place was amazing, and the Ministry of Sound DJ was providing the perfect musical backdrop to the first phase of the party, the hour or so before the BBC2 broadcast.

Pencil was there to greet his guests, dressed as usual in vintage Levi's and his pale pink shirt. He had taken more painkillers than was perhaps advisable, but Pencil did not want his big evening spoiled by pain. He watched Vicki Ruthven arrive and go and join Paul Ruthven and Dr Campbell. As always Pencil thought Vicki looked sexy, the perfect MILF, and he knew that he was in danger of developing another obsession. Pencil was obsessed with perfect tidiness and order; obsessed with being fit, having the perfect body; obsessed with making as much money as possible, and was now close to obsession with pornography. Every time he arrived back at his apartment, he could not wait to get onto a porn site or a Sky adult channel, the desire to masturbate taking control of his mind. And when he couldn't get online or have access to Sky, he obsessed over the thought of fucking Vicki Ruthven; wanked himself red at the thought of getting naked with his store merchandiser. It was an obsession that needed to stop, but Pencil knew that if he did get it under control, then something else would get a hold of him, something more damaging like drinking or gambling. Now, however, with his plaster cast removed, he could concentrate on other things, be more mobile, more busy, and not just spend time with his sad little porn fantasies.

At five to nine, the DJ announced that the music would be stopping soon and invited guests to fill their glasses and get some food before the TV was switched on and people began getting themselves positioned to watch the programme as the glamorous waitresses busied themselves, making sure the food and drink was supplied to all who wanted some. As the theme tune began on the TV, lights were turned down and the bustling room fell into a focused silence.

In Northwood, Colm Elliot and Susan Lamont got comfortable in their big old sofa in front of the television and settled down to watch *Pencil's 7/7 Recovery: An Intimate Portrait*. Elliot had spent the day finalizing the presentation he was due to give on Tuesday at MI6 on his work on suicide bombers, and it was perfect timing to watch a programme about a young man who had suffered greatly at the hands of such terrorism.

For fifty minutes, the programme and its sensitive voice-over followed Pencil's private and public life. There was the horrible moment when his foot had been broken again and he had been rushed to Whitechapel; there was the touching scene when Pencil and his Arsenal colleague who had made the bone-breaking tackle had met in hospital and Pencil had hugged the man to show that there were no hard feelings; there was the grand opening of Pencil Four with its celebrity guests and Pencil back on crutches, and then the show slowed down and Colm and Susan sat watching as Pencil arrived that very morning at Whitechapel to have his cast removed and his drive across London to his meeting with the Arsenal coach. Suddenly, like peeping Toms, the British public were witness to the decision, made jointly by Pencil and his head coach, that his battle was over, that the star-spangled football career of Pencil Kane was at a premature end. The show ended with the two men embracing, tears in their eyes, and a shot of a badly limping Pencil getting into his DP Crew-driven car and speeding away from the Arsenal training complex, the theme tune and credits leaving half a country in silent tears.

Susan couldn't speak, was simply happy for Elliot to take her in his arms and hold her tight.

For two minutes, the gathered guests in Pencil One remained stationary in stunned silence, before the lights were turned up ever so slightly, ever so dramatically, and Pencil Kane stood before them.

'Pencil would like to say a few words if that's okay with you guys,' he began, holding a mic supplied by the Ministry of Sound DJ. There was no need for any agreement; the crowd was at one with their host.

'Today was a big one for Pencil, but don't be kidded by that little show. Pencil has known for many months that his football days are over; his God-given talent has gone. So, guys, no tears, no sadness for me. Pencil is very lucky. Pencil has other talents and thanks to you lot, Pencil can now get on with being the best shopkeeper that ever lived, and Pencil will not relax until we're having our openin' party for Pencil Ninety-Nine.' The small gathering started to cheer; tears were being wiped aside and people were hugging and embracing each other as Kane asked them all to raise a glass to Pencil Ninety-Nine.

CHAPTER 29   TUESDAY 25 APRIL 2006

The sound of silence woke Gary Ruthven at just after seven that morning. He had left the curtains open overnight and early morning sunshine was threatening to invade his bedroom. Shifting in the large bed, he checked the time on the bedside clock and reckoned that the grass cutting on the golf course would be starting soon, meaning little chance of getting back to sleep. Rising, he paddled to the en-suite bathroom and as he emptied his bladder caught sight of his naked reflection in the large bathroom mirror. His gym work and swimming had got his waist back to its original 32 inches and the tan he had been acquiring during his sabbatical made him look at least five years younger than he was. Pulling on a pair of boxers and an old grey T-shirt, he went down the marble staircase to the house's small kitchen and put a kettle on, needing his early morning cup of tea.

He was just into his third week of his agreed six week break from RCS and had been in San Roque for two weeks. This was a week he had been looking forward to for some time as the Open de Espana golf championship was being held on the newer of the club's two courses later in the week. Already the place was a buzz of excitement as many of the European Tour's top golfers had been arriving and practising at the club. Marquees had been pitched and temporary stands built for spectators and Gary really looked forward to watching the competition unfold from such close proximity.

The stresses of the last year were lifting from his shoulders; he had cash in the bank and although he was yet to put his financial action plan in motion, some degree of stability had returned at least to that aspect of his life. As for his marriage, that matter remained to be resolved and although he was looking forward to Vicki joining him in Spain, he was in no way certain of any outcome. They had become closer in recent months, particularly when they had handled the issue with Emma and her desire to quit her law degree at Leeds. The girl was now back at university and, according to her at least, working hard towards her end of year one exams.

After a shower, Gary dressed in jeans and a light cashmere sweater and made his way across the fairways of the old course to the beautiful old clubhouse for his breakfast. There, he could read the morning papers and watch the preparations for the golf tournament as a multitude of people busied themselves about the place. Just after eleven he caught sight of the Spanish golf legend Seve Ballesteros whose company Amen Corner were running that week's event. The world famous golfer had a home on San Roque and his brother was one of the club's professionals, a difficult character who had given Ruthven a couple of challenging lessons that in fairness had helped improve Gary's game. As he watched Seve and his entourage pass through the workmen and their preparations, his mobile phone vibrated in his pocket and when he looked at the screen, he was surprised to see that the caller was Lucas Hunt.

'Hello,' he answered tentatively.

'Gary, it's Lucas. Can we talk for a few minutes?'

'That depends on the subject matter, Lucas.'

'It's about these bloody shares and Julia's claim against you,' offered Hunt carefully.

'Her nebulous, factually inaccurate, time – and money – wasting claim? What about it?' Gary did not want any of his precious sabbatical taken up by this topic or indeed this call.

'Well, I have just spoken with her and she has decided to drop the claim,' continued Hunt, conscious that his former friend was not sounding patient.

'That's fucking big of her, Lucas. Did she discover the truth?'

'She is now aware of all the important facts,' conceded Hunt.

'What, and you have not had a pillow held over your face?'

'So, my reason for calling is to ask if you can talk to Dan and Carole; ask them to reinstate their offer to purchase our shares.'

'Your shares, Lucas. Your wife never had any fucking shares, remember?'

'Well yes, indeed, my shares.'

'That's better, Lucas. Now, let me think about that for a second.' Gary held his phone to his chest and counted slowly to ten before continuing. 'Okay, Lucas, I've thought about it.' He enjoyed keeping the old man waiting.

'And?' pushed Hunt.

'And, my answer is simple. Go fuck yourself, Lucas.' And with that he cut the connection and threw the phone down on the table in front of him.

After his late breakfast, Gary wandered outside the clubhouse, watching well-known players and their coaches practice their putting, their chipping and their bunker play. The talent on show was incredible, and he watched as a crowd gathered as Seve got into a bunker to show a leading pro how to hit a shot. Of the three shots modelled by the Spaniard, one flew into the hole and the other two finished inches away. This had the crowd clapping before the player receiving the advice took his shot and flew it into the hole to join Seve's ball. The crowd went into raptures as Ballesteros climbed from the bunker and headed across the car park which had been turned into a tented village, his stellar reputation enhanced even further.

The golf circus had lifted Ruthven's spirit after his call from Hunt, and as he headed back towards his house that overlooked the twelfth fairway he decided to call Carole and let her know that 'Hunt the cunt', as Vicki was now calling him, had been in touch.

The loan shark sat with his back to the wall in true Mafia style and was making the terrible mistake of underestimating Delroy Powell. The meeting had been hastily arranged and Delroy had arrived with his two most trusted and capable crew members with the primary aim of renegotiating his dumb client's debt.

'The fing is Delroy, my boy, if I was to let your client get away with not meetin' his obligations, then I would look like a dumb fuck and every other twat would stop takin' me seriously. You get my drift?' The loan shark was probably forty and had obviously lived on a diet of nerves and cigarettes, if his skinny frame and brown teeth were anything to go by.

'That's the thing, I don't get your drift. After all, who is going to know about our revised arrangement?' replied Powell, not quite sure if this was going anywhere.

'Well, my boy, nobody will know, 'cause it ain't goin' to happen. Your client is gonna pay sixty-five grand by tomorrow, or the debt reaches seventy and a couple of my lads are gonna 'ave to get a bit heavy.' The loan shark looked at two of his big guys and raised his eyebrows before stating, 'This little meetin' is at an end. See ya tomorrow.'

Delroy leaned over the table that stood between them and replied in his best stage whisper, 'I came with good intentions, and I am leaving with a bad taste in my mouth. You may not live to regret that.' And with that he turned on his heels and left followed by his crew.

Outside the pub, they sat in Delroy's car for a few moments, reflecting on what had just happened.

'So, where does that get us?' Powell asked of his people.

'Looks like we've got a problem,' replied his number two, a former heavyweight boxer who had got himself out of the fight game before he had incurred any brain damage.

'Wrong answer,' replied Powell. 'It looks like our skinny loan shark has got a problem, as I am not taking that shit from anyone. Let's get back and put a plan together; we don't have much time.'

Dan Jenner sat in his beautiful Holland Park house and considered his approach. Sure, he wanted the shares that Lucas Hunt held in RCS, but not enough to be prepared to pay what he had originally offered. Dan had been in business long enough to know that there was no place to go if you developed a reputation as a soft touch. Picking up his mobile, he called Carole who was at work, and suggested that she offer Hunt his original price minus five percent for their delay in selling. Carole had laughed at this but had taken great pleasure in calling Lucas and confirming their final offer.

When Carole called Dan back fifteen minutes later it was to confirm that Lucas had agreed to accept their offer and that Rosie Calder had already faxed the paperwork to Hunt for signing.

'Good job. A slight delay in getting what we wanted, but a tidy little saving. That will teach those two a lesson,' reflected Dan to his wife.

'I wouldn't be too sure that Julia will be made aware of the true facts,' suggested Carole.

'Perhaps that's just as well, we don't want her getting all upset with Gary again. Who knows what the psycho bitch might do next.'

'That's true. Hopefully, this will put an end to that little war.'

'Mmm, I wouldn't bet on it. Do you want me to call Gary and give him the good news?'

'Please, I need to get back to a meeting. This place is bloody ragged without Ruthven. Whose idea was it to let him have six weeks off?'

'The firm will benefit in the long run, sweet pea, mark my words.'

'I believe you. Though right now, we could do with him back.'

With Carole gone, Dan tried Gary's phone but it went to voicemail, so he left a simple message informing him that the Hunt shares had been repatriated. He then gathered his things and headed to his nearby health club for one of his twice weekly gym workouts.

Julia Hillman was not in any frame of mind to be concerning herself with the price that her husband had accepted for his 12.5% stake in RCS. She was too preoccupied, as she sat in the bathroom of their remodelled cottage and looked again at the result of her latest pregnancy test. Trying not to overreact, she took care to meticulously follow the procedure of a second test. Five minutes later, she was calming herself by taking long, deep-breaths, trying to come to terms with the enormity of the moment. Placing both tests into a small bag and stashing them in her bathroom cupboard, she went in search of her husband.

Lucas was sitting at his laptop in their small study trying to find a way of making the offer he had just accepted for his shares look better than the actual reality when his wife was suddenly behind him.

'Shit, Julia. You gave me a fright sneaking up on me like that.' A few seconds earlier and his wife would have seen him working on his spreadsheet, manipulating numbers. But his wife said nothing, and simply put her arms around her husband to give him a tight hug, tears welling in her eyes.

'What is wrong?' asked Lucas, suddenly concerned.

'Nothing is wrong. It's just the opposite, in fact. At last something is very right,' offered Hillman, as a smile broke out on her tear-stained face.

'What?'

'I'm pregnant, Lucas. The treatment has worked, and I'm bloody pregnant.'

'Honey, that's fantastic news,' smiled Hunt as he stood and took his wife in his arms, secretly hoping that the tide might now begin to turn in their tumultuous relationship.

Pencil Kane reckoned that at some time in the near future his young body would react in some way to the happenings in his life over the last twenty-four hours, but for now Pencil was far too busy to even consider taking time for reflection. After the party at Pencil One, which had finally wrapped up at midnight, he had been driven home and had gone straight to bed, not even taking time to shower or watch porn. His driver had been at his door to collect him and take him to his lawyer's office at eight that morning, where he had spent two hours refreshing his statements given to the police in early preparation for the forthcoming trial of the bastards who had tried to extort Pencil's money from him.

From the lawyer's office, he had been driven to the London Studios on the South Bank where he later appeared on *This Morning* and was interviewed by Fern Britton and Phillip Schofield. It was a television show that Pencil was far too cool to have ever watched. Both presenters were very nice to Pencil and if the messages of goodwill that were flowing into their studio from the British public were anything to go by, then Pencil was once again right up there as one of the top ten most famous people in the country.

By the time Pencil was leaving the London Studios with two giant DP Crew guys, a large crowd had gathered and Kane was cheered and photographed all the way to his silver Mercedes with its blacked-out windows. If Pencil was honest with himself, he was loving this level of fame and popularity and just hoped that he would be able to cope when all the fuss died away and he was no longer famous, because Pencil Kane was sharp enough to know that was what would happen. Meantime, he was due to have lunch with his agent at Langan's Brasserie in Mayfair and he hoped that someone had tipped off the press and that another crowd would be awaiting his arrival.

He was not disappointed, and when he was eventually led to join Paul Ruthven at their table, Pencil Kane had a big grin on his handsome face.

'You're causing a bit of a stir in London today,' smiled Ruthven as he stood to welcome his client with a handshake.

'Pencil appreciates all your efforts, Paul, he really does,' began Kane, taking his seat and accepting a menu from the waiter. 'And Pencil promises not to do too much loud cursing at this fine eatery.'

'Glad to hear it. How has your day gone; how was *This Morning*?'

'It was kinda cool. You know Pencil has never seen that show,' he whispered.

'Why doesn't that surprise me. How is the foot?'

'It's okay, man. I guess it's more relaxed now Pencil has retired from football, but this brace thing's beginning to fuck Pencil right off.'

'So, to sum up, what our early research indicates is that the concept of martyrdom may well be something of a myth; a myth that most terrorist organisations are happy to cultivate. The truth may be that many suicide bombers were suicidal anyway and merely targeted and exploited unstable individuals. If that is the case, those in MI6 or the SIS who infiltrate communities in order to identify and negate potential threats will need to widen their net, broaden their investigations.'

Elliot concluded his presentation to a group of ten very senior officers from the Met, MI6 and the secret service. There was silence for a few moments and then a generous round of applause.

'Thank you, Detective Chief Inspector; a very thought-provoking and insightful presentation. Can we now open the discussion up for questions?'

'Of course,' replied Elliot, not too sure what would follow, but for the next thirty minutes he was impressed by the reflection, focus and presence of those in the room and when the session was over, he was given the assurance that he would be called upon to share his research team's findings more widely across the various security organisations.

Leaving the MI6 building on Albert Embankment, Elliot headed towards Vauxhall Underground station and switched on his phone to call Bellamy and let her know how the meeting had gone. Hannah answered first ring, obviously eager to get his news.

'So, do they think our little team has gone crazy?' she began.

'Not at all. They were surprisingly open and thoughtful on the matter and I think we will be asked to share our findings more widely. Indeed, we might even get asked to further develop our research.'

'That sounds great. Any sticky moments?'

'No, not that I can think of. They seemed genuinely engaged and curious.'

'Blimey, boss, you might get a medal for this little brainstorm of yours.'

'Two hopes on that front, Sergeant. Bob Hope and no hope,' replied Elliot, using another of his odd little sayings that Bellamy had heard before but didn't quite understand. She would need to start writing them down in case they were lost to posterity.

'So, what are you doing now?'

'Heading for the Underground. Should be back in Marylebone in an hour or so.'

'Good, we've got another suspicious death coming our way.'

'Ah well, that'll keep us out of trouble. See you shortly.'

CHAPTER 30   WEDNESDAY
                                 26 APRIL 2006

Carrying only a small rucksack that contained a Public Law book, a hastily prepared sandwich, her purse, passport and ticket printed out in the law faculty library, Emma Ruthven arrived by coach at London's Luton airport. How they could possibly call this airport London was a mystery to her; the place was miles from London, so why the stupid title?

Dressed in tight, her dad called them 'spray-on', jeans, and a big woollen jumper, she took the escalators to passport control and then spent ten minutes going through security. It felt odd being at the airport without any other members of her family, but loneliness was something she had got used to during her time at Leeds. Sure, there had been her brief and totally stupid fling with one of her younger lecturers, a situation that she had managed to keep from her parents when she had been summoned home for 'crisis talk', but she had not taken to Leeds or her course and just hoped that she'd be smart enough to pass her exams when she sat them next month. Passing would at least give her some wriggle room in her proposed negotiations with Gary and Vicki.

Her Monarch flight to Gibraltar was called on time, and she was surprised how full the flight was, having totally forgotten the fact that the bloody golf was at San Roque again this year. They had been at the house last year to celebrate her mum's fortieth birthday and had found the entire Sotogrande area overrun by golf types. Sure, some of the younger guys were quite fit, but did they all have to dress in such stupid clothes? Golf clothes design certainly needed a rethink.

She tried to reread her public law stuff as she ate her cheese and ham sandwich and hoped that there would be a taxi across the border in Spain after she took the short walk to border control from the airport. She had read somewhere that Gibraltar was one of the ten most dangerous airport landings in the world, with its short runway and frequently windy and misty conditions, but that didn't bother her at all and if anything only added to the excitement of her little excursion.

She also hoped that she wouldn't find her dad entertaining some woman at the house. How embarrassing would that be? It was possible. After all, he had been living apart from her mother for some time now. Although she and Molly had never been told the real reason for the split, it had to be something serious for them still to be apart. Well, if there was a woman involved, her dad would be the bigger loser and if, as she had been told, he was having a solo sabbatical, then she knew he would be pleased to see her. In her dad's eyes she could do no wrong; when her mum got on her case, when she knew she was up to some trick or another, her dad could always be relied upon to calm things down. Which was why she had made the decision to come and see him for a few days; have a break from Leeds and discuss with Gary what she had planned for next year at university.

She got a taxi without difficulty, and twenty minutes later it was turning off the N340 and into the driveway leading up to the San Roque Club. As the cab approached the busy gatehouse, she suddenly felt nervous. What if he did have a woman with him? What if he was not at San Roque at all? The latter was okay, she knew where the spare key would be, and a few days on her own here would not be a bad gig.

He was taken as cleanly as had been planned. Had not known what had hit him and could feel the van in which he was now being held accelerate away at pace from the small lane at the back of his house. Yes, the small lane at the back of his house. Where the fuck were his team; how the fuck could this be happening to him? Fucking heads would roll for this. Balls would be broken. Fuck sake, what was going on?

Ten minutes later the van was driven into a large lock-up and the engine killed before the side door was slid open and the loan shark had the sack covering his head removed to enable him to look straight into the jolly face of Delroy Powell.

'Sorry about the drama, man, but we wanted a private word with you, away from your boys, if you get my drift,' began Powell, hiding any anxiety that he was feeling more than well.

'You're one dumb fuck for doin' this, my boy. It's somethin' that you are goin' to regret big time,' came the man's bravado-filled reply.

'Yeah, yeah. As you can see, I'm pissing my pants.'

'What do you want, man?'

'I just want to repay my client's little debt, which as you rightly said when we last met, is due to be repaid today.'

'Well, there was no need to go to all this trouble. Should've just brought the 65k in a paper bag to my pub, man, then we'd all have been happy.'

'Therein lies your problem. We ain't going to be paying you no 65k. We needed you here to negotiate a proper repayment,' explained Powell, keen to get this over with.

'No negotiations. Told you that before, my boy, or are you kinda hard of hearing?'

'You're consistent, I'll give you that, so I'll explain the options as clearly as possible. That sound okay?'

'Well, I'm here now, so why not, my boy?'

'Option one is simple. You accept what's in my little bag as full and final settlement, nothing more is said and we all go back and get on with our busy little lives. Oh, and you undertake to never lend money to any of my clients again, under any circumstances. Clear?'

'It's clear, my boy, but ain't goin' to 'appen. So, I hope option two is better.'

'Option two is shorter. You refuse option one and are taken from here to a place of execution, buried in concrete and are never seen or heard of again.'

'Yeah right, and you've got the balls to carry out that little trick? Think not, my boy. Is there an option three or can you just pay up and we can all get out of here? You see, my mobile has a tracking device attached, so my team are probably outside now and we could be in for a fuckin' bloodbath, my boy.' The loan shark hissed this last part through clenched brown teeth.

'There's no option three, and your mobile is lying crushed in your back lane. And, if you call me your boy one more time, option one will be deleted from the offer as well.'

'How much cash in your bag, my—?' he asked, thinking twice about completing his question.

'Thirty-five grand, used notes, all ready to walk out the door with if you are good with my terms.'

Powell watched the man carefully as he weighed up his situation, not sure if Delroy was really going to have him killed or not, trying to find a way out while keeping his stupid gangster pride intact.

'If I agree, no other fucker will know?'

'That's why we sidetracked your team, wanted to save your face. You can go back now, say the debt was paid, get on with your grubby little business.'

'Show me the cash,' he asked quietly.

'Not before I show you this,' replied Powell, pulling his shooter from his coat pocket.

'Okay, now show me the money.' The loan shark had gone two shades lighter than pale.

Powell reached for his bag and held it open for the man to see the contents.

'Thirty-five?'

'Yep, but you're not going to have time to count it, I'm afraid. It's deal or no deal time.'

'And you'll drop me back home?'

'That's not going to happen. Deal or no deal?'

'Deal, but I better not see you again. I might not be so calm.'

Delroy turned to his two crew members. 'What do you think?'

The two giants slowly climbed from the van, leaving Delroy to bid his farewell to the loan shark. 'Nice doing business with you, and remember to leave my clients alone in future or the ending might not be so amicable.'

With that he stepped from the van and pulled the door firmly shut, leaving the loan shark inside with his bag of money.

Outside the lock-up, Delroy and his crew climbed into his waiting Audi, and as it was driven slowly away he told his ex-boxer to call the guys at the site and tell them that they could pour the concrete; that the space would not be needed after all.

Walking carefully around the side of his house, Gary Ruthven was startled to hear music coming from beside the pool and see one of the sun umbrellas now extended to its full height. With fear making his heart thump against his rib cage, he gingerly sneaked to the next wall in order to see what the fuck was going on, who was availing themselves of his private property, his much loved garden. He then saw her as she reached up from her sun lounger and began sipping from her wine glass.

'Emma, what the bloody hell is going on?' he began as he strode across the perfectly manicured lawn to where his daughter lay topless, enjoying the April sunshine.

'Dad, I wondered when you were going to get back,' replied his daughter as she jumped from the lounger and made to hug her father.

'Put a T-shirt on, girl. I'm in enough bother without being seen hugging my big-titted daughter,' he smiled.

'Dad, they're not that big,' protested Emma, taking time to study her breasts.

'Just put them away for the moment and tell me what the hell you are doing here.'

Emma did as she was told and pulled on a white cotton top that displayed the graphic *F*ck me I'm famous* on the front, a T-shirt her dad would no doubt frown upon at some point soon.

'Thought I would pop down and see my favourite dad; take a couple of days away from boring law and recharge my batts before exam time,' she began as she settled herself back on the sun lounger.

'Did you indeed? And does your mother know that you're here?'

'Of course not. What good would that have done?'

'Jesus, Emma. What am I going to do with you?'

'Nothing, Pops. So why not go get yourself a nice glass of wine and come back and we can have a nice little catch-up,' proposed Emma, and Gary left her to go to the house and change into his swimming shorts and a T-shirt.

Five minutes later, with glass in hand, he rejoined his daughter by the pool and as he settled himself down on a second lounger, simply stated, 'Now, young lady, this had better be good.'

Pencil Kane had come to the conclusion that it was not very cool for him to still be a virgin. *Fuck*, he thought, *if the people around Pencil knew that was the case, they would rinse him beyond any level of rinsing that Pencil had ever had.* And now, there were a few rumours appearing in the press and magazines that were even suggesting that the current darling of the great British public might even be gay. Not that Pencil had any issues with gay people, it was just something that Pencil did not want to become known for. Sure, he had OCD, and sure he liked his perfect clothes and his pristine pink shirts, but Pencil was into pussy. More into pussy than anyone could possibly imagine.

So, Pencil would have to fix it, would have to find himself someone to lose his freaking virginity to. But who? Yes, there were always women around, fans and the like, but he would need to be careful; didn't need some broad bedding him and then running off to the press with her story. Perhaps Delroy could sort it for Pencil, find a high-class hooker that Pencil could be seen with, could fuck and dispel the rumours. Yes, that would do. He would get Delroy on the case, get fixed up with some skirt that could be trusted to not go running to the press with her story.

Just then, there was a tap on the door of his small office at the back of Pencil One and Vicki Ruthven entered, asking if Pencil had ten minutes to take a look at a couple of new products she was considering for his stores. Pencil, as always, was in awe of Vicki; couldn't believe how lucky he was having this beautiful MILF work for him. Pencil Kane and Vicki were close, perhaps she could be the one to advise Pencil on his dilemma?

So, as Vicki was showing him this new product, Pencil was hatching a plan in his mind. A plan that would get Vicki to his apartment one day soon, so that Pencil could explain his predicament, get his trusted friend's advice. *Yes,* thought Pencil Kane, *that would be safer than Delroy.* Powell did not need to know that Pencil was still to pop his cork with a broad.

Meanwhile, across London, the loan shark had managed to extricate himself from the van and catch a cab back to his pub, where two of his team were waiting in fear for their boss's arrival, keen to understand where he had been all morning.

'Boss, we've been worried about you,' one of them began as the man entered the pub carrying the bag of cash he had received from Delroy Powell.

'Glad to 'ear it my boy, glad to 'ear it. As you can see, I'm fit and well and 'appy to have settled my little dispute with my footy client.'

'On your own?' asked the second of his team incredulously.

'This may surprise you, boys, but I can still look after myself. I'm still capable of doing a little bit of business without you two goons to wipe my arse.'

'It was just when you texted to say meet you here and you know, when we found your phone run over by a car in your lane, flat as a pancake, we was a little bit worried.'

'Nice to know it, boys, but I am good. Now, someone get me a drink, it's well past whisky time.' The loan shark took his usual seat with his back to the wall and waited for his drink to appear, giving the appearance of being far more in control than he was actually feeling. He had been done over, had got a hiding and been shit scared that his number was up, that he had been for the concrete grave, never to be seen or heard of again. The big question he was now asking himself was what to do about it? Would Powell have done him over like he had said? Did he now need to go to war with the black cunt, destroy the cocky fuck before the news got out and his reputation took a nosedive and his business hit the skids?

With nobody to have this particular conversation with, he decided to bide his time, keep his counsel and see if any noise hit the streets. If it did, war would be his only option. If it didn't, then war was probably his only option. Meanwhile, he decided to enjoy his whisky, lick his wounds and just be grateful for the fact that he, at least, still had the comfort of having a bag containing thirty-five grand in used notes.

Leaving Belmarsh Prison later that afternoon, Julia Hillman was in a better frame of mind than she had been for some considerable time. Her father, delighted with the news of her pregnancy, had agreed to most of the funding she had requested in order to get their charity project off the ground; funding that she had argued was needed to launch the thing properly. She could now begin to implement her plan, which included a press launch in the House of Lords, no less, to be attended by as many famous names as her budget could muster.

Lucas was waiting for his wife by their car, the remnants of a sandwich lunch down the front of his slightly tattered cashmere sweater.

'Hi, honey,' he began. 'How did it go? How was Malcolm?' he continued, opening the passenger door to enable his wife to clamber into the BMW.

'He was fine,' replied Julia Hillman as she leaned over to wipe the crumbs from her husband's chest.

'What did he say about the baby?'

'He was really pleased. Seemed to put him in a good mood regarding the charity proposal.' Julia talked as she adjusted her seat and pulled the seat belt across her large chest, wondering as she did how much bigger she would get during her pregnancy.

'So, did he approve your budget?'

'Most of it. I agreed to make do with eighty percent, let him feel that he had won a little of the battle.'

'And will that be enough for what we have planned?' With his job at RCS now long gone, Lucas was totally focused on working with his wife on her charity project.

'Yes, it will be more than adequate. I had built in a cushion, had anticipated that he would want to adjust the numbers downwards.'

'That's terrific, well done.' Lucas started up the car and began guiding it carefully from the prison car park, keen to be away from this place, to be heading back towards their home in Hampshire.

'Thanks, and I've been thinking about Gary Ruthven...' She changed the subject much to her husband's disquiet. Lucas had been hoping that they could now move away from that particular topic. Put it behind them.

'Really? Do you really want to go there?'

'I do, Lucas, and with him thinking he has got rid of me, I think that there's one last thing that I can do to fuck the shit-head's life good and proper.'

'Really, and what might that be?' Lucas was struggling to concentrate on his driving.

'Yep. I am going to tell Tandy's husband what the fuckers got up to,' she finally stated categorically.

'That doesn't sound like a rational thing to do, Julia. Why would you want to do that?' Lucas was conscious of the fact that he was raising his voice, sounding hysterical.

'Because I can, Lucas, and that will be a checkmate move. End the game once and for all.'

Lucas Hunt looked at his wife, took in the expression on her face and realised properly for the first time that his wife, the woman who was now carrying his child, was more than a tiny bit insane.

'Let me be clear, Julia. You are not going to do that. This thing has got to stop now before it destroys anything else.' Hunt had pulled their BMW to a halt and had turned to look at Julia, trying to determine if she had understood his message.

'Too late for that, Lucas. My mind is made up. Gary fucking Ruthven will regret messing with us for the rest of his shit-head life. Now can you please drive, I need to get home. I've got a lot of work to do.'

Dressing to take Emma out to dinner in the harbour at Sotogrande, Gary Ruthven was reflecting on his afternoon discussion with his daughter. Although sorry that she wanted to quit Leeds University and move back south, he was at least pleased that she was going to continue with her law degree by transferring to Oxford Brookes. All she had to do was achieve decent grades in her forthcoming exams and a place would be hers.

What he was less than pleased about was her brief affair with one of her lecturers. That had come as a bit of a hammer blow. Sure, he knew Emma was good-looking, could turn heads when she entered a room, but one of her lecturers? Vicki would want to sue the university when she found out about it, and she would need to know. Ruthven was long past keeping things secret from his estranged wife, was determined to live his life in *adult* where possible, from now on.

Emma was waiting for him when he eventually came down from his bedroom, keen to get into Sotogrande. Looking forward to her dinner in their favourite Belgian restaurant, to the steak she always had there. Gary had hired a small car and as they drove the ten minutes to the harbour, his daughter turned to a topic he had been keen to avoid.

'So, Dad, are you and Mum intending to get back together sometime soon?'

'Not sure yet, Em. We are planning to get together down here in a couple of weeks, see where to take things from there,' replied Gary honestly.

'Are you going to tell me what happened?'

'Nope. It's between your mum and me, and we need to sort things if we can.'

'After all the stuff that I shared with you this afternoon, you're bringing the shutters down, just like that?' she asked, clicking her fingers for effect.

'Guess I am, Emma. As I said, it's private.'

'Mum told me she wants you back. Said you are still the one.'

'Oh yeah?'

'Yeah, she said that on a scale of one to ten, you are the one.'
Emma laughed at her joke.

'Very good, but I am still not going to tell you what happened.'

'Guess you must have had an affair. What else could it be?'

'Emma, can we change the subject?'

'Mol and I have often speculated; wondered if you got up to
stuff when you were away. Out on your travels with the beautiful
Carole.'

'Emma, I swear, nothing has ever gone on between Carole
and me. She's a great friend and that's all for Christ's sake.'
They had reached the harbour entrance and had to wait for a
lugubrious security guard to lift the security barrier, and allow
them into the narrow street leading to the harbour front.

'Well, I'm still guessing that you failed to keep your pecker in
your pants and got caught.' Gary had found a vacant space and
was glad of the small car as he manoeuvred into the slot.

'Well, you can guess as much as you like, but you are getting
no details from me.'

As they exited the car, Ruthven received a text from Lucas
Hope, asking him to call as a matter of urgency. *Fuck that*, he
thought, as he walked with his daughter towards their restaurant,
nothing can be that urgent.

CHAPTER 31

THURSDAY
27 APRIL 2006

'Hello.'

'Hi, Tandy, it's Gary. Gary Ruthven.'

'Hey, Gary Ruthven. How are you doing?'

'I was very good thanks. I am in Spain having a sabbatical from the business.'

'I heard the "was" in there, is something wrong?'

'Yes, I think something could be very wrong.'

'And that's the reason for your call? Here was me thinking you might be about to invite me for another sleepover at the Hempel.'

'You know that I spoke to you about the bitch who threatened to go to Vicki about what happened between us?'

'The cow whose husband used to work for you?'

'That's the sweetheart.'

'Why do I think that I'm not going to like this, Gary?'

'Well, the thing is, she still has this running vendetta against me. Has tried a few other tricks, like suing me for a hundred grand.'

'Did she win?'

'No, Tandy, she didn't win. She had no claim, no case.'

'Well, that's good to hear, but I'm still scared, Gary. Why the call?'

'The thing is, her old man has just called me and she is

threatening to call your husband. Tell him everything that happened between us.'

'Threatening? What does that mean?'

'Not sure. Lucas, that's her husband, is trying to stop her. Feels the whole thing has gone on long enough.'

'And what if he doesn't manage to stop her, Gary? What if she does call Tomas?'

'That's why I'm calling, Tandy, to alert you. This woman is dangerous.'

'Christ, Gary. What did you do to the woman?'

'That's the mystery. I've hardly ever met her. Probably no more than five times and one of them was at her wedding.'

'Tomas will go ballistic, Gary. The fallout could be nuclear.'

'I'm so sorry, Tandy. I will do everything I can to stop her.'

'Think you better get on with that, if you value your kneecaps, your life.'

'Shit, Tandy. What were we thinking about when we got together?'

'Not sure much thinking came into it, Gary. It was lust, pure lust.'

'Speak for yourself.'

'I was. Make this go away, Gary, before we both live to regret it, whatever *it* was for you.'

It was a lovely morning in London but Lucy Campbell was not enjoying the sunshine as she tried to pick up speed, tried to get the better of the final hill as she neared the end of her run. She was due to run in a charity event with her sister Lesley in Harrogate in three weeks' time and was determined to be fit enough to do the thing properly. She was in no doubt that Lesley would be in training, would be determined to beat her little sister and Lucy did not want that to happen.

She had tried to persuade Paul to join her on her morning

runs, but the ex-footballer claimed that his knee was no longer capable of coping with the pounding that running entailed. As she topped the hill and began her final sprint towards her imaginary finishing line, she hoped that her future husband was not planning on letting himself go to seed, like the other fat ex-footballers she saw occasionally on television.

Letting herself into the flat, she could hear Paul in the kitchen preparing their breakfast, Sky Sports News blasting from the television. Seeing her enter the kitchen, he killed the volume and closed the gap between them and took her in his arms, her sweat putting damp patches on his white T-shirt.

'God, you turn me on when you look like that. It makes me want to strip you and lift you into the shower and have my wicked way with you,' he began, kissing the top of her head.

'And you're hesitating because?' she replied, taking him by the hand and leading him through to his large bedroom.

Thirty minutes later, both now late for work, they bid each other farewell and went their separate ways. As Paul walked, he thought of their wedding, which was now scheduled for October in the beautiful Rudding Park in Harrogate. Never before had he thought that he would be looking forward with such anticipation to his wedding, to taking any woman as his wife. But with Lucy, October could not come quickly enough. He then turned his thoughts to his business and smiled at the thought of the ridiculous compensation that he had just negotiated on behalf of Pencil Kane following his retirement. Realistically, the young man did not need to do another day of work in his life; he could live comfortably from the interest alone. That, of course, assumed that interest rates remained at current levels and that was not something that his brother was prepared to bet on.

Just then, his mobile rang in his pocket and taking it out, he was surprised to see that it was his dad calling.

Vicki Ruthven had been surprised by Pencil's suggestion that they meet that morning at his apartment to go over their merchandising forecast for the autumn season. So, she had taken great care to dress for the situation, make sure that the young man would still find her attractive. She often caught him looking at her and knew that he secretly lusted after her. For her part, she felt that she was now over her crush on the boy, had put her erotic dream about them fucking on the mirror-topped table to the back of her mind and focused on reconciling with Gary.

Pencil was in grey shorts and a navy Arsenal training top when he let her into his apartment, thankful to her for getting to his place on time. He offered her tea or coffee and eventually led her to a couple of big white leather sofas that dominated the room. The place was immaculate. The perfect pad of the OCD bachelor.

'Thanks for coming here, Vicki. Pencil is kinda hoping that you can help him with something that he needs to fix, all confidential like.'

'Oh yes?' replied Vicki, a little surprised by this opening.

'Pencil is not sure where to start, is thinking that this might not be a great idea.'

'Why not try me? I'm sure it can't be that difficult.'

'Okay, Pencil wants, Pencil needs, some advice and guidance on a personal matter and thought you would be the ideal person to help.' Vicki smiled. Kane was clearly struggling to get to the purpose of this little chat.

'You see, Vicki, Pencil is still a virgin and needs your advice about how to rectify that thing.' He could no longer meet her eyes, was now totally embarrassed.

Vicki was not sure how to react; this was perhaps the most bizarre thing that had ever happened to her. She tried to remember that thing that Gary always told the kids when they were going for interviews and the like. What was it? *Think, breathe, speak* – yes that was it. So, for a few moments she tried to think and breathe before eventually trying to speak.

'Okay, and how do you think I might be able to help?'

'Well, Pencil trusts you, is sure that you won't just rinse him.'

'Right, so why don't you just go out and get yourself a girlfriend like everyone else? Take your time, go through the motions?' she asked as gently as possible.

'Because Pencil doesn't want a girlfriend, Pencil just wants to lose his cherry,' he replied, looking all of twelve by now, probably regretting having ever started this discussion.

'Okay, so what about a hooker? Get Delroy to fix you up,' she suggested.

'Pencil thought about that, but didn't want Delroy knowing about the virginity thing.'

'Well, he doesn't need to know does he? Just tell him that you want him to organize a no-strings attached fuck.'

'But surely she would know, the hooker like?'

'Not sure it works like that, Pencil. No one needs to know, just tell her you want her to take charge, do what you're told. Like painting by numbers.'

'You sure? See Pencil don't need any negative shit getting in the papers.'

Vicki then had her light bulb moment – this was what it was all about. Pencil was afraid of the potential publicity if things went wrong. Suddenly she felt sorry for the young man, the young man who had been through hell and done so much of his growing up in public over the last ten or so months. Then she had an idea and asked Pencil if she could use his bathroom.

When she came back, she had stripped down to her sexy underwear and when Pencil saw her, his eyes almost popped out of their sockets. Crossing the room to where he was sitting, she took his hand before whispering, 'Come with me, Pencil. It can be our little secret.' And with that she led the limping young man to his bedroom, his cock already rock hard in his shorts.

'Let me be absolutely clear, Julia, you are not going to do this. It is time to put this stupid Gary feud to bed.' Lucas was standing in their remodelled kitchen and had been rehearsing his little speech all morning, ever since he had plucked up the courage to call Ruthven and tell him of his wife's threat.

'And what will you do if I don't, Lucas? Come on, this will be good,' Julia goaded him.

'I will not let you bring ruin on this family. You have caused enough bad energy and I will not let you continue to do so.'

'You will not let me?' Julia Hillman let out a laugh. 'You will not fucking let me? Don't be a dopey fuck, Lucas. Since when did you start wearing the trousers in this relationship?'

'Since you became pregnant with my child. And if you defy me on this, then I will pack my bags and be out of this house in ten minutes.'

'Pregnant with your child? That's a cracker, Lucas. Pregnant with your child thanks to the clinic and a wedge of my father's money.' Julia stopped, suddenly aware that she had crossed a line, said something that she now wished she could withdraw. His expression said it all. She had very probably just ruined one of the best moments in her husband's life and all because she wanted revenge on Gary Ruthven. And for what?

'Lucas, I am so sorry, that was quite unforgivable of me,' she began, trying to close the gap between them, wanting her husband to take her in his arms and accept her apology.

Lucas moved away from her before replying, his face white with fury.

'Promise me that you will bury this Ruthven vendetta once and for all and we can discuss the rest later.'

'I promise and I'm so sorry for what I said about our baby.'

'As I said, we can talk about that later. Right now, I need to go for a walk, get some fresh air.' And with that Lucas Hunt left the kitchen, pulled on a light gilet and left the house, leaving his wife feeling absolutely distraught.

Paul Ruthven tried to connect with his brother, but his phone kept going to voicemail. He then tried Vicki with the same result. Jesus, didn't anyone answer their mobiles these days? He then called Lucy who was probably still on the Underground and asked her to call him urgently. Just as he reached the entrance to his office, it was Lucy who returned his call first.

'Hey, thanks for getting back. I've just had my dad on the phone. My mum has been rushed into hospital, they think she's had a stroke.'

'Christ, Paul. I'm sorry. Any more details?'

'No, he's at the hospital now, waiting for more information.'

'Okay, let's wait and see. I'll keep my phone switched on. Call me as soon as you hear from him and we can take things from there. Stay calm.'

'Thank you,' replied Paul, cutting the connection, conscious of the fact that she hadn't said anything reassuring like don't worry, things will be alright.

His office manager got him a strong cup of tea and he then went to his office meeting room and pretended to be going about his business as normal. In reality he was just thinking about his mother and their pretty difficult relationship, wishing to God that he had been a kinder, more patient son who had visited his parents more often. Thoughts and memories flooded back. Memories of his childhood in Scotland as he tried to live up to his talented and clever big brother and his parents' obvious expectations. Yes, football had been his escape, his chance to shine at something Gary had not been good at, get some much wanted praise from his parents. However, no matter what he did, what he achieved, he still got nothing from his mum. His mum who just wanted him to be like Gary and go to university; get a degree and a profession. In her eyes, he had always been the second son, and as far as he was aware that had never changed. He had secretly hoped that things might have been different with Lucy, his beautiful and brilliant wife-to-be; that she would have more than met his mother's standards, her expectations that she had of her sons' life partners. And now even that might be gone for good. Christ, she might not even be alive for his wedding in six months' time. Just then his mobile rang. It was Gary returning his call from Spain.

Pencil's initiation into the world of full-blown adult sex lasted for almost two hours, and Vicki had to admit that the experience had, eventually, been quite enjoyable. Sure, his first stab – she winced at the term – had ended somewhat prematurely as the experience had obviously been a bit too much for a young man used to wanking along to porn movies. However, with a little gentle coaching and advice, the boy seemed destined to become something of a natural and sensitive lover. And, she thought as she sat in the back of a cab that was heading to Marylebone station, his powers of recovery were quite remarkable. Before leaving she had agreed with Pencil that what had happened had to be considered a one and only occurrence and he had seemed incredibly appreciative and sensitive about the situation.

Paying the taxi, she entered the bustle of Marylebone station and spent a few moments checking the large screens for the time of the next train to Beaconsfield. With ten minutes to spare, she bought a copy of *The Times* from WHSmith before grabbing a one-shot latte from the AMT kiosk, passed through the ticket barrier and headed for platform 4. It was just after 2pm, so she would be home in under an hour and would have plenty of time to compose herself before Molly got home from school. Walking along the platform, she felt she was walking with a new swagger, conscious that a few men were admiring her figure, her smart appearance, and was beginning to feel just a tad guilty that she was loving the moistness in her pants. Now she was even with Gary, she could concentrate on their reconciliation, forgive his affair with Tandy on the grounds that she now had her own sordid, sexy little secret.

Rummaging in her large Mulberry handbag, she found her phone, considering it safe to rejoin the outside world. The number of missed calls and voicemail messages was a surprise. Couldn't a girl spend the morning breaking in one of the country's most famous young bachelors without being hounded? She smiled and dialled Gary's number first. Moments later, she was sitting on the half-empty train, trying to come to terms with the sad and disturbing news of her mother-in-law's stroke.

Medically, Catherine Ruthven could recover many of her pre-stroke faculties and could indeed live for many years. However, as Lucy Campbell received a brief summary of Catherine's condition from Paul later that afternoon, she thought it was probably best that she begin to prepare him and the rest of his family for the worst.

'Okay, to begin with I think we should plan to be on a plane to Scotland early this evening. I'm no expert in this area, but I think that you and Gary need to brace yourself for the worst. The next twenty-four hours will be critical, so you should be there for your dad.'

'Fine. Let me see what flights are available. Are you sure you want to come?'

'Of course I want to come. Let me arrange cover and I'll meet you back at your place by three-thirty.'

'Thanks, Lucy. I'll get onto the flights straight away.'

'I think that's best. Have you spoken to Gary?'

'I have. He'd been out on the fairways of San Roque following Colin Montgomery when I was trying earlier,' explained Paul.

'Sounds like fun. And Vicki?'

'Gary tracked her down. She had been in a business meeting all morning.'

'Sounds like less fun. Okay, I'm going to go and get organised. See you at half past three.'

Hanging up his office telephone, Paul reflected momentarily on how focused and structured Lucy was in these situations. There was little to no time for sentimentality, just clear-headed thinking, practical and professional. He then briefed his office manager on flight requirements and began checking on his diary for tomorrow. Pencil had asked him to go with him to the Arsenal training complex at London Colney, where he was planning to say his goodbyes to his teammates and the Arsenal staff who had been so good with the young man for the last ten years in general, the last ten months in particular. Sorry that he would have to miss that, he called Pencil to explain the situation, surprised that the young man was still at home and not out overseeing things at one of his stores. That done, and flight tickets booked, he packed his things away for the day and headed for his apartment to pack some things and await Lucy's return from Whitechapel.

What was it his dad used to say to him when he was plotting and planning his young football life? It was something like 'life is what happens when you are busy planning your life', and Paul could think of nothing more suitable to explain what had happened that day.

Pencil rode in the back of the car with Delroy Powell, headed for Pencil Four, and could still not bring himself to believe what had happened that morning with Vicki Ruthven. After an embarrassing start, when Pencil had not been able to control himself and had shot all over his bed covers, the woman had been great; had made the thing seem natural and had gradually given him everything he could've wanted, even more. Now Pencil felt cool again. His cork had been popped; he was no longer a virgin.

'So, Pencil, how you feelin' about being an ex-footballer, man?' asked Delroy, bringing Pencil Kane back to the present.

'Guess that's what Pencil is now, Delroy. Hadn't really thought about it. Pencil is good. Busy seems to be the answer to everythin', so the stores will just have to be Pencil's new football, his replacement. How's your Crew business doin'?' He had been too busy to keep up-to-date with Powell's business venture recently, although he was aware that Delroy seemed a bit more distant, seemed to have much on his mind.

'It's good. Might be a bit more to it than I'd first thought; bit more dangerous if you get my meaning,' replied Powell, looking out of the smoked windows at the London traffic.

'How so?' asked Pencil.

'Well, all football boys aren't as smart as you, Pencil. Not clever with their money, man. Seem to go from one fuck-up to the next.'

'Like what, man? Give Pencil an example.'

Delroy then explained the situation that he had just had with the loan shark, avoiding naming names, but giving Pencil all the other details. Kane sat silent for a while before responding to what his old friend had just told him.

'But you were bluffing about killing the fucker, right?' he asked eventually.

'Not too sure if I was, man. It was tricky and luckily it didn't get there.'

'Come on, man. You were going to top the fucker and have him buried in concrete? Jesus, Delroy. Really?'

Delroy caught his driver's eye in the mirror, aware that he was listening to every word being exchanged between him and Pencil in the back seats of the car; aware that he needed to say the right thing, give the right answer if his credibility was to remain intact.

'Guess, if the fucker had got out of hand, man; it wasn't a time for empty threats,' he replied.

'Pencil needs to know, Delroy. Would you have topped the fucker?' Kane had turned in his seat and was looking Powell straight in the face.

'No other option, Pencil, and the world would be a better place.'

'Pencil needs to think about this, Delroy. This is mad fuck dangerous stuff.'

'It is, but look at it this way. If those cunts that tried to extort your dosh knew that there would've been serious fucking ructions if they got caught, that matters would be dealt with firmly, think they'd have tried?'

'Not sure, Delroy. The stupid fucks got caught anyway,' reflected Pencil, following Delroy's point but still uncomfortable with this shocking turn of events, still seriously worried about Pencil's perfect public reputation and the damage this sort of shit could do to it.

'Well, I'll tell you, Pencil, they'd have stayed well away from you. We need to protect ourselves from scum like them; scum like the fucking loan shark.'

'Shit, Delroy. You're really saying you'd have topped the fucker. That what you're really saying, man?'

'Guess I am, Pencil, guess I am. And you know what?'

'What, Delroy?'

'I really think it would've been the right thing to do.'

Pencil was not cool with this, but didn't reply; felt that he needed to keep Pencil's thoughts to himself, probably ask Paul Ruthven for his advice on this scary shit. Pencil was happy that the police were there to protect him; didn't want no gangster shit growing up around him and his business.

Paul and Lucy had found a space in car park B of Edinburgh's sparkling new Royal Infirmary hospital in the city's Little France district. The powers that be had decided that it made sense to bring all of the city's hospital provision and the University of Edinburgh Medical Faculty under one gigantic roof on the southern outskirts of Scotland's capital.

'Looks like a bloody airport,' observed Ruthven as they hiked towards the main entrance from the massive car park area, having come to the hospital straight from Edinburgh airport following their flight from London Heathrow.

'It's the way things are going these days I'm afraid,' offered Dr Lucy Campbell, who was privately rather sad at the demise of her old hospital in the city centre, a site that was now being turned into luxury apartments.

'Mmm,' replied Ruthven. 'Best not judge the book by its cover then.' He took Lucy's hand and they entered the new hospital via a couple of large swing doors and followed the signs for reception, passing as they walked an RBS bank, a WHSmith, a hairdressers and a couple of coffee shop franchises.

'It's even like an airport inside,' he laughed as they approached a massive reception desk, his humour a cover for the nervous anxiety he was feeling in the pit of his gut.

At the desk, Lucy took control, knowing how these places worked; how to get themselves through the complicated labyrinth of corridors and onto their scheduled meeting with his dad.

Five minutes later, they were ushered into a small room in the intensive care ward where Paul hugged his ashen-faced father, who looked as though he had aged ten years since they had last seen him. After a few moments of general greeting, it was Lucy who decided to get to the point; ask the questions that were in the air between them.

'So, what's the latest on Catherine's condition?'

'The doctor is with her now, says that he'll come and brief

us in a wee while,' replied Peter Ruthven quietly, his lawyer authority seemingly drained from him in this big, unfamiliar place.

'Okay. And is she still unconscious?' continued Lucy.

'She is. Well, at least she was an hour or so ago.'

'Have you heard anything from Gary?' It was Paul's turn for an update.

'He called me from Malaga a couple of hours ago. He is aiming to be here first thing tomorrow with Emma who was in Spain with him,' replied Peter. 'And Vicki is planning to be here with Molly around lunchtime tomorrow. Where are you all going to sleep?'

'Don't worry about that, Dad. We'll get things sorted later. Now, tell us what happened.'

'Not sure really. We were both up early as usual. I was getting ready for the office and I think your mum was busying herself outside with the dustbins. Today is collection day.' Peter was answering them in a daze, obviously in shock at what had gone on, the sudden illness of his long-term partner.

'When she came in, she said she was feeling a bit odd, was having difficulty talking and couldn't move her right arm. I didn't know what to do. She seemed to be getting gradually worse so I dialled 999 who were great, very calm and gave me instructions while we waited for the ambulance to arrive. In the ambulance, she seemed confused and agitated. When we got here, she was drifting in and out of consciousness and not responding to anyone. They then sent Catherine for a CAT scan, which has shown a bleed on the brain.'

Just then the door opened and a slim Asian doctor, stethoscope round his neck, entered the room, introducing himself to Paul and Lucy and asking them to take a seat. The doctor then, with brisk efficiency, briefed the small group on Catherine's condition, explaining that she had suffered a major bleed in her brain that was causing pressure that was not, at this time, amenable to surgery. He then explained that Catherine was being admitted to the stroke unit where she would be kept comfortable, supported with oxygen and a drip, and that the next twenty-four hours were going to be critical to the prognosis. Lucy then asked a couple of direct medical questions, enabling the doctor to be quite precise about what he considered the likely outcome.

The bottom line was harsh but straightforward. Catherine Ruthven's chances of survival were at best slim, that her chances of making any sort of recovery were virtually non-existent. The doctor left with Lucy, who was keen to have a private word as Paul turned and once again embraced his father who was obviously trying very hard to hold back tears, his marriage in tatters, his life as it had been only that morning in ruin.

CHAPTER 32   FRIDAY 28 APRIL 2006

Gary Ruthven parked his car opposite the golf clubhouse and walked across the now deserted public putting green and found a bench, dedicated to some long-gone husband and wife, and sat taking in the view of North Berwick beach and distant harbour.

Out to sea stood the famous Bass Rock, populated to capacity by seabirds the species of which he had long forgotten. Ruthven recalled a childhood boat trip around the giant rock with Paul, his dad, and his Granny Ruthven. A small woman with her grey hair tightly bunched behind her head, Gary had forgotten how worried his gran had been that the boys, if they didn't sit still, might cause the boat to capsize.

How easy it had been for him to leave this beautiful place behind as he had chased his dream in London, had made a new life for himself and not given much thought about who or what he had left behind. And now his mother lay unconscious in a hospital bed, possibly – no, probably – never to recover enough for Gary to tell her how grateful he was for everything that she and his dad had done for him, to tell her how much he loved her.

A young woman had entered the beach at the harbour end and was walking purposefully, throwing a stick for her dog, a large black lab, as it frolicked among the breakers. The woman looked relaxed and happy, appeared fully in the moment with her dog and Ruthven was suddenly jealous of her freedom, her apparent happiness. That said, it was probably just a myth, the woman's happiness. She had probably just had a row with a husband or partner and stormed from their home with her dog, now walking to calm herself down, asking herself what the fuck she was doing spending her life with such a loser. Ruthven wondered when it was that he had become so cynical, so dark about things, so fed up with his life, so tired. Christ, he had been on vacation for three weeks, should be feeling the benefit of having his batteries recharged, but no, he couldn't even enjoy the view, enjoy watching a beautiful young woman walk her dog on this lovely beach without thinking the worst.

Slowly standing, he walked back towards his car. He was due to collect Vicki and Molly from the airport and take them to the hospital and join the rest of the family as they waited patiently for the next bulletin on his mother's condition, her tenuous grip on life. Sitting in his hired BMW, he checked his phone for any messages and answered a couple of texts. As he started the car, the young woman with the black Labrador walked past and smiled a friendly, pretty smile at Gary. It was a smile that broke his heart, brought a deluge of tears to his eyes.

There was an undoubted buzz about Arsenal's training complex at London Colney later that day. The club had reached the European Champions League Final for the first time in its history and were due to play world famous Barcelona in Paris in just nineteen days' time. And, with only three Premier League fixtures remaining, the season's grand finale could not come quickly enough.

Pencil Kane had requested that his farewell to staff and players be kept low key, but with the famous Pencil, that was a lot easier said than done. For a start, the BBC had insisted that the omnipresent documentary crew be there, and there was a fairly large press contingent awaiting his arrival with Delroy Powell, an arrival that had been timed to coincide with the end of that day's training session.

Pencil was nervous and had not been sure what to wear for the occasion, eventually deciding on his Arsenal tracksuit and trainers. He was met by the head coach and after a private meeting in his office, was led to one of the players' lounges where a large group of players and coaching people were there to greet him. As he entered, a music system was turned on and began pumping out the theme tune to Pencil's TV documentary series. Players and staff were then on their feet applauding Pencil as he entered, limping without the aid of a stick.

The head coach then said a few kind words in his heavily accented English, before handing the microphone to Pencil and inviting him to say a few words.

'Pencil has not got much to say really, other than that this is the saddest day of my life so far. Yes, even sadder than 7/7 as back then Pencil still believed that this,' he stopped to indicate the entire training complex with his waving left hand, 'Arsenal thing would still be Pencil's life. But life moves on, and it's not to be for Pencil. So, let me finish with three things. First, a massive thanks to our fantastic head coach. You have been like a father to me and Pencil will never forget that. Second, thanks to the rest of the coaching staff; you've taken Pencil the boy and turned him into Pencil the man.' One of the players then shouted, 'When did that happen?' causing loud laughter.

'Be clear, boys. Pencil is now a man!'

'We've seen your knob in the showers, Pencil. You sure about that?' Another burst of laughter.

'Anyway, to all the coaches, a big thanks.' A burst of applause then followed before Kane could continue. 'Finally, I want to thank the rest of you wankers, for your great banter, support and encouragement. And, if you don't come back from Paris with that giant trophy, be fucking careful when you open your lockers next season, that rat trick really worked for me.' Pencil then handed the microphone back to the head coach who had to wait until the cheers had stopped before he could present Pencil with a small silver trophy from the club.

Pencil then spent the next hour mixing with the gathering, having his photograph taken with so many of the players, most of them knowing that whatever they might achieve in their football careers, they would never be as famous as young Pencil Kane.

Catherine Ruthven's condition had deteriorated rapidly causing her to lapse into a fully comatose state later that afternoon, and despite the best efforts of the top class medical team in the Edinburgh Royal Infirmary, she was declared dead just after 4pm.

Gary Ruthven, his estranged wife Vicki, and their daughters Emma and Molly, were there along with Paul Ruthven, Dr Lucy Campbell, and Catherine's distraught husband, Peter, when the heart-breaking news that they had all feared was confirmed.

An hour later, the shell-shocked Ruthven family repaired in a convoy of three cars to Rose Cottage, the family home in Manse Road, Dirleton, east of Edinburgh. Gary had driven his father's car with Molly, while Vicki and Emma had travelled with Peter in Gary's hired car allowing Lucy and Paul to hurry ahead and get the house open, a kettle on and a few sandwiches made.

Later, it was somehow decided that Emma and Molly would take their dad's old room, Paul and Lucy would have Paul's room, while Gary and Vicki had booked themselves into the famous Greywalls Hotel just a few minutes up the road in Gullane. No one seemed to question these arrangements or the fact that Gary and Vicki had actually been living apart for months.

With sleeping arrangements made and tea and sandwiches served, the small group then had to develop a plan for dealing with the tragedy that had so suddenly befallen them. So, as Peter Ruthven went off to have a shower, and probably spend some private time grieving for his dead wife, Vicki and Lucy sat in the small dining room putting together a list of things that needed to be attended to. This allowed Gary and Paul to take themselves for a walk, out of the house and around the village green to the Castle Inn where they both had a very much needed wee dram of whisky, still reeling at the thought of Catherine's death, no need for any conversation between them. Two very close brothers silently stunned, neither of them sure what to say or sure what this sudden death might mean for them or their family.

JUNE 2006

CHAPTER 33 MONDAY 5 JUNE 2006

It was a pleasantly warm and sunny late morning as Tomas Brozek stepped out of his Bentley Continental and walked up the steps to the entrance of the world famous RAC Club in central London. A second generation Polish immigrant, Brozek was very proud of what his family had achieved since his father had arrived as a penniless refugee back in 1942. Dressed, as always, in his immaculate suit, white shirt and silk tie, he cut a dashing, handsome figure as he entered the building and made his way to the downstairs bar for his lunchtime meeting with one of his oldest friends.

Ordering a refreshing Gordon's & Tonic from the bar, he found a quiet table and sat to await his friend's arrival. It had not been a good morning and he was considering his options, processing how he should react to the information he had received by text only an hour earlier. At forty-four, he had known that Tandy would be a challenge when he had married her eight years earlier. Fifteen years his junior, from a wealthy background and with a considerable reputation as a wild child, he had nevertheless been happy to put the divorce from his first wife behind him and enjoy the roller coaster ride that she was. Her occasional flirtations and affairs were tolerable in that they allowed him the degree of freedom that his first marriage had not, but the deal had always been clear – privacy was paramount.

And now this woman had texted him to tell him that his beautiful, sexy and fun-loving wife had managed to get herself pregnant and had aborted the child that she had conceived during her fling with Gary Ruthven, a guy he had met and liked. Not that it mattered who Tandy screwed. As long as she always came back to him, why did he need to know? What was in this woman's head that led her to think that she should take it upon herself to inform him of Tandy's indiscretion? Seeing his old friend arrive, he decided that he was not angry with his wife. God, he wished that she had felt able to come to him and share her problem. Nor was he angry with Ruthven. After all, what healthy man could refuse his beautiful wife when she turned her charms in his direction? No, he realised, he was absolutely furious with this Julia Hillman woman, this asshole who had taken it upon herself to pour her poison onto his mobile phone. Rising to shake his friend's hand, he made a mental note to himself to get one of his people to track this bitch down, dig the dirt on her, before he would decide on what action to take against her.

Detective Chief Inspector Colm Elliot was on vacation and had persuaded Susan to join him in a somewhat nostalgic trip to the north Antrim coast in Northern Ireland. There, he planned to visit some of his few remaining relatives and play the renowned golf courses of Royal Portrush and its near neighbours. He had rented a lovely old cottage overlooking the sea near Ballycastle and as he waited for Susan to get ready for their day, he sat poring over a report that had just been published on the failings of the emergency services during the 7/7 London bombings the previous year. That the report was damning did not surprise him too much. After all, what was to be expected? Sure, preparations could be made, contingencies planned for, but when four young

British men decide to go into the London transport system and blow themselves and fifty-two others to death, what planning could be made for that?

Elliot and Bellamy were now spending about half of their time on duty working with their research group on the suicidal suicide bombers project, and were building a considerable reputation for their provocative and thoughtful insights. The project had given Elliot a new lease of life at work, had made him realise that the grey hairs now flecking at his temples were of some value. His lifetime experiencing the trauma of human cruelty could at least be put to some good use.

'So, how do I look?' Susan had emerged from the cottage bedroom, dressed in cropped chinos and a pale pink cable cashmere sweater, ready for a walk on the beach and their visit later to Elliot's brother, Liam, at the care home he had been living in since his alcoholism had ruined his marriage, his business, and his relationship with his kids.

'You look great,' began Elliot, closing the report and standing, ready to be out in the fresh summer's day.

'You think I'll be warm enough?'

'It's Ireland, Susan. Best bet is to cater for all weather possibilities. You know what they say over here. If you can see the mountains it's raining, if you can't, it's about to rain.' Elliot smiled and kissed Susan on the lips before adding, 'So, best take a rain jacket.'

They drove the mile or so from their cottage to the town and parked near the tennis courts. From there, they crossed the River Margy by a footbridge, stopping halfway across to watch fish jumping in the centre of the river. Stopping to remove their shoes, they then walked the crescent-shaped beach, set against the beautiful backdrop of the Fairhead cliff formation away in the distance. At the end of the beach, they stopped to take in the rock formations that were known as Pans Rock and the Devil's Churn, with its scary underwater tunnel.

Returning to their car, they decided on a cup of tea from a seafront café before their visit to Liam, a visit that Colm was feeling anxious about. It had been a long time since he had seen his big brother, and he was not holding out much hope of a loving reunion.

The care home warden had told them that Liam was out sitting in the garden and after a few minutes they eventually tracked him down to a bench with views over open countryside, farmland speckled with the occasional sheep. Susan stood back as Colm tentatively approached the balding and wizened man that his brother had become, ravaged by the addiction that he had inherited from their father.

'Liam?' he opened quietly, shocked to see the blank look on his brother's face when he turned in response.

'Who's asking?' came the grumpy, near aggressive response.

'It's Colm, your brother.'

'Ah, don't have a brother. Did once but he left me behind long ago.'

'Well, I'm here now, Liam, and have brought my friend to meet you.' Susan stepped towards the man and offered her hand.

'Hi, Liam. I'm Susan, Colm's partner.' Liam Elliot looked Susan up and down. Once a womaniser, always a womaniser.

'Always had an eye for a good-looking woman did Colm. Glad he's not lost the knack.'

'So, Liam, how are you? How are things here?' Elliot junior tried to find some space on the bench but his brother was not for moving, not for giving ground.

'Me? I am just champion, champion of the world. In fact, luckiest fucker alive, that's me.'

'Glad to hear it. They looking after you okay?'

'What the fuck do you care?'

'Well, that's no way to talk in front of a lady, is it, Liam?'

'If she don't like it, she can fuck off and take you with her. I didn't ask you to visit now, did I?'

'Thought you might like to come out with us for the afternoon. Have lunch somewhere nice, be civil to one another, like we used to be as boys, as young men.' Colm was determined to try as Susan watched this sad scene with a hint of tears in her eyes.

'I'm just fine here, little brother. Not one for going out to lunch these days. So unless you've brought me a nice wee bottle of Bushmills, suggest you take your bonny girl there and fuck off back to wherever it is you came from.' At that, Liam Elliot turned away from his visitors and began staring out towards the fields once again.

'Are you sure, Liam?' But his brother ignored the question.

They hardly spoke on the way back to Ballycastle, Susan realising how painful the encounter with his brother had been for Colm. Before they had left the care home, Elliot had checked that things were okay with the warden and had settled the bill for any extra expenses that Liam had incurred over and above the expensive monthly direct debit that he paid for his brother's keep.

Meanwhile, back in London, Julia Hillman and Lucas Hunt were emerging from their Harley Street clinic into mid-afternoon sunshine, almost unable to contain their mutual excitement about the news that they had just been given, indeed seen with their very own eyes.

'Twins, how about that?' asked Lucas, taking hold of his wife's arm and leading her down the street, not really too sure about where they were actually headed.

'Bloody hell, Lucas. That's come as a bit of a surprise, bloody twins.' Julia Hillman was walking fast, already compiling a list of things that she needed to reconsider now that she knew that she was having two babies and not just the one she had been planning for.

'Where shall we go? How about tea at the Ritz, treat ourselves.' Lucas was as partial to tea and cake as he was to tea and Hobnobs.

'We'd never get into the Ritz, Lucas. They've got that shit-head booking system in the summer, that or they'd be overrun by tourists. Let's get ourselves home, go over our preparation for the launch on Wednesday. Shit, how on earth are we going to be able to launch and run the charity now that we're going to have twins?'

'Do you think we should have asked him for the sex of the babies?' Hunt asked, tripping on a paving stone and almost pulling his wife to the ground as he stumbled.

'Jesus,Lucas. Can't you go anywhere or do anything without having an accident?'

'Sorry, honey. I'm just a little bit excited.'

'Well, be careful.'

Their charity, StartOver, was due for its public launch in the House of Lords in two days' time and Julia Hillman had roped in an aging television actor, known for his political campaigning, and a former Conservative MP to front the launch. Press packs had been prepared and sent out and eighty hand-picked guests and initial sponsors had been invited to attend. Malcolm Hillman had been upset when his daughter had told him of her grand plan for the launch, but there was little that he could do to get Julia back under control from his cell in Belmarsh.

Suddenly keen to get home, Lucas hailed a cab and soon they were entering Waterloo station and searching for the time of the next train to Petersfield. As they stood on the station concourse, they made an incongruous couple, Lucas all dishevelled and untucked, Julia with her smart suit and baby bump already beginning to show. Looking at her husband, her heart suddenly skipped a beat. What the hell would he say or indeed do when he found out that she had eventually sent the text to Tandy Brozek's husband informing him of her disastrous affair with Gary Ruthven? Indeed, what would he say about the war she was now waging on Vicki Ruthven and her young boss? Thinking of the twins she was now carrying, she decided that perhaps it was now time to put her hatred of Ruthven to bed for good and quietly hoped that it was not too late to do so.

'Hello, Gary. It's Tandy, can you talk?'

'I can. How are you?'

'I am well, going off on vacation next week.'

'Somewhere nice, I assume.'

'Friend's yacht off the Greek islands. Should be great.'

'Sounds fun, but I guess that's not why you called.'

'No, although it is always nice to hear your voice.'

'That feeling is mutual. What can I do for you?'

'Just a heads up, to let you know your bitch has contacted Tomas about us.'

'You're kidding me?'

'Nope. Sent him a text this morning.'

'Christ, I'm sorry, Tandy. How was he?'

'Very calm actually, with me anyway. Same goes for you, although I wouldn't like to be in her shoes.'

'Really? Why do you say that?'

'He's got some people finding out about her. He's as mad as I've ever seen him.'

'But you say that he's okay with us?'

'So he says, but I don't think you should expect a Christmas card.'

'But Julia Hillman?'

'Mmm, not sure he's made his mind up yet. We'll see.'

'But you're okay?'

'Yes, Gary. I'm okay.'

'Really glad to hear it.'

'Be good, Gary. Bye.'

'Bye, Tandy.'

CHAPTER 34   TUESDAY 6 JUNE 2006

Heads were turning as Carole King walked between the busy tables to join Gary Ruthven for an early breakfast in the Wolseley in Piccadilly that fine Tuesday morning. He had wanted to get Carole alone and away from the prying ears of the office to share with her the news of the decision that he and Vicki had made the previous weekend. Their food ordered, coffee and tea in front of them, Gary got quickly to the point.

'Thanks for the early start. I wanted you to know before it gets out elsewhere that Vicki and I have decided to get back together,' he stated calmly across the small table.

'God, Gary. I'm really pleased to hear that. And you're both sure? Certain it's the right thing to do?' Carole reached across the table and put her hands on top of his, a gesture of caring for her great friend.

'We've been apart for a long time, had the chance to get used to being without each other, and now feel it's right to give things another go.'

'And your stupid fling with Tandy what's her name?'

'All in the past I hope, but if things had been right between us in the first place, I guess I wouldn't have been too keen on a bunk-up in the Hempel.'

'Mmm, you could be right. How's Vicki and the girls?'

'Vicki is pretty calm about it. Wants us to do it gradually, take things one step at a time. Make sure we're doing the right thing.'

'So, when will you move back to Beaconsfield?'

'Not sure yet.'

'And the girls?'

'They don't know yet. We're going to wait a couple of weeks, tell them together once Vicki and I have got used to the idea.'

'When did you realise that getting back together would be okay?'

'Funnily enough, it was on the day that my mum died. We stayed the night together at Greywalls. Were kinda sad about things, but both felt that maybe it was time to try again. Obviously, we then had to focus on the funeral and all that stuff, so decided to park things for a while.'

A silence fell between them as they tackled their breakfast, trying to avoid getting crumbs everywhere. After all, they both had a long day at RCS ahead of them. Eventually, it was Gary who restarted their chat.

'What are you thinking right now?' It was a question that they often challenged each other with.

'Truthfully?'

'I hope so,' replied Ruthven.

'I was thinking about us. Thinking about what might have been if this had happened a couple of years back,' offered Carole, her beautiful big eyes staring at Gary.

'Ah well, that seems to be the story of my life. Full of what might have beens.'

'I guess, but you do know how much I loved you back then, before Dan came on the scene?'

'I guess I chose not to think about it. Felt it was too risky to do so.'

'Yes, I suppose it was.'

'And now we'll never know.'

'Know?'

'What might have been, Carole.'

Pencil was not a happy bunny. In fact, Pencil might have been better described as being fucking furious. He was standing outside the new Pencil Five store in central Birmingham looking at the damage that some twat had caused to his new window. The store was due to open in three days' time and some pathetic graffiti artist had taken it upon himself to call into question Pencil's sexuality by covering the majority of the glass with the legend: 'Is Pencil a poof? Does the Pope wear a hat?'

Getting Delroy Powell on speed dial, Pencil waited for his security guy to answer his call, wondering, as he waited, where all this anti-Pencil shit was coming from.

'Delroy, Pencil's got a quick question for you,' he began on getting connected.

'Hey, Pencil, my friend. And what might that be?'

'Pencil would like to double-check that he's paid his bill this month.'

'What bill, Pencil?'

'The fucking hefty bill that Pencil pays the DP Crew for personal and fucking premises security, that's what fucking bill, Delroy,' Kane near shouted down the line. He then went on to explain what had happened and demanded that Delroy get his ass up to Birmingham and get an investigation underway, that he find the crazy fucker who was casting these shitty aspersions against Pencil.

With that call over, Pencil entered the store. The place was looking great, would be a terrific new addition to his rapidly expanding chain. Vicki Ruthven was there to greet him with a kiss on the cheek, and Pencil could not help recalling their time together at his flat, when this beautiful lady had taken him to his bed and patiently introduced Pencil to the fantastic world of sex. Pencil had gone a bit crazy since, dating a string of younger models, but was yet to repeat the fabulous experience that he had had with Vicki.

'Bit of an anti-Pencil thing going on with you at the moment,' she began as she nodded towards the pink graffiti on the window.

'Pencil will make them fuckers pay for that. Will get Delroy and his crew to sort this out well and proper.'

'No police?'

'Nah, Pencil needs this sorted pronto, and the police will not take this shit too seriously. Delroy, on the other hand, gets paid a lot of wedge to cease stuff like this.'

'Your shout, boss, but be careful. You don't want your brand tarnished.'

'Pencil knows that, Vicki, but these fucks are rinsing me with this gay shit all the time and Pencil wants it stopping.'

'You want me to put in a good word for you?'

'It's not funny, Vicki, and as you know, that's not the point.'

'I know that, Pencil, but it's still kinda funny.' Vicki smiled and left the young man to his fury. She had a store to ready for Friday's grand opening.

'Let me get this straight. Her father murdered her stepmother and is now banged up for life in Belmarsh?'

'Yes. And now she's about to launch a charity, with the help of Daddy's money, that will help offenders set up their own businesses. Hopefully stop them reoffending and heading back to prison.'

'That's no bad thing. The bitch can't be all bad then. Anything else?'

'Well, she's married to some old bloke. A geezer who used to work for Gary Ruthven.'

'Used to? What happened there then?'

'Ruthven sacked him. Less than amicably by all accounts.'

'Okay, anything else?'

'Well, apparently she's up the duff.'

'To the old bloke?'

'Yes.'

Tomas Brozek sat at his tidy desk and rubbed his palms together like he was about to start praying; contemplating what he had just heard and what impact it might have on him and his desire to exact some form of revenge on the woman. Rising, he walked to the large panoramic window and looked out over the empty football stadium. How he loved this place, empty or full, the most dramatic theatre of them all.

'So, Delroy, what have you got on this afternoon?' he eventually asked.

'Going up to Birmingham. Pencil's got a bit of an issue at his new store. Needs me to have a look.'

'When will you be back?'

'Not sure. Why?'

'I want this woman followed. Every move scrutinized, no stone in her life left unturned.' Tomas returned to his desk, his attention back on Delroy.

'Can you tell me why?'

'No, Delroy, I can't tell you why. Just get me a full report on her by Friday lunchtime.'

Delroy Powell then left to be driven to Birmingham. He really liked Tomas Brozek, had been delighted when the man had decided to invest in the DP Crew, when others including Pencil Kane had turned him down. That said, he certainly wouldn't like to cross the geezer and in some way felt sorry for this Julia Hillman woman. Whatever the fuck she'd done, Delroy would not like to be in her shoes.

Paul Ruthven was at risk of being run off his feet. With the domestic football season now over, every one of his clients had made at least a couple of calls to him to see what was going on, to check if there was any chance of a lucrative transfer or new contract. Officially, the transfer period had not opened yet, but unofficially it was like a crap shoot. He now had fifteen players signed to his agency, more than he had wanted, and the majority were tied up on medium to long-term deals with their current clubs. Two were likely to be transferred with large fees involved, and two were free agents and attracting some of the bigger Premier League clubs, prepared and wealthy enough to offer big money deals for up and coming young players.

Happy that he could get things under some sort of control, at least in relation to the four transfers that were likely to happen, he decided to walk home before his scheduled meeting with Gary in the Masons Arms. Since his mum's death he had hardly seen his brother, who was now fully re-engaged at RCS and seemed to be throwing himself into his job with his old levels of dedication and commitment. That said, Paul was surprised that Gary had not yet returned to his home in Beaconsfield, as he had been convinced that a reconciliation had been on the cards during the sad time that they had spent together in Scotland. Time would tell, and he would no doubt get an update on that front when he had a drink with his brother later. Just then his phone vibrated in his pocket and Paul responded, expecting to hear Pencil's voice on the other end. However, it was Vicki calling on Pencil's number from Birmingham.

'Pleasant surprise, Mrs Ruthven. How are you?'

'I'm okay, thanks, Paul, but I'm calling to give you a heads-up this end regarding something that your star client is proposing. Hoping that you'll be able to talk some sense into him.'

'Fire away, Vicki. I've got a feeling this isn't going to be great.'

Vicki then outlined her earlier conversation with Pencil, the young man's frustration at the growing 'Pencil is Gay' campaign and his plan for getting Delroy Powell and his crew involved to sort the issue quickly.

'Christ, somebody's really got it in for him, obviously jealous of Pencil's success,' reflected Ruthven after listening to Vicki's brief.

'I guess it's the price that you pay these days. Celebrity culture stuff.'

'You're right, but I don't need him getting Delroy to kick the shit out of someone on Pencil's behalf.'

'Having the shit kicked would be getting off lightly, Paul. The DP Crew boys are getting quite notorious.'

'Okay, leave it with me. I'll have a word with him. By the way, how are my favourite nieces?'

'They're good, I think. Emma is due back from Leeds shortly and Molly is now a woman of leisure after her exams.'

'That's not going to last very long. Not with you as her mother.'

'That's true,' laughed Vicki, not quite sure if there was a barbed message in there somewhere.

Two weeks after his release from Belmarsh Prison, Jimmy the Jynx Johnstone had been contacted by Malcolm Hillman's daughter, Julia, and offered one of five trial places on the new StartOver programme. Malcolm Hillman had taken to the young Glaswegian and had suggested to his daughter that the young man, who had taken painting and decorating NVQs while in prison, could be an ideal candidate for the new charity.

The way that StartOver worked was quite simple: a former inmate would be funded to start their own business and be supported by one or more of the charity's experienced mentors. Thus far, Jimmy had grabbed the opportunity with both hands and now had an order book for his external paintwork business that ran a couple of months ahead. The young man was almost anal in his attention to detail and if his mentor had any criticism of his performance to date, it related to how long it took him to do a job. Customers, however, were delighted with both price and quality and his mentor was happy to leave things on the basis that Jimmy would surely begin to speed things up at some point.

That Julia Hillman had begun to take a private interest in Jimmy was something of a surprise, but as always with people, Jimmy knew that there would be a payback at some point. After all, who did anything without the need for a payback?

When Julia Hillman's request came, it was a little bit of a surprise to him. She wanted him to put his alternative paintwork skill to use; his secret work as graffiti artist the Jynx was to be used as a high profile and highly controversial campaign against the former footballer and 7/7 national hero Pencil Kane.

And so, despite the fact that Jimmy the Jynx Johnstone had no issue with Pencil – indeed the opposite was true and he carried real respect for the boy – he began a secret night-time mission that suggested Pencil was gay, and so far he had produced seventeen prominently placed claims on the ex-footballer's sexuality. For each piece of graffiti, the Jynx was paid £150 in cash and all he had to do in return for the money and his artwork was to make sure that he didn't get himself caught.

With his latest work on the Pencil Five window in his new home town of Birmingham complete and even getting mentions on local radio, Jimmy decided to take the day off, take the time to get himself tidied up before travelling to London the next day, where he was due to be held up as a stellar working example of how StartOver can work when the charity had its formal launch in the House of Lords.

'Two guys in a bar. One says "Your round" and the other looks at him and replies, "You're not so slim yourself."'

Gary laughed out loud. Paul rarely remembered the jokes that he picked up from his young clients, so it was unusual for him to be telling one.

'Is that a hint?'

'Yeah, I'll have another pint of bitter please.'

Paul was delighted at being told that his brother and Vicki were going to get back together. Despite the separation, he had always assumed that the couple, two of the people that he loved most in the world, would eventually get back together. As he waited for Gary to return from the bar with their beer, he wondered what effect this would have on his relationship with Vicki, on her work at the Pencil stores project.

'And Lucas Hunt's wife's still causing you grief?'

'She is, and I think it's time for me to put an end to it,' replied Gary, sliding Paul's pint glass towards him and sitting back down opposite his brother.

'How're you planning on doing that?' asked Paul, beer froth on his upper lip.

'Not sure yet, but she needs confronting. Stopping.'

'She needed stopping a long time ago; she's done you some real damage.'

'I know, but I thought it was over when their shares got bought back. But, no, she had to keep going, had to tell Tomas Brozek. Have you ever met him?'

'Not yet, but press speculation suggests that one of my players could be wanted by his club. If so, we're bound to meet soon.'

'Hope that's not too awkward.'

'Hmm, and I hope you're not thinking of doing anything daft about Julia.'

'Ach, you know me, wee brother, and I don't do daft stuff.'

'That's the problem, I do know you.'

'Aye, I guess you do. Should you not be getting home to the lovely Lucy?' Gary looked at his watch. He needed to be moving too, had a ton of stuff to get done before a meeting at RCS in the morning.

CHAPTER 35

WEDNESDAY 7 JUNE 2006

Despite the fact that the morning's newspapers were filled with speculation about England's chances of winning the football World Cup in Germany, Pencil Kane was much more focused on what Dan Jenner was pushing for in terms of the expansion of the Pencil store concept.

'But Pencil can't imagine what it will take to open another twenty-five stores in the next year, Dan. How the fuck is Pencil going to manage that?' Dan was there to persuade Kane and his agent, Paul Ruthven, that the time was right for rapid expansion, that they should be aiming for fifty stores across the UK by the end of 2008.

'You've done the hard bit, Pencil. You've created five fantastic new concept stores, the rest is easy. We just need to get the right team in place to get out and replicate the brilliant model that now exists. Each store will do more than two million in revenue next year, with a twenty point margin. Scaling up will mean that we will clean up.'

'So, fifty stores will do a hundred mil?'

'Give or take, and rake in a twenty mil margin. That would put a value on the business of approximately one fifty million. You'll be the richest twenty-year-old in the country.'

'Paul, what do you think Pencil should do?' Kane looked at his trusted adviser, suddenly aware of an excruciating pain in his foot.

'You okay?'

'Yeah, it's just this freaking arthritis. It hurts Pencil like fuck some days.'

'Sorry Pencil, but to answer your question, I honestly don't know. This is so far out of my comfort zone, I'd need to understand the whole thing a lot better,' offered Ruthven truthfully.

'That makes sense,' interjected Dan. 'This could be the biggest decision that we make for this business. We shouldn't make it lightly; should get the professionals in to advise us.'

'Pencil would like that, Dan, and trust me that is nothing to do with you, man. Pencil trusts you two guys.' Kane looked in pain and stood away from the table that they were sitting at and began stretching his right leg and foot out in front of him.

'Can I get you anything, Pencil?' Dan was also getting up from the table, ready to go and find any painkillers that he or Carole might have in the house.

'Pencil is fine, man. Just a touch of cramp or something.'

'If you're sure?'

'Pencil's sure. Let's wrap up, agree what's next and I'll be on my way.'

'Okay, let me get some guys in from the bank. I know a great guy at RBS. They are very keen to do business these days.'

'Pencil hopes they're not too keen, Dan. Pencil wants really good impartial advice on this plan.'

'Leave that with me, Pencil. I'll make sure that they understand the brief.'

With their meeting over, Paul Ruthven and Pencil left Dan in his beautiful house and headed outside to their respective cars. Before departing, Paul turned to Pencil, concern for the young man etched on his face.

'You want me to fix you an appointment with Dr Campbell? Get her to have a close look at that foot.'

'That might be a good idea. It's been really bad the last couple of days.'

'Okay, consider it done. Now, before we go, tell me about what you're doing regarding this "Pencil is gay" thing.'

'Nothing much. Pencil has asked Delroy to get it sorted.' Kane was opening the rear passenger door of the waiting DP Crew car, ready to be on his way.

'Sure that's the right course to take?'

'Let's see what they come up with, Paul. It's the final episode of Pencil's documentary in a few weeks' time and Pencil wants this shit fixed before then.' He was now in the back seat, mobile phone in hand, ready to go.

'Promise me you'll do nothing until we've had a chance to talk about what Delroy finds out,' pleaded Ruthven, leaning in the door, his left hand on the roof of the Mercedes.

'Pencil promises you that, Paul, so don't worry.'

'It's my job to worry, Pencil. It's what I get paid for.' And at that Pencil smiled one of his charismatic smiles, so glad to have Paul Ruthven on his side.

Lucas Hunt was dressed in his smartest suit yet still managed to look like he had just got out of his bed. Not that how he looked was anywhere near the front of his mind as he left the train at Waterloo and headed outside to find himself a taxi cab. Julia had stayed the night in London, keen to be at the House of Lords really early to ensure that everything was ready and perfect for the official launch of StartOver later that afternoon.

What was at the foremost edges of Hunt's consciousness was the fact that he had just had a very uncomfortable call from Gary Ruthven informing him that Julia had broken her promise to him by contacting Tandy Brozek's husband about his wife's affair with Gary. Ruthven had been rude and to the point, telling him that if he didn't stop his wife's vendetta, then he would. Ruthven had then gone on to say something about that not being pretty and coming down there and burning their fucking house down. Lucas had sort of lost the thread at that point, his anger at his wife's betrayal taking over.

Now, he had to get to the launch and act as if nothing was wrong. Pretend all was well with him and his fucking stupid bitch of a wife. The fucking stupid bitch of a wife who just happened to be carrying his twin babies.

His brain fuzzy with fury, he saw the taxi rank and hurried towards it, stepping off the pavement and right into the path of an oncoming London bendy bus.

The River Room in the House of Lords is available for hire at the discretion of the Lord Speaker and is reserved almost exclusively for functions on behalf of UK registered charities if sponsored by a member of the Lords. That Julia Hillman had managed to obtain permission to use the room for the formal launch of her StartOver initiative spoke volumes about her tenacity and single-mindedness. She had set her heart on a House of Lords launch, and when Julia Hillman set her heart on something, she invariably got what it was that she wanted.

Dressed in her smartest business suit, purchased especially for the day from Harvey Nicks – her dad would surely accept the cost as a legitimate business expense – she looked at her watch and wondered where the hell her shit-head husband could be. Surely he was not going to be late on today of all days? The River Room had been set out theatre-style with four rows of House of Lords hardback chairs all facing a large screen and two lecterns that would allow the speakers to present in a presidential fashion to guests and invited members of the press. To the side of the room, twelve seats had been reserved for the charity's first five guinea pigs and their current mentors. Julia Hillman watched as the Jynx entered, dressed smartly in a shiny navy suit, and stood self-consciously looking about the place, seeking out his mentor. At some point she would need to pay him for his latest work of art, a pink declaration that had actually made the national press that very morning. Just the thought of that made her smile, inwardly pleased at how much nastiness she was actually capable of.

Seeing the TV actor enter, Julia Hillman went to greet him like he was an old friend, although they had only ever talked on the telephone. The man was best known for a long-running eighties BBC sitcom, and looked just a little frayed around the edges as Hillman introduced herself and led him towards one of the lecterns. He would speak after the MP, who would speak after Julia Hillman had welcomed people to the launch, making sure that everyone in the room knew that she was the brains and the energy behind this new charitable organisation.

So, at just after 2pm, Julia Hillman asked for the room lights to be dimmed and stepped up to the right-hand lectern. Behind her, the newly designed StartOver logo appeared on the large screen and the room fell into an anticipatory silence. Hillman took a deep breath and looked around the room one last time in the hope of seeing Lucas, before commencing her well-rehearsed introduction.

'My lords, ladies and gentlemen, it is my privilege to welcome you all today to the launch of our new initiative. In the UK, some eighty thousand people are released from prison every year and sadly official statistics show that some sixty-five percent of them will have reoffended within two years of their release. That is more than fifty thousand reoffenders, who have in some way or another failed to be rehabilitated whilst in prison.'

Julia Hillman was pleased by the way her opening had grabbed the attention of everyone in the room, and took a moment to look around, let the anticipation build, the audience really believe that they were to be in at the beginning of something substantial in prisoner rehabilitation in the UK. Her roving eye landed on the Jynx, who seemed to be shifting uncomfortably in his seat, probably realising the irony of the figures she had just presented.

All in all, the presentations lasted forty minutes, and by the time Julia Hillman and her guest speakers made themselves available to the floor for questioning, she was more than pleased by how things had gone, although she was now furious that her shit-head husband had somehow managed to miss her moment of glory. Most of the questions were friendly and easily answered, mostly by Julia Hillman, who needed no more self-important pontification from her two guest speakers. So when the shit from *The Sun* newspaper asked her directly if she would be standing there today if her father had not murdered her stepmother, the room fell into an eerie silence and all eyes turned to their host for her reply. Julia Hillman took her time, sipped from her water glass as she tried to hide her indignation at being asked such a thing, before replying in a calm manner.

'Probably not, although I can say this.' She stopped for effect before continuing slowly, 'If that sad and tragic death means that just one tenth of people leaving prison can be helped to live a better and crime-free life, then at least something positive will have been taken from the tragedy.' The stunned audience took a few moments to react, before breaking into a hearty round of applause.

Colm Elliot had just finished a scrappy but thoroughly enjoyable eighteen holes of golf on the Ballycastle links when his mobile phone rang and he was surprised to see that the call was from Paul Ruthven.

'DCI Elliot.' He answered the call formally, curious as to why the ex-footballer would be calling and hoping that it had nothing to do with the wellbeing of Pencil Kane.

'Good afternoon. It's Paul Ruthven here. Not sure if you'll remember me, but...'

'Oh, I remember you, Paul. I'm just wondering why you might be interrupting my holiday.'

'I'm sorry. Would you prefer me to call back when it's convenient for you?'

'No, it's okay. I've just come off a golf course, so you're only keeping me from a well-earned pint.'

'If you're sure, I'll try to be brief.'

'That'll help.'

'Well, I'm not sure that you're the right person but I still had your card, and needed some advice regarding something that's cropping up around Pencil Kane.'

'I'm all ears,' confirmed Elliot, pulling his sweaty golf glove from his left hand.

Ruthven then explained the situation with regard to the graffiti campaign being waged against his young superstar client, adding that he was worried that Pencil was at risk of taking things into his own hands and not getting the police involved.

'Do you think that there might be a link to the extortion case?'

'Not for me to say really. It's just beginning to get out of hand and Pencil liked you; might listen to a bit of sound advice,' offered Ruthven.

'Well, that's good to know. Have any threats or demands been received?'

'I don't think so. Can't be certain. Pencil is a bit cagey about it all.'

'Well, I'm due back in Blighty on Friday. Can you get him to meet with me on Saturday morning? You tell me where and when.'

'Yes, I'll do that. Let me talk to him and get back to you.'

'Good, I'll wait to hear from you.' Elliot broke the connection and headed for the clubhouse and his pint of stout, hoping that Ruthven was just being over cautious and that Kane would not do anything rash before they met at the weekend.

The journalist from *The Sun* had been surprised to be asked to stay behind for a private chat with Julia Hillman and watched with interest as the woman slipped a white envelope into the hands of one of the people who had been introduced as an initial member of the StartOver initiative.

Moments later, Hillman was by his side, leading him to a quiet corner of the room.

'So, what can I do for you, Mrs Hillman?' he asked, keen to be out of this place, desperate for a cigarette.

'Two things. First, I was less than amused by your question earlier. Did someone put you up to it?'

'I know us journos have a reputation for being lazy, Mrs Hillman,' he began.

'It's Julia Hillman. My married name is Hunt,' she corrected him.

'Whatever, but I like to do my research, and feel, if you're genuine about all this, then there's a pretty good story here.'

'And do you? Think I'm genuine, that is,' she asked.

'I think so. Not totally convinced.'

'What makes you skeptical?'

'This big fancy launch. Why not just get on with it quietly?'

'The project needs sponsorship and mentors. This place gives the initiative gravitas,' explained Julia Hillman.

'I guess it might. What's your second thing?'

'Ah, yes. But first the protocol. This needs to be treated in confidence. Nothing attributable to me.'

'I work for *The Sun*, Julia Hillman. I'm used to that.'

'Good. Then I might have a nice juicy scandal to interest your newspaper.'

'I'm listening.'

'Okay. It's about a very messy extra-marital affair involving the wife of a top director at one of London's leading football clubs,' she began.

'And you can verify this story?'

'Oh yes,' confirmed Julia Hillman with great relish.

Despite the very best efforts of a crack team of A&E doctors in St Thomas's Hospital on the Lambeth Palace Road, Lucas Hunt died from his injuries at just after 4pm that afternoon. The bendy bus driver had been given no time to react, and the limp body of Hunt, who had felt the full impact of the first blow to the top of his skull to the horror of dozens of shocked onlookers, had been dragged for twenty-five feet entangled with the front wheel of the large vehicle.

Remarkably, paramedics were on the scene within minutes and the painstaking process of getting the victim stabilized at the roadside before his short ambulance ride to the nearby hospital took the best part of an hour. On arrival at St Thomas's, Hunt was then transferred to an emergency operating theatre where surgeons assessed his injuries before the realisation struck and they knew that there was in fact nothing that they could do to save the poor man.

The process of identifying the dead man was now well underway, but the fact that he had only been carrying cash, a return ticket between Petersfield and Waterloo, a smashed mobile phone and an invite to an event at the House of Lords, made the exercise more difficult than normal.

'Hey, Pencil. It's Delroy.'

'Delroy, Pencil is hoping that you've got some news for him.' Kane had just arrived back at Pencil Five in Birmingham, delighted to see that the graffiti had been removed from the window of his latest store.

'I think that we might be making headway,' offered Powell, happy with the progress of his team's swift investigation.

'In what way, my man?'

'Well, I think that we've identified your artist. Now know who's been doing the graffiti.'

'Pencil thanks fuck for that. Who is the bastard?'

'Scotch bloke, goes by the name of the Jynx.'

'And you've talked to him?'

'Not yet. Seems like he's out of town today, due back tomorrow.'

'So, what's the plan?'

'That's why I'm calling, Pencil. We need to decide what to do with him.'

'Pencil wants to know why he's been doing this. We need to find out why.'

'Okay, let's arrange a little meeting with the Jynx. Let me get back to you.'

'Pencil wants it to be somewhere private, and, Delroy, make sure he's in one piece when we meet. I don't want any damage done to the little fuck just yet.'

'Leave it with me, Pencil. It'll be somewhere south of Birmingham, probably close to the M40. I'll call you back soon.'

'Just let Pencil know where and when, Delroy, and we'll take things from there.'

Happy with this turn of events, Pencil turned his attention back to his new store, excited to get the place opened on Friday.

CHAPTER 36   THURSDAY 8 JUNE 2006

By the time that the knock came to her front door, Julia Hillman had been going out of her mind. From the launch at the House of Lords, she had gone to lunch at Claridge's with her sister and an old schoolfriend who was now doing some pro bono marketing work for StartOver. Repeated calls to Lucas were met with a 'call failed' response, and she had decided to forget about the shit-head until she got home, which had been after 8pm. Finding no sign of her husband in their house, she had called a few friends before eventually getting in contact with the local police in Petersfield and reporting Lucas as being missing.

It was just after 2am when Julia Hillman led the two young police constables into her kitchen, now fearing the worst as the WPC asked Julia if there was anyone else in the house, and if not, was there anyone she could call to come and join her there.

In a clipped, matter-of-fact manner, the WPC then informed her that they believed that her husband, Lucas Hunt, had been killed in a road accident that afternoon in London. Hillman took the news calmly, having expected the worst news possible when it had been the police at her door and not her husband.

A call was made to Julia Hillman's mother, who lived a short distance away, and one of the police officers left to go and pick her up from her home.

'So, how did it happen?' she eventually asked the WPC who had taken the time to make the stricken woman a cup of hot tea.

'To be honest, we are not actually sure. However, it seems that your husband was run over by a London Transport bus as he rushed towards a taxi rank.'

'My God, poor Lucas. Was he killed instantly, outright?'

'I'm sorry, Mrs Hunt, but I don't have that sort of detail, and until your husband has been formally identified, there is not much more I can tell you.'

'You mean it might not be Lucas?'

'No, we are not saying that. From the details we have, we are as close to being one hundred percent sure that it was your husband who was involved in the fatal accident.'

'Dear God, what am I going to do now? I'm pregnant, with twins. We only found out it was twins on Monday. Lucas was so thrilled at the prospect.' Tears now began to pour down Julia Hillman's face. What was she going to do now?

The Jynx was pissed. He had started drinking on the train back from London and had visited at least three pubs on his staggered journey back to his small flat. Trying to find the keys to his home, he was confused; they were not where he usually left them – in the bottom of his dustbin, under an old brick, under the bags of trash. *Shit*, thought the Jynx, *where's my fuckin' keys*? With the trash bags now on the path, he tipped the dustbin upside down, only for the heavy brick to fall out and land on his right foot.

'Holy fuck,' muttered the Jynx, his head spinning, losing his balance and falling onto the ground, the bin on top of him.

'Looking for these by any chance?' asked the voice from above him.

'The fuck you got ma keys fur?' slurred the Jynx, in an attempt at his toughest Glaswegian.

'Was lookin' for you. Needed to have a little chat.'

'I'm too pissed to chat tonight, so geeze ma keys and fuck off. Ah need to sleep, pal.' The Jynx was now on his unsteady feet and reaching for his keys, trying to grab them from the big black guy in front of him.

'Think not, though we should go inside. Don't want to wake your neighbours.'

The Jynx was then gripped from behind by a person unknown and half carried up the stairs to his open front door, where he was unceremoniously dumped into his small flat.

'The fuck is this about? Somebody no like my paintin' work or what?'

'You could say that, yes. Somebody is not happy with your paintwork, assuming that we've got the right bloke, of course. Assuming that you are the famous Jynx, the Jynx that has been dragging my client's name through the mud.'

With that, Jimmy the Jynx Johnstone threw up all over the pristine and very expensive jeans that Delroy Powell was wearing.

Carole King and Gary Ruthven were working on a pitch document for Nike in the second meeting room at RCS later that morning when Gary's PA Jenny interrupted their session to inform them that David Lane was on the line and wanted a quick word with either one of them. Carole asked Jenny to put his call through, saying she would take it as Ruthven was not looking too keen to do so.

Moments later, the telephone in the room rang and Carole took the call in her usual professional tone.

'Good morning, David, it's Carole here and I'm with Gary. What can we do for you?' she asked, switching on the speaker phone facility.

'Thanks for taking the call, but I thought that you would both want to know that I've just heard the sad news that Lucas Hunt died yesterday.'

'God, how awful. What happened?' Carole asked, looking at Ruthven, who had turned a whiter shade of pale.

'Apparently, he was involved in a road accident. The poor bloke got himself run over outside Waterloo station, on his way to some House of Lords event.'

'And how is his wife, David?' continued Carole, struggling to come to terms with the news.

'She's being comforted by her family. It's all been a big shock. Especially with her being pregnant and all that goes with that.'

'David, it's Gary here,' Ruthven finally spoke. 'How are you? You guys went back a long way.'

'Pretty upset. We've not been too close since he left RCS. I think he felt that I'd betrayed him in some way,' replied Lane thoughtfully.

'Mmm, I guess it all got a bit messy,' reflected Ruthven, conscious of the fact that he had spoken to Hunt only yesterday, just as he had been arriving at Waterloo.

'Sadly, that is how life works sometimes. When did you last talk with Lucas?'

'Yesterday actually,' answered Gary, caught off guard for a moment, aware that Carole was now staring at him with widened eyes.

'Really?' asked Lane.

'Yes, he was on a train on his way into Waterloo.'

'Bloody hell, Gary. You might've been the last person to talk to him. How was he?'

'A bit rushed, a little distracted. He seemed worried that he might be late for his appointment, although he never said what his appointment was.'

'All very tragic. Do you guys want me to keep you informed regarding funeral and the likes?'

'I guess you'd better, David.' Carole took control back, and was watching Ruthven as her friend struggled to come to terms with this tragic accident.

'Okay, I will. Thanks for taking the call.'

'No problem, David. I just wish that the news had been something different, something better.'

With Lane gone, Carole turned her attention back to Ruthven, who had recovered some colour to his complexion despite the fact that his eyes were showing that his thoughts were elsewhere.

'Are you okay?' she asked quietly.

'Not really. That is a bolt from hell. Poor old Lucas. What a thing to happen.'

'Indeed, but let me get us some fresh tea and coffee, and then you can then tell me why you were speaking to him yesterday.'

The blacked-out Mercedes carrying a nervous Pencil Kane pulled into a parking space at the very back of Warwick services on the M40 a few minutes later. Pencil, his foot sore and a little stiff after the drive from London, climbed out and clambered quickly into the back of the black Ford Transit that was parked parallel to the recently arrived Mercedes.

Delroy Powell smiled at Pencil and motioned for one of his two crew members present to pull the sacking from the man's head. And as the Jynx's eyes grew accustomed to the light, Powell began formal introductions.

'Pencil Kane, meet the Jynx; Jynx, meet Pencil Kane, the man you've been dedicating so much of your artistic skills to.'

'Dinny know what the fuck you're talking about, pal. Been sayin' that fur oors now,' opened Jimmy the Jynx Johnstone, who was well capable of looking after himself, was not going to be easily intimidated.

'Pencil wants to know why you been doin' it, man, and Pencil is very busy, not got a load of free time for your Jocko bullshit, man.' Kane spoke quietly with just a modest hint of menace in his voice.

'The Jynx is a big fan of yours, Pencil. Why would ah wanna do you harm?'

'Really, you're going to fuck these boys about? And there was Pencil making sure that they didn't do things like pull your nails out with pliers before Pencil arrived.'

'Should we get started now?' Delroy asked, lifting a pair of rusty old pliers from the floor of the van.

'Why not? You get on with it while Pencil goes to take a piss, man.' Kane moved to open the door, but the Jynx was not that silly, knew that these fuckers were serious.

'Ah just got paid to do them, don't go. Let's do a deal, Pencil. I'll be glad the thing is over and done way.'

'Who said anything about a deal?' Powell began, smiling at the man and his fear.

'You want the thing stopped, you need to ken who's behind it. Me? I'm just the paid skivvy, the hired help. You want it stopped you need a name.'

'And Pencil wonders what you want in return.'

'I dinny want nothin', Pencil. Just want to get back to ma day job. Left in peace to see out ma parole.'

'Pencil's not too sure that's possible. Feels some punishment might be needed.' Kane was playing along; knew that if this Jocko gave him the name behind this campaign, then he would let him off, free to get back to his life.

'Her name is Julia Hillman; her old man was in Belmarsh with me, murdered his wife or somethin'. She runs a charity, helped me get on the straight an' narrow when I left the clink, then got me to do some extra work, bit of graffiti an' that.'

Delroy Powell was dumbstruck by the coincidence and nodded to Pencil that he needed a private word outside the van.

Moments later, as they sat in the back of the Mercedes, Powell told Pencil that he and his crew had Julia Hillman in their sights. Something to do with Gary Ruthven.

'Ruthven's wife works for Pencil. You think that's the connection?'

'Could be, but I doubt if our little Scotch friend will know. What do you want done with him?'

'Pencil wants you to let him go. He's as much a victim of this woman as Pencil, poor little fucker.'

'You sure?'

'Pencil is sure, man. Dump him out, let him find his own way home. Pencil is out of here, man. Thanks for getting things clearer.'

'What about this woman?'

'Pencil needs to think about her. Needs to talk to Vicki Ruthven.'

'Okay, Pencil. You're the client.'

'Pencil is, Delroy, so let's not forget that.'

The sun was shining as Gary Ruthven took himself away from the RCS office to try and come to terms with the news about the death of Lucas Hunt. Until Julia Hillman had arrived on the scene, they had been good friends and colleagues. As he walked across London in a somewhat random manner, he remembered the time when they had met, a boozy lunch in a restaurant somewhere in London to explore a short ad film that Hunt's agency had pitched for. Lucas had drawn his ideas on the paper tablecloth and Gary had taken the thing back to his office in Hammersmith, his only notes from the meeting. The film had been made and had gone on to win a number of national awards and their collaboration had continued for many years. Ruthven had valued Hunt's experience and his often wise advice, and on many occasions they had discussed ideas and suggestions over a round of golf at Hunt's home course down in Liphook.

He had seemed the ideal Chairman for RCS and for a number of years they had taken the business forward, with the help of Carole, who always seemed suspicious of Lucas and his talents. Vicki had not been a big fan either. How would she react to the news of his sudden death?

In Piccadilly, he stopped in Waterstones and bought a blank card in which he planned to send his condolences. After all, Lucas had written to him when his mother had died. Not that Gary felt any sympathy for Julia Hillman. That woman was a fucking accident waiting to happen. The nastier and more vindictive she got, the greater the mess in her life became. Shit, what was she going to be like after this? What if she discovered that Gary had been the last person that her husband had talked to before his death?

Finding the bookshop cafe, Ruthven got himself a cup of tea and found a table and sat contemplating what to write in the card, the words struggling to form in his head, his mind a confused mix of sadness for Lucas and accumulated anger at Julia Hillman and her on going and mysterious vendetta against him. Drinking his tea, Ruthven watched the other customers as they came and went from the café, going about their business, their minds on whatever it was their minds were on that day. Thinking of Vicki and their impending reconciliation, Gary felt sad, could feel himself getting close to tears. First there had been Tandy Brozek and their aborted child, then his separation from Vicki and his daughters, then the sudden death of his mother, and now this shock with Lucas. How could his life have gone so wrong and what part had he played in this latest string of events?

Standing, leaving the card unwritten, he stuffed it into his inside pocket and headed out of the store. He needed to call Vicki and hear her voice; needed to arrange for them to meet, see if there was any possible way of speeding up their reunion.

The Jynx was feeling like a great weight had been lifted from his shoulders, had been worried that his criminal graffiti work would get him banged up again, returned to Belmarsh or somewhere worse like the Bar L in Glasgow. Realising that he was in the Warwick services and some way from Birmingham, he checked what money he had left from the one fifty that Julia Hillman had given him the day before. He had sixty quid left, but did not want to spend that on getting home, so set about getting himself a lift from one of the many trucks that were parked up nearby.

First though, he went to the services toilets to check his appearance, which he was surprised to see was not too bad given the circumstances. His face washed, some mints bought to reduce the stale smell of booze and puke, the Jynx then returned to the truck area of the services, looking for somebody who'd be happy to let him hitch a ride back to Birmingham.

Half an hour later, he was in the warm cabin of a truck and heading north and away from his scary confrontation with Pencil Kane and his gang of heavies. The big question on his mind was what to do about Julia Hillman. Should he tell her that he'd been rumbled? Or should he just keep quiet, let Pencil Kane get in touch with her, deal with her in whatever way he wanted?

Whatever, he could do nothing about it now. He had no phone and needed to get back to his flat, get back to his new business, worry about the Hillman woman later.

To Carole it seemed like every other car that her taxi passed that evening was flying the St George's Cross flag and she was not quite sure why or where all this sudden display of patriotism had come from. Leaning forward in her seat she almost needed to shout for her cab driver to hear her question.

'What's with all these flags on cars?'

'It's the World Cup, love, innit?'

'Ah, the football,' she reflected, getting back into her seat and re-doing her seat belt.

'Not that it's gonna do that bunch of losers much good. Got

no chance,' expanded the driver, although Carole was no longer interested. She hated football, always had, and was thankful that her husband was not a big fan either.

Her thoughts then returned to the news that had confronted her so far this week: first Gary and Vicki's reconciliation and now the sad death of poor old Lucas. Sure, she had never been close to the man, never really liked him if she was brutally honest with herself, but to die so suddenly? A bloody tragedy. Dan had asked her if she had wanted to cancel their trip to the theatre; she was due to meet him in Drury Lane, but she had decided it would be good to get out, take her mind off things.

Since the departure of Hunt, and then David Lane, the positive energy at RCS had returned and with Ruthven now back in harness after his sabbatical, the place was thriving once again. New projects seemed to be flying in through their door and with expansion plans now all but cancelled, it was great that the agency focus was once again back on doing great work for their clients. Dan had managed to find the firm a good and experienced CEO who was due to start at the end of August, so Carole hoped that their bad year or two was now well behind them.

How things would be once Gary was back with Vicki was another issue that was troubling her. How she had loved that man; how often had she lay awake at night thinking, hoping that one day they might get together. Then Dan had appeared on the scene and how she now loved their life together; their wealth was beyond her understanding and the fun that they had together was way beyond anything that she had ever anticipated. And now the love of her life was going back to his wife, would once again be out of reach, no longer there to tempt her into something that she knew she would regret. No, Dan deserved her loyalty. Life with him was almost serene and that enabled Carole to get on with her career, and do pretty much as she pleased. Ruthven and his recent tendency towards chaos was not what she wanted, was something that she was no longer attracted to.

Not long ago, RCS had been about Gary, Lucas and herself, and now Hunt was dead and Gary had managed to reinvent himself as a tosser. *What a lucky escape,* she was thinking to herself as the cab pulled up outside the theatre and there was Dan, her dear and lovely husband, standing waiting patiently for her to arrive.

In Ballycastle, Colm Elliot and Susan Lamont were busy packing their cases, getting ready for their return trip home in the morning. Every time Elliot left Ireland he wondered if this would be the last time he would visit. Some strange thing challenged him inside his head and he was not really sure where the feeling came from. Deep down, however, he knew that he would be back, would one day have to return to bury his brother, and from his encounter with Liam earlier in the week, there was a good chance that that task would come sooner rather than later.

Bellamy had called him earlier, and it looked like he was heading back to another busy spell, and on Saturday he was now scheduled to meet with Paul Ruthven and the famous Pencil Kane at Ruthven's office in Fitzroy Square. That would be interesting. He had liked Pencil when he had been investigating the extortion case, and he hoped that he could make the young man see sense on this latest issue.

Just then, he looked up and Susan was standing at the door to the cottage bedroom, a skimpy towel in front of her, covering her nakedness.

'Come on, DCI Elliot. I need some action of the truncheon variety,' she said seductively, and that was not a request that Elliot could consider refusing.

CHAPTER 37   FRIDAY 9 JUNE 2006

New Street is perhaps the most famous shopping street in Birmingham, starting with the Bullring at one end to the grand Town Hall at the other. Narrow streets with brilliant names snake off New Street to reveal real hidden gems and on one of these, Needless Alley, Pencil Five stood gleaming and ready for its grand mid-morning opening. Crowds had been gathering since before daybreak and the DP Crew members on duty were taking care to ensure that everything was kept polite and proper, under firm instruction that there should be no heavy or offhand behaviour.

Members of both local and national press mingled with photographers and a couple of TV crews on the opposite side of Needless Alley, awaiting the arrival of the famous young store owner and any of his invited celebrity guests. Vicki Ruthven instinctively knew that something was wrong when her taxi dropped her off at the top of the lane and a number of reporters broke away from the larger group and headed in her direction. The first to reach her was a woman she had seen at other events around Pencil, but Vicki was shocked by the reporter's opening broadside.

'Mrs Ruthven, what do you have to say about the reports in *The Sun* this morning about your husband's affair with Tandy

Brozek?' A miniature recording machine was pushed towards her as a number of others arrived, keen to hear her reply.

'Not sure what you are talking about, so if you'll excuse me, I've got a job to do,' she replied, trying to stay calm, wondering where on earth all this shit had suddenly come from. Trying to make her way towards Pencil Five, she found her path blocked by an increasing mob of reporters and was happy for the arrival of two big DP Crew members, who began shepherding her towards the store entrance.

'Come on, Mrs Ruthven. You must have something to say!'

'Any comment on Tandy Brozek's abortion?'

'Are you and your husband still living together?'

'How long has the affair been going on, Mrs Ruthven?'

Not a second too early, she was suddenly inside the store where she was met by near silence from the people already there to finalise store preparations. Delroy Powell took her by the arm and suggested that she go through to the back office, which doubled as a busy stockroom. Ordering a cup of tea for Vicki, he picked up a copy of *The Sun* that had been left by one of his crew and followed her through to the quiet haven.

'Christ, where did that come from?' she asked, tears in her eyes, and Powell handed her the newspaper. The headline on the front page read: TOP SOCCER BOSS'S WIFE IN LOVER ABORTION SHOCK! Slowly and deliberately Vicki read the article, an article that was short on words but long on the implication of its claims.

'Did you know about all this?' asked Delroy sensitively.

'Of course I knew. It happened a long time ago; was the reason for Gary and me separating,' she replied, her eyes still on the newspaper, her world in tatters. Then her thoughts turned to her daughters.

'Christ, Delroy. I'll need to call my daughters; this will break their hearts.'

'Better get on with it. I'll connect with Pencil. He'll need to know what he's coming to. It's going to be a shit show out there.'

In London, Tomas Brozek was in deep consultation with his lawyers. He had been alerted to the article last night and had failed to get an injunction stopping its publication. Now, and with the cat well and truly out of the bag, it was a matter of trying everything possible to limit the damage. For Brozek, the news getting out about the affair was bad enough, but as a prominent member of the Polish Catholic Community, the abortion was a bigger embarrassment. It was also clear to him that he would have to take steps to end his marriage to Tandy, an action that he was really sad about, but one that nevertheless he would need to take.

Then there was the thorny question about who had leaked the story to the press. The person, whoever he or she may be, would be well protected as the legal source of the story, but Brozek and his people would get past that fireguard and make sure that the fucker got what was coming to them.

Waiting for his lawyer to call back, he was intending to issue a writ against the newspaper and its owners, his mind turned to Julia Hillman and the report he was expecting to receive from Powell that afternoon. Surely it was too much of a coincidence that this woman had contacted him only on Monday and the story was now in the national press?

Just then his mobile rang; it was Tandy getting back after trying to contact Gary Ruthven.

'Did you speak to him?'

'I did, and he's in bits that this has got out,' she began sheepishly.

'I bet he is. Does he have any clues about who might be behind this?'

'He can only come up with the one name,' replied Tandy.

'Julia Hillman?'

'Yep.'

'She'll be the one in bits, if I find out she's done this to us.'

'I think she is already. Her husband was killed in a road accident in London on Wednesday.'

'Ah well, God does indeed operate in mysterious ways.'

'Mmm, anything else you'd like me to do?'

'There is indeed.'

'What?'

'Start packing your things, Tandy. My lawyer will be in touch.'

Gary had been on his way to his family home in Beaconsfield when he had received the call from a very disgruntled Tandy. Her husband was trying to determine who it was who had sold the story to *The Sun* and she was as keen as he was to find out. After a short exchange, they had landed on Julia Hillman as the most likely candidate with Tandy asking him yet again what it was that he had done to the woman.

Reaching the gates to the house, he tried to open them with the small remote control device that he kept in his car, but the gates refused to budge. Climbing from his BMW, he walked to the tall pillar and pressed the buzzer that he knew Molly would be able to hear in the house. There were lights on, so somebody was clearly in the house, but he got no response to his increasingly aggressive buzzer pressing.

He then fetched his phone and first called the house number, again without success. Calling Molly's mobile only got voicemail, so he returned to the entrance button, and this time his daughter's voice responded.

'Dad, can you just go away and leave me alone? Mum and Emma will be home later, contact them. But I don't want to see you or speak to you ever again.' And with that she was gone.

Walking back to his car, Gary climbed back in and reversed away from the entrance before slowly driving away from the house, tears welling in his eyes, his heart broken.

Not sure where to go, he headed down the A40 and pulled into the little road that ran across the common in Gerrards Cross and parked up in a layby that overlooked the large duck pond. What a fucking mess he had made of everything. Was there any point in going on? Why didn't he just end it now? Kill himself and be done with the .whole fucking crappy mess that he had created. He then started to cry, sobbing for the things that he had now almost certainly lost in life – his wife, his daughters, his mother, his business, Lucas, the child that Tandy had been carrying… indeed, every ounce of self-esteem that he had ever possessed. The sobbing began to hurt, his chest started to get tight. What a fucking mess he had made, and how that cunt Julia Hillman had punished him for his mistakes, for each of his stupid fucking cock-ups!

Recalling his studies on transactional analysis, he tried to bring some sanity to his thinking by searching for some adult way of dealing with his situation. But it was too difficult, too hard to rid himself of the anger he felt at Julia Hillman and the self-loathing that he now had for himself. Knowing that he was not brave enough to kill himself, he decided there and then that he needed to get away from all this, go someplace where he could find some perspective, get some advice about how to begin to rebuild his fucking fucked up life. And there was only one place to go. He needed to get to Scotland and see his father.

Pencil arrived at Pencil Five in his blacked-out Mercedes and accompanied by a very attractive member of the girl band of the moment. The waiting crowds were ecstatic and Pencil and his partner went about the task of mingling and signing autographs. He looked as if he had no care in the world.

Inwardly though, Pencil was far from cool. Pencil was really worried for Vicki Ruthven and the shit that had hit the headlines that morning. Now he knew why Vicki had been living apart from her husband; now he knew why she had been more than okay with taking Pencil to bed and probably giving him the introductory fuck of his life; now Pencil knew what pain the woman had been going through; and now Pencil wanted to find the bastard who had gone to *The Sun* with the story. And when he found the person Pencil wanted to have them crushed – crushed like the piece of vermin that they were.

After forty minutes of flesh pressing, Pencil entered the store and ten minutes later his girl band partner cut the large ribbon and declared Pencil Five open for business.

CHAPTER 38   SATURDAY 10 JUNE 2006

Detective Chief Inspector Colm Elliot had found himself an unoccupied meter, parked his car and made his way on foot to Paul Ruthven's office at 10 Fitzroy Square. Before entering, he stood for a few moments enjoying the fine architecture of the area and watched as a young mother played with her two young kids in the gardens at the centre of the square. He loved London, so much more than he had ever imagined that he would, and felt more at home in this place than he ever had back in Northern Ireland.

Pressing the entry button, he waited for a minute or so before the large black door was opened by Ruthven himself, a welcoming smile on his face.

'Sorry to keep you waiting. There's nobody in this building on a Saturday. Really appreciate you coming,' he began a little nervously. The last twenty-four hours had been traumatic for the Ruthven family, but with Lucy now in Beaconsfield with Vicki and the kids, and Gary back home in Dirleton, it was time for things to calm down on that front.

'Is your man Pencil here yet?' asked Elliot, conscious that he was perhaps sounding more Irish after his few days back there.

'He is, and I think ready for a proper discussion on how to deal with this thing.' They had climbed the wide stairs to the first floor and Ruthven held the door open to let the detective into his office.

Pencil rose and shook hands with Elliot.

'Nice to see you again, Mr Elliot. Pencil just wishes the circumstances were better.'

'Part of my job, Pencil. The downside of being a copper I suppose.'

'Pencil appreciates you coming to see us.'

'It's a pleasure, and how's that foot of yours?'

'Not great to be honest, sir, but Pencil knows how lucky he is to be alive.'

'I guess so, Pencil, but nevertheless, it must be a fucker to live with.'

'It is that, sir,' smiled Pencil as they each took a seat around the meeting room table.

Ruthven and Kane then took their time to outline the entire situation to do with the 'Pencil is Gay' graffiti campaign, as Elliot listened silently, taking only the odd note in his small black notebook. When they had finished, he closed his book and sat silently for a few moments.

'Okay,' he eventually began to respond. 'And this Jynx character confirmed under some duress that Julia Hillman was indeed his paymaster?'

'Yes. Though when you say duress, Pencil would like to be clear he was not harmed in any way. Pencil would not have that,' clarified Kane.

'Mmm, some might say that being abducted from your home and driven for miles with a sack over your head could be construed as duress, Pencil, but let's leave that aside for the moment.'

'Okay. Then yes, he did confirm that Julia Hillman was the paymaster.'

'Does he know why she asked him to do this?'

'Nope. Pencil thinks the bitch put him under duress, with his parole and all that.'

'Duress and paid him one fifty per piece of graffiti,' suggested Elliot.

'That's fair, but Pencil would be sad to see the Jynx back in the slammer.'

'And do either of you two know why she did it?'

'Not until yesterday, but if you saw *The Sun* and the story regarding my brother, then perhaps she was using Pencil to get at Vicki?' replied Ruthven.

'Perhaps. She's a strange lady, Julia Hillman.'

'She's one bad fucker, and she needs stopping before someone takes the law into their own hands,' offered Pencil firmly.

'She does, and I'm glad that you came to me for advice. It'll be nice to see her again, I've got such fond memories of the last time we met.' And with that Elliot stood to leave. A trip to the country would be right up his street and he was sure that Bellamy would also be delighted to reacquaint herself with the delightful Julia Hillman. Walking back to his car he dialled his colleague's number, not sure if she would be taking calls on an off-duty Saturday. His call, however, was answered within three rings.

'Sergeant Bellamy, how are you this fine day?'

'I was great until ten seconds ago. What can I do for you, boss?'

'Oh, I was just wondering if you might fancy a wee drive down to Hampshire with me.'

Every time that he thought about what had happened in his life, tremors seemed to flood through his body, tears well in his eyes. His father had suggested that he try to take a nap after his all-night drive to Scotland; he was clearly close to exhaustion. Lying on top of his old bed in the family cottage, his mother no longer alive, Gary was feeling like there was no way back from this horrible black place. Peter Ruthven had been calm and had taken his son's news with a sigh and a shrug of his weary shoulders, and his son wondered why he had been so selfish, why he had decided that his dad was the only person he could talk to? Surely his father had enough on his plate following Catherine's stroke and sudden death?

Putting his right forearm over his eyes, he began to cry again, the continued uncontrollable release of everything that he had been holding in for such a long time. How could he have possibly screwed everything up? He had simply sleepwalked from one bad decision to the next, barely taking time between his cock-ups to consider what the fuck he had been doing. He had called Carole during his drive north and although she had listened and expressed some sympathy, she was not going to be the one to let him off the hook, ending their call by asking when it was exactly he had decided to stop being a decent bloke and start being a useless tosser! Those were her exact words and frankly, he could do nothing but agree with her. He had become a fucking useless tosser!

His dad knocked on his bedroom door and entered the room carrying a small tray with two mugs of tea and a few ginger nut biscuits on a plate. Pulling a chair towards the side of the bed, Peter took a seat and placed the tray on the bed between them.

'Still crying then? Maybe it's time for you to stop feeling sorry for yourself and start thinking about how you might start sorting this mess out,' he began in his very deliberate but perfect east-of-Scotland accent.

'I'm not crying for me, Dad. I'm crying for the people I've hurt.'

'Well, if you're intent on giving me the bullshit, I don't see the point in talking.'

'It's not bullshit. I mean what I say.'

'I believe that's what you think, but you've always done what you wanted to do in your life, and the rest of us just had to get in line with you.'

'Really? That's what you think? What you think of me?' asked Gary, sipping his piping-hot tea.

'It's not what I think, it's what's always happened. Sure we were delighted with what you've achieved, but try and get in your way, try to get you to see things differently? Nah, you were never one for that. Always knew best, Gary.'

'So you and Mum resented me too?'

'Jesus, don't be such an arse. Of course we didn't, we just recognised early on that that's how you were wired. And, given that, we were still mad about you; still able to love you as you were, as you are.'

'I've always been this selfish?'

'Selfish isn't how I'd put it, no. You've always been very focused. Lived your life on your terms.'

'You're right, of course, but I didn't get that trait from you or Mum,' reflected Gary, suddenly feeling very cold, his emotional stress leaving him empty and shaking.

'Traits don't matter. I've been a bit like you in my time. Followed my career, let your mother look after you guys.'

'Yeah, but you didn't go off and have an affair behind Mum's back. Didn't put your family at risk by chasing a sneaky fuck or two.'

'Don't judge a book by its cover, Gary. We were all young once. You're not the only attractive young man to have his head turned by a good-looking woman.'

'Not you, Dad, surely?'

'Gary, perfection is a hard bedfellow and life has too many twists and turns for it to be a realistic target.'

'But I'm not trying to be perfect. Never have.'

'Just as well, given recent events.' Peter Ruthven was not looking at his son, but gazing out the bedroom window, recalling a time long past.

'Can I ask you something, Dad?'

'Depends what it is,' replied Peter, turning back to his son.

'Are you ashamed of me?'

'What right have I to be ashamed of you, Gary? Christ, I'm worried about you, worried about your lovely wife and my beautiful grand-daughters, and want to help you get back on your feet, but ashamed?'

'You should be. I've let everyone down.'

'So, you've decided that I should be ashamed? You really are a bloody arse, Gary. Finish your tea, get yourself tidied up a wee bit. We're going for a walk, a talk and a couple of beers. I've really had enough of your self-pity. It's time for you to get a grip.'

With that Peter Ruthven was up from his seat and gathering their cups. It was obvious that he was on a mission to sort out his son.

Elliot and Bellamy had found the Hunt address with ease but had real difficulty in finding somewhere to park in the narrow lane in which the house stood.

'Looks like there's a party or something going on in Chez Hunt. Hope we don't ruin it for them,' began Elliot as he climbed from his car and stretched his legs and arms.

'Would hate to do that, boss,' agreed Bellamy, who was privately looking forward to Elliot's latest jousting match with the not-so-delightful Julia Hillman.

However, when the front door was eventually opened by a woman Elliot recognised as Hillman's mother, it was obvious that the gathering was not of a celebratory nature.

'Good afternoon. I'm Detective Chief Inspector Elliot from the Metropolitan Police. Would it be possible for me and my colleague to speak with your daughter?'

'Is it about Lucas's death?' asked the woman quietly.

'I'm sorry, but I don't know about that. Can we speak with Julia Hillman?'

'She's here, of course, but she is in no fit state to speak to the police or anyone else.'

Just then, Julia Hillman was at the door, instructing her mother to leave this to her before turning her well-loaded venom on Elliot and Bellamy.

'What the fuck are you two shit-heads doing here?' she began in a strong stage whisper.

'Look, if we're interrupting something, we're sorry for that. However, having come all this way, we'd appreciate the opportunity to ask you a few questions on a matter currently under investigation.' Elliot tried to sound reasonable.

'For your information, my husband was killed on Wednesday and our families are here today to plan his funeral, so if you don't do one, I will not be responsible for my actions. Do you get my drift?'

'Let me just say that in the circumstances, we'll pretend that we didn't hear that threat, Julia Hillman. However, we do want to speak to you urgently regarding a campaign that we believe you have been orchestrating against one Pencil Kane.'

'Don't know what the fuck you're talking about. Now just do one like I said.' And with that the door was closed firmly in the faces of the two police officers.

'Guess that's our little chat over, Sergeant Bellamy,' smiled Elliot as they stepped away from the door and began walking back down the short garden path towards the lane and their parked car.

'Let me get on to the office. See if we can get some info on what happened to her husband,' offered Bellamy as she took her phone from her light jacket pocket.

'Okay. And I'll find us some place to have a coffee, and we can decide what to do next.'

Sixty miles away in Beaconsfield, another smaller family gathering was taking place and rather like the Hunt family gathering, tears and tissues were very much in evidence. Dr

Lucy Campbell had arrived last night and helped Vicki as she had tried to calm Emma and Molly down after the dreadful revelations about their father had appeared in the newspaper. Their phones had been bombarded by texts from friends and foes alike, many making bitchy and sarcastic remarks about their dad and his sordid little affair with society beauty Tandy Brozek.

In truth, Emma was less upset than Molly, and was more angered by the fact that her dad had not told her about the affair when they had spent a couple of days together in San Roque. After all, she had told him about her fling with her lecturer, so why had he not had the balls to tell her about Tandy? Vicki had told them that she had found a way to forgive Gary and had actually been planning to get back with him, let him return to their family home. Molly found that sickening and had, on numerous occasions, stated categorically that if her dad returned to their Beaconsfield home, then she would leave; would run away and they would never see her again.

After four that afternoon, Vicki and Lucy called the girls to the kitchen and over a cup of tea, it was Lucy who decided that perhaps they had spent enough time crying over this horrible situation.

'Okay,' she began a little tentatively. 'Your mum and I have been talking, and think that we've spent enough time moping about and feeling sorry for ourselves. There's a big wide world out there and it might be a good time to get out of the house, go do something silly, take our minds off this situation.'

'Like what exactly?' asked Molly moodily. She was not really sure why Lucy was there. After all, wasn't she likely to be on Gary's side, given that she was going to be stupid enough to marry the other Ruthven brother?

'Don't be so bloody rude, Molly. Lucy's only trying to help,' interjected Vicki.

'I only asked what she had in mind,' replied Molly.

'Fine, but no rudeness. This is bad enough without that.'

'Okay. Sorry, Lucy.'

'Thank you. So any suggestions about what we might do, where we might go?' asked Lucy, keen to move things on.

'How about we go up to London? Stay in a fancy hotel for the evening, send the bill to Dad?' It was Emma who got the suggestions ball rolling.

'Nice one.' Molly smiled for the first time since the news had broken.

'Good. Any other suggestions?'

After a few other ideas were kicked around, the group settled on going to Stoke Park, booking a couple of expensive rooms for the night and indulging themselves in the club's magnificent spa. So, an hour later, the small group clambered into Vicki's Mercedes and began the relatively short drive to the place that ironically only a few months earlier had been the scene of Julia Hillman's wedding to Lucas Hunt.

Later that evening, Gary and Peter Ruthven arrived home after perhaps a pint of beer too many and ate fish and chips covered in vinegar out of newspaper wrapping as they watched England's football team stutter to victory in their opening World Cup Group B match against Paraguay. It was Carlos Gamarra who broke every Scottish heart as he put David Beckham's left-wing free kick past his own goalkeeper for the only goal of the match.

'Ah well,' reflected Peter Ruthven as he tried to tidy after their makeshift meal, 'and I thought things could get no worse.'

'What you talking about, Dad?' asked Gary, who was pleased with the result.

'Bloody England getting a lucky win. It's all we'll be hearing about on the news, reading about in the bloody newspapers.'

'Don't be like that. After all, your grand-daughters are English.'

'Aye, they are. And that's another of your grand cock-ups.'

'Dad, come on,' teased Gary.

'Come on, my arse. As I've always said, I'm not biased.'

'I know. You don't care who beats England.'

'Exactly.'

Gary watched his dad as he left the room and reflected that despite all the crap that he had brought upon himself, some things would never change and at that moment that was at least something Gary could be pleased about.

His phone was vibrating on the small bedside table, so he sat up in his familiar old bed, found the device and decided to take the call.

'Gary? It's Tandy. Can you talk?'

'Of course I can. How are you?'

'I'm not good. Been banished to my parents. Where are you?'

'At my parents too. Well, I guess it's just my dad's now.'

'In Scotland?'

'Yep. Tell me what's happened. I thought you said Tomas was okay.'

'He was until our sad little tale ended up in *The Sun*. Now he's going to divorce me.'

'Shit, Tandy. I'm so sorry that this has gone so toxic.'

'Ah well. What are you going to do?'

'God knows. Vicki and I had been planning to get back together. But with everything now so public, I guess that plan might be fucked as well.'

'Any more thoughts on who might have sold them the story?'

'Not for certain, but if I was putting money on it, I'd still be backing Julia Hillman.'

'For her sake, I hope you're wrong. Because if it was her, she's a dead woman. Tomas will have her wiped from the planet for this.'

'He'll need to join a queue.'

'Are you in that queue?'

'Something's got to be done, but I'm not sure if I'm up for killing the bitch.'

'I wouldn't worry about it. She'll be dealt with, sooner or later.'

'Christ, what a mess.'

'It is, and seems like a shitload of fall-out for just one night of passion.'

'Mmm… Rinsed, for one night. That should be my epitaph.'

MAY 2007
EPILOGUE

EPILOGUE   MONDAY 7 MAY 2007

Still buzzing from the adrenaline created by the business that she had just concluded, Julia Hillman stepped out into the early evening London sunshine and headed purposefully for the Underground.

If she was lucky, she would be home in less than two hours and be able to spend some time with her young twins, Malcolm and Lucas, have a glass or two of wine and get to bed reasonably early for a change.

Reflecting on the fact that she had just bawled out two of her relatively incompetent subordinates, one by telephone and one face-to-face, Julia Hillman chuckled to herself. That would teach the shit-heads, show them not to mess with her again.

Crossing the busy street, she headed up a small alleyway, her heels clicking loudly in the enclosed lane, and only hesitated slightly on seeing three young men, faces half covered in blue hooded jackets, coming towards her down the alley.

Panic struck, however, when they surrounded her and one tried to grab her leather handbag, the last gift she had received from her dead husband. Striking out, she tried to scream but by now another of the gang had a gloved hand over her mouth. Now terrified by their obvious youthful strength, she saw the knife late and could not believe what was happening to her as she felt the first efficient and excruciating stab pierce her light clothing and enter between two of her left ribs.

As she began to fade into unconsciousness, the gang released her, letting her fall against some railings, and as she slipped to the ground, the tallest of the gang leaned over her and whispered in her right ear, 'That's what being rinsed feels like, Julia Hillman.' They were the last words that she wanted to hear – the last words that she would ever hear.

The gang, without speaking, then retreated back out of the lane and into the busy London rush hour, ensuring as they ran, that they kept themselves hidden behind their blue hooded jackets. A large white Ford Transit, its rear doors open, gathered the gang in before speeding off into the traffic. The Ford would be found two hours later, but no forensic evidence would be lifted from the vehicle – the perfect crime, the perfect getaway, and not a single drop of evidence.

By the time Detective Chief Inspector Colm Elliot returned to his team room after his Starbucks coffee, he had an initial suspect list beginning to formulate in his mind. Hannah Bellamy was alone in the room, going over the CCTV footage for the umpteenth time, no further forward in her deliberations.

'Has Atkinson given up already?' asked Elliot, handing Bellamy a container of very hot latte.

'Not yet. I've sent him down to my office to get my file from our last dealings with our now dead friend,' she replied, pressing the rewind button on the machine and stopping the film just before the actual stabbing.

'Thoughts on suspect list?'

'One or two, but with this woman it could be very long.'

'Indeed, but what's your starter for ten?'

'Well, there's Pencil Kane, Gary and Vicki Ruthven, and

Tomas Brozek and his ex-wife for starters,' began Bellamy, using her fingers to recall her initial suspect list.

'Christ, you're right, this list could be endless. Julia Hillman was one of the nastiest, most difficult people I've ever come across.'

'No excuse for an execution, boss,' offered Hannah on reflection as she turned back to the screen.

'Good word for it though.' Elliot nodded at the screen before concluding, 'An execution is exactly what happened in that lane.'

Just then Atkinson arrived back in the room carrying a neat green folder containing pages of meticulous notes from their previous dealings with the Hillmans.

'That didn't take you long,' said Bellamy without turning away from the screen.

'No, but have you ever considered therapy for that OCD thing you've got going on down there?' teased the young detective constable.

'No, but have you taken good care of your PC plod uniform, dick for brains?'

'Now, now, children, let's focus on the task in hand,' intervened Elliot, not entirely unhappy with his team's banter.

The three then spent another hour meticulously going over the CCTV film, each committing every last detail to memory. Elliot then sent the other two home with the instruction that he wanted them in bright and early next morning to begin a thorough investigation into the execution of one Julia Hillman. With his guys gone, Elliot picked up Bellamy's folder and headed for his office, confident that his sergeant and her meticulous notes would give him something concrete to get them focused on in the morning.

Since her divorce from Tomas Brozek, Tandy had been seeing Gary Ruthven on a regular basis. Their one night of passion that had caused so much grief in their lives had been turned into a regular and quite special fuck fest that she was really enjoying. Indeed, Ruthven was due that evening and Tandy was really excited at the prospect of another long session with her handsome Scot. When her phone played its silly tune, she rushed across the drawing room of her new and somewhat expensive apartment in Pimlico, expecting the caller to be Ruthven confirming that he was on his way.

However, the caller's number was withheld and when she answered she was surprised to hear her ex-husband on the line.

'Bet you were not expecting me,' he began in his quiet, calm way.

'You're right of course, Tomas, but it's good to hear from you.'

'Sure, just thought I'd call and let you and that boyfriend of yours know that I've just heard that Julia Hillman was murdered in London earlier this evening.'

'Oh my God, Tomas. Are you sure?'

'Quite sure. Heard from my contacts and there's just been an announcement on the late London news. Stabbed by a gang of hoodies as she left the offices of that charity of hers,' explained Tomas without any trace of emotion.

'How awful. What will happen to her young children?'

'Thankfully, not a problem that we have to worry about.'

'Yes, true, but all the same.'

'Anyway, thought you and Ruthven would want to know.'

'Thanks, but he's not here. We're not a full-time item, you know.'

'Not a concern of mine. Take care, Tandy.' And with that the connection was broken.

The news upset Tandy. After all she had long predicted that Julia Hillman was unlikely to make old bones, and now she was dead. Entering the kitchen, she pulled a bottle of wine from the wine cooler, opened it and poured herself a large glass, silently hoping that the woman's death was not the work of her ex-husband or more likely one of his cohorts.

Just then the entry phone buzzed; it would be Gary. And how, she wondered, would he react to this dreadful news?

Malcolm Hillman sat in his cell in Belmarsh Prison struggling to come to terms with the devastating news that had been delivered to him earlier by the Assistant Governor. How could such a thing have happened; what had Julia done to deserve such a tragic end to her relatively young life?

Sure, she was, or had been, a difficult character and been able to antagonise most people she came into contact with. But this? To be murdered in central London in broad daylight? Tears began streaming down the old man's face, destroyed by the knowledge that he had brought this ill fortune on his family and now sure that this was where the entire thing would end.

Climbing from his bed, he fumbled in the near darkness for his toilet bag and soon found the razor blade he had been stashing for such a moment. Kneeling beside his bed, he said a few prayers for the safety and well-being of his remaining family. Then, climbing onto his bunk he pulled up the left sleeve of his prison-issue pyjamas, closed his eyes and then slashed open the main arteries of his left wrist. Yes, they would find him soon, but thankfully, he thought, it would be too late, his pain would be over for good.

Jimmy the Jynx Johnstone arrived back in his home city of Glasgow just before midnight. Stepping from the train in Queen Street station, he hurried along the platform, handed over his ticket, slung his overnight bag over his shoulder and hurried out into the wet evening and found the taxi rank.

Instructing the driver to take him to the address of his family home in the Parkhead district of the city, he was delighted by the way things had panned out and just wanted to get inside the tenement building and make sure that the three blue hooded jackets and three pairs of leather gloves were destroyed in the large furnace in the boiler room in the building's basement.

As the taxi approached its destination, the Jynx flipped open his phone and began typing a simple message that he had been instructed to send the moment he reached the safety of his family home.

The message prepared, he then carefully reread it before pressing the send button. Climbing from the taxi, he paid the driver and stood for a few minutes enjoying a final cigarette before entering the building and climbing the three flights of stairs and knocking on the Celtic green door of the flat. His eldest brother Pat opened the door and let him enter without a word. He had been expected and the family were just glad to see him home.

A short time later, Pat and the Jynx went to the basement, where they made sure that the contents of his overnight bag was completely destroyed. The perfect crime, the perfect getaway and not a single drop of evidence.

TUESDAY 8 MAY 2007

The bedside clock indicated the time in luminous green as 0315 as Colm Elliot sat bolt upright in bed, sweat streaming from his forehead. Turning to his right, he saw that his sudden movement had not stirred Susan, so he quietly climbed from the bed, pulled on an old Iron Maiden T-shirt and tiptoed out of the room and headed for their small study. There, he clicked on his reading lamp and found the copy of the CCTV film of Julia Hillman's execution and moved to push it into his tape machine. Switching on the television, he found the remote and pressed the mute button.

After watching the entire film in slow motion, he flicked the thing forward to watch a repeat of the final five seconds as the three people in blue hooded jackets retreated up the lane before disappearing from view. His heart now thumping in his chest, he replayed the scene one more time, just to be sure. And sure he was. Colm Elliot knew for certain who one of them was. Not the one with the blade, but the big fucker who took time to lean over and whisper something to Julia Hillman as she lay dying against the railings in the lane.

Elliot switched off the equipment and turned his reading light off. He needed a cup of tea, needed to think very seriously about what he was going to do with this discovery. In his years as a detective, he had faced many dilemmas, but as he quietly filled the kettle, he doubted if he had ever faced one as difficult as the one now confronting him.

At six, he shaved and showered and got dressed for his day before writing a note for Susan, leaving their house and heading on foot for the station and a very early train into central London. In his office in Marylebone, he jotted his outline plan down on a spare piece of notepaper, before calling Bellamy and telling her that he would be out of the station until sometime after lunch.

He then found the number that he had kept stored on his mobile phone and dialled, hoping for a reply and keen to be putting his plan into action.

The Ritz Carlton in Dubai, with its low red pantile roof, stood proudly on the beach as a monument to a time when building in the great new city was a lot more modest than the Manhattan-type skyscrapers now sprouting up all over the reclaimed desert. Dr Lucy Campbell and her husband Paul Ruthven had come to the place as part of their elongated honeymoon, a promise that they had made to each other when they had tied the knot in Harrogate the previous autumn.

It was getting close to midday hot as they returned from their long walk along the beach and headed back up the sand towards the hotel and the freshly squeezed lemonade that had become their customary lunchtime drink. Finding their sunbeds, they settled down, brushed the wet sand from their feet and simultaneously checked their phones for any messages or missed calls.

Intrigued to have a missed call from Colm Elliot, Paul Ruthven left Lucy to order their drink as he went to find somewhere quiet and cool to return the detective's call. Elliot's phone hardly completed its first ring cycle before it was answered.

'Good of you to call me back,' was Elliot's opening welcome.

'Not a problem. Sorry for the delay, my wife and I are on vacation in Dubai; we were out walking on the beach.'

'Seem to recall you disturbing a holiday of mine a while back. So, sorry for the disturbance.'

'Not a problem. What can I do for you?'

'Well, I was hoping that you could arrange for me to meet with Pencil Kane. Sometime today if possible.'

'Nothing wrong I hope.' Ruthven was suddenly anxious.

'Just part of a new enquiry. Guess you've not heard.'

'About what?'

'Julia Hillman was murdered in London yesterday evening.'

'Holy shit. What happened?'

'Later. Meantime, I need to talk with Kane.'

'But surely you can't think that Pencil would have anything to do with such a thing?'

'I would hope not, but can you arrange for me to see him soonest?'

'Okay, let me call him and get back to you.'

'Thanks.'

Sadie had been cutting Pencil's hair for at least five years and now stood behind the young superstar in her modest London shop as Pencil tried to give her instructions on how he wanted his sideburns cut.

'Pencil would like Sadie to leave this left side an inch longer than the right side,' he explained earnestly.

'I can't do that, Pencil. It would look kinda stupid,' she argued.

'Why not, Sadie? It's what you did the last time!'

'Ha, very funny, Pencil, and I thought you were being serious.'

'Pencil is always serious, Sadie, you should know that by now. Pencil will just have his usual trim,' he replied, smiling in the mirror at the girl as he wondered, not for the first time, how good his hairdresser would be in bed.

Just then, Pencil's phone vibrated in his vintage Levi's pocket, causing him to stop his haircut and check who the call was from.

'Can't Pencil have peace to get his haircut by the lovely Sadie?' he asked on noting that Paul Ruthven was the caller. But Ruthven was not in a jolly mood as he explained the purpose of his call from Dubai.

The offices of RCS were in a sombre mood when Uli Muller stepped into meeting room two to join Carole King and Gary Ruthven. The fact that Muller was still with the firm a year after he had been investigated by David Lane for running a parallel business with his wife in the now closed Hamburg office was a strong indication of how things had got back on a level footing at the agency.

The three of them were there to finalise a pitch that they were due to make to BMW in Munich the following week; a pitch that would be made in German by Uli and Carole and in which they all had high hopes of success.

Before they began, however, Gary informed the small group of the news of Julia Hillman's death and for a few minutes they reflected on the tragedy that had befallen their former colleague Lucas Hunt and the young family he had never known. Just then Gary's PA Jenny entered and handed him an email note.

'Christ,' he began. 'Just when I thought things couldn't get any worse.' Ruthven passed the note to his colleagues. It was a short email from Vicki Ruthven informing them that it had just been announced on the London news that Malcolm Hillman had taken his own life in Belmarsh prison.

Across London, Detective Chief Inspector Colm Elliot sat alone at the meeting room table in Paul Ruthven's office in Fitzroy

Square awaiting the arrival of Pencil Kane. For an experienced campaigner like Elliot, it was unusual for him to be feeling anxious, but anxious he was. Just then Kane arrived in the company of Delroy Powell, who took a seat in the reception area as Pencil entered the meeting room and gave Elliot his most charming smile as he offered his hand.

'Mr Elliot. As always, Pencil is very pleased to meet you again.'

'I wish I could say the same, Pencil. Unfortunately I can't on this occasion.'

'Should Pencil be worried, Mr Elliot?'

'Mmm, that depends, Pencil.'

'On what, Mr Elliot?'

'On how honest you are with me in the next five minutes.'

In San Roque, Vicki Ruthven had just completed her morning run but was unsure about taking her swim. The pool was not heated, and was still just a little too cold for her liking. As part of her pending divorce settlement with Gary, they had decided to keep the house and share its use, which was at least something as she had become very fond of the place. Leaning over the flower bed beside the pool, she began deadheading some of the exotic plants that Ruthven had planted and was well into the task when she heard the telephone ring inside the house. Walking quickly across the still damp lawn, she pulled open the doors and rushed to answer the call.

'Pencil wants to know when his top merchant is coming back to work,' Kane began without waiting for a greeting.

'I'll be back soon enough. Just need to get my equilibrium back. You of all people should understand that,' she replied in her now regular flirty manner with Pencil.

'Pencil's glad to hear that, but thought you'd like to know that I've just had a meeting with that copper, Elliot.'

'Christ, Pencil. That was quick. What did he want?'

'He knows, Vicki. The fucker knows what went down with Julia Hillman,' said Pencil quietly, thoughtfully.

'And?'

'And nothing. He's got no evidence, will not find any.'

'So, how do you know he knows?' Vicki was shaking with fear as she pulled a chair across the marble floor and sat down.

'Says he recognised Pencil's limp in the CCTV pictures, but that's fuck all.'

'How did he leave it?'

'Told Pencil to be good, to stay out of trouble.'

'And that's all?'

'That's all.'

'Blimey, Pencil. I hope you're right about no evidence.'

'Pencil is right, Vicki, but you need to get rid of the text that the Jynx sent you from Glasgow.'

'Don't worry, Pencil, that's long gone.'

'And the texts from Brozek?'

'Untracable old telephone that's now at the bottom of the Med, so relax, Pencil.'

Sergeant Hannah Bellamy was reading the initial autopsy report on the death of Julia Hillman when Elliot entered her office an hour later.

'Hello, boss. I guess you're about to fill me in on where you've been all morning.'

'I guess I am, Bellamy, I guess I am.'

Ten minutes later, they were joined in Bellamy's office by Detective Constable Mark Atkinson.

'Well,' began Bellamy. 'It looks like you were right after all, DC Atkinson.'

'In what way?' asked the bemused young detective.

'DCI Elliot and I would like you to write up our initial report for the CPS on the Julia Hillman killing.'

'Oh yes, and what's our conclusion?'

'It's simple. We believe that Julia Hillman was the unfortunate victim of drug-crazed youths looking for quick cash to support their addiction. As you rightly suggested yesterday, another pointless, stupid waste of an innocent life.'

'Really? That's your conclusion?' Atkinson asked, looking from Elliot to Bellamy.

'Indeed it is. Obviously, we will do what we can to find the gang, but...'

Bellamy looked at the ashen-faced Elliot, who simply nodded his agreement before taking his leave and heading to his own office, his mind swirling with a phrase that his poor, sad dad used to use.

The phrase was, 'Enough is enough.'